Má

No Uaiq áq

BELFAST'S DOME OF DELIGHT
City Hall Politics 1981–2000

Máirtín Ó Muilleoir

Published by
Beyond the Pale Publications
BTP Publications Ltd
Unit 2.1.2 Conway Mill
5-7 Conway Street
Belfast BT13 2DE
Tel: +44 (0)2890 438630 Fax: +44 (0)2890 439707
E-mail: info@btpale.ie Web site: http://www.btpale.ie

British Library Cataloguing-in-Publication Data.
A catalogue record for this book is available from the British Library.

ISBN 1-900960-08-7

Typeset in 10 on 13pt Times
Printed by
Colour Books Ltd, Dublin

Cover illustration: specially commissioned from John Kennedy.
Cover design by *emty graphics*.

The phrase 'Dome of Delight' was first coined by Jim McDowell who
we duly acknowledge and thank for its use in the title of this book.

Tíolacadh/Dedication

*Do na laochra siúd uilig gan iomrá a thug aire dá
gcomhairleoirí Sinn Féineacha*

*To all those unsung heroes who took care of
their Sinn Féin councillors*

Also by Máirtín Ó Muilleoir:

Comhad Comhairleora
Krauts
Holy Cow Sin Ceann Mór
Ceap Cuddles

I, Too

I, too, sing America.

I am the darker brother.
They send me to eat in the kitchen
When company comes,
But I laugh,
And eat well,
And grow strong.

Tomorrow,
I'll be at the table
When company comes.
Nobody'll dare
Say to me
"Eat in the kitchen,"
Then.

Besides.
They'll see how beautiful I am
And be ashamed -

I, too, am America.

Langston Hughes

(From *The Collected Poems of Langston Hughes*. Editor Arnold Rampersad, Associate Editor David Roessel. Vintage.)

Contents

Foreword

Máirtín Ó Muilleoir's political memoir should be required reading for everyone from Irish schoolchildren to the high-and-mighty who seek to transform Northern Ireland from war to peace. Even Ireland's best friend in the world, President Clinton, needs a look at this account to balance his recent unconscious slip that the parties in Northern Ireland are just 'a couple of drunks' addicted to outmoded disputes.

This adventure story is often funny, suddenly sad and always intense, a journalistic account of Ó Muilleoir's ten year crusade to make Belfast City Hall safe for republican and nationalist politics. It seems narrated on the run – guerrilla warfare with words and wit as weapons. It captures well two decades of transition from exclusion to inclusion. At first, despite their democratic mandate, Sinn Féin councillors found themselves demonised like few elected officials on the planet. The Unionists closed meetings rather than sit with the 'Shinners', tabled their motions, stacked all committees, blew toy trumpets, walked out to prevent quorums, denounced the Irish language as dead. The Sinn Féin offices at City Hall were bombed as recently as 1994. One of their councillors, Alex Maskey, shot in the stomach at home, was called 'leadbelly' by the laughing daughter of Ian Paisley when he returned to City Hall.

This vile and petty arrogance was rooted in the blind assumption that Belfast City Hall was an impenetrable bulwark of a 'Protestant state for a Protestant people'. Sinn Féin was regarded as a cabal of demonic godfathers whose entry into politics was categorised as only 'a new dimension in urban terrorism' by *The Sunday Times* (August 3, 1975). 'Knowing they will never persuade the Catholics to vote for them at ballot box', *The Times* reported, certain unnamed 'military intelligence analysts' predicted that Belfast republicans would use the control of food 'to force the Catholics community to support them'.

But today Belfast City Hall has changed. In 1983, the voters of West Belfast proved the British press wrong by choosing Alex Maskey as Sinn Féin's first elected councillor since 1920. By 1999, the nationalist bloc including republicans commands a majority of the City Council and – who knows? – there may be a Mayor Maskey in the new millennium. 'We had to eat in the kitchen for a long time but now I'm happy to say that Sinn Féin is in the City Hall dining room with everyone else', Ó Muilleoir sums up with satisfaction.

This upbeat account should bring little comfort, however, to armchair analysts who uphold the pragmatic ideal of working within the system, *i.e.* constitutional politics. The Unionist venom was aimed at punishing Sinn Féin voters by blocking services as simple as providing children with swings at Whiterock leisure centre. And being an elected representative meant risking death. As Ó Muilleoir recalls, 'I walked in the valley of death and I was shit scared. Before every (council) meeting I would don my Sinn Féin-supplied flak jacket, though I could never work out which was the front... In ten years, barely a month went by without a gun or a bomb attack on Sinn Féin members and their families... a horrific price so that republican rate payers would have their views represented at City Hall'.

This change at Belfast City Hall has been caused by many forces, among them a growing nationalist voting population, the peace process, and the pressure of American and European diplomats and investors. But it could not have happened without the likes of Ó Muilleoir and his relentless tactics based on wit. Once his humour failed him, and he found himself kneeing a provocative Unionist councillor in the groin during a City Hall confrontation. He acknowledges that his personal lapse into the physical force tradition 'brought an end to the intense loyalist barracking of Sinn Féin' but otherwise he embraces the nonviolent guerrilla strategy of exposing the Unionists where they are most vulnerable. In particular, Ó Muilleoir and Sinn Féin were very effective in exposing the ratepayer-subsidised junkets that privileged Unionist politicians took for granted. 'No destination was too far away when it came to (unionists) searching for tips on how to conduct the business of local government', Ó Muilleoir remembers.

Ó Muilleoir is a de facto nationalist, and I half-suspect that he secretly prays for city-state status for Belfast, if not that of a full-fledged Republic. If he sounds like a civic booster, the label fits better than those the Unionists have hurled at him.

When I first interviewed Ó Muilleoir in 1995, I was briefed that he was a 'very independent' member of Sinn Féin. He was indeed. His vision for Belfast, he said, was Barcelona. 'The Europeans are more used to proud, assertive nationalists and cultural diversity. The Brits don't have any of that. Yes, Barcelona is on the land of Spain but they have their own language, their own regional government, their own television, industry and finance. People come there from all over the world', he said passionately.

But when I first visited Belfast City Hall in that same year, it was still more grey-domed centre of the Spanish Inquisition than a lovely new Barcelona by the sea. Symbols of the Empire, from Union Jacks to battlefield paintings of the Somme, adorned the imposing interior. The Mayor at the time was Hugh Smyth of the Progressive Unionist Party, a gentleman whose party enjoyed traditional links to the Ulster Volunteer Force.

However, it was a time of change, partly caused by the Mayor's need to project a pluralist political atmosphere to the U.S. trade delegation I accompanied. Rather than excluding and demonising Sinn Féin in front of American visitors, it was a time when the token presence of a Shinner or two was mandatory in meetings with American officials who might be bearing gifts. In fact, the next time I met Hugh Smyth was during the Stormont peace talks. He waved me over for coffee with Gusty Spence and I brought along Sinn Féin's Pat Doherty, thus integrating the coffee shop like the old days in the segregated American South. Unfortunately the PUPers drew the line at photographs of this cozy inclusivity. It wasn't time, they said. In any event, another royal citadel had been breached by republicans carrying briefcases, and fraternising was sure to follow.

Ó Muilleoir's memoir is a precious resource for historians and politicians who have given little respect to Sinn Féin as a political phenomenon. The question they should ask is how and why Sinn Féin has managed to overcome so many obstacles to become the largest political party in Belfast today and an indispensable force in the Irish peace process? Bluntly, why is Sinn Féin still around? Its steady success, measured in electoral results, defies most conventional wisdom and contains positive lessons for other movements seeking to move from military to political struggles for social justice.

During the so-called 'Troubles', Sinn Féin was regarded by British and American strategists as nothing more than a front for the Irish Republican Army. For good measure, any Sinn Féin political potential was throttled by official censorship, harassment and incarceration, political vetting, and financial support directed to the traditional Catholic Church and the more moderate Social Democratic and Labour Party (SDLP). And as the party has continued to gain strength and recognition, it has had to cope with persistent pressures to divide its ranks, co-opt its leadership, and smother its republican heart in the coils of compromising tokenism. The most powerful governments in the world want Sinn Féin as a junior partner in pacifying a partitioned Ireland. As one official explained the policy to me, 'we will give them less than they want but enough to keep them in talks'. Yet Sinn Féin has survived all forms of containment and counter insurgency so far.

Why? Ó Muilleoir's memoir gives plentiful evidence that republicans have carried out their electoral campaigns and peace initiatives as 'the moral equivalent of war', a term invented long ago by Henry James. From whence does his passion and unity arise? Why doesn't Sinn Féin follow the official script and split up, burn out, settle for gadfly status and enlightened colonial state and enjoy the glittering benefits of 'co-optation'?

The answer might lie in the blood of martyrs, in the rich experience of Irish Nationalists, in the political and organisational skills of a people long denied their use. Ó Muilleoir implies the revision of Mao Tse Tung's famous claim that 'political power grows out of the barrel of a gun'. Instead it may be that nationalist political power will grow out of guns remaining silent. It remains to be seen. Who knows? This story of how Sinn Féin broke the barriers of Belfast City Hall may be a preview of how the organisation – and its nationalist partners – will break the barriers of forming an inclusive executive in Northern Ireland, and beyond that an Ireland that achieves unity, democracy and equal economic opportunity. It's a challenge, to be sure, but one which anyone with the mad civic courage to wear a flak jacket to City Hall should be able to overcome.

1.

House of Horrors

A ccess to the stately debating chamber at Belfast City Council is via a long corridor bedecked with portraits of former Lord Mayors, transforming the spacious City Hall first floor corridor into a unionist version of a house of horrors which would have done the old Barry's Amusements Arcade in Bangor proud. The po-faced pictures of the ex-Lord Mayors weren't erected solely on the basis of their dubious artistic merit; they also served as a unionist totem, marking out the City Hall as the fiefdom of not-an-inch Protestantism.

They were certainly enough to knock the fear of God into a novice ambassador from the independent republic of Andersonstown as I found out when I ran the gauntlet of former first citizens on the way to my first meeting of Belfast City Council in November 1987.

I had been elected two weeks previously along with colleague Fra McCann in a double whammy of victories for Sinn Féin at by-elections caused by the resignation of Alliance Party husband-and-wife council team, Will and Pip Glendenning, but this was my first taste of the Council in action. Press reports painted the Council's monthly meetings as a bearpit of bigotry. I wasn't to be disappointed.

Laid out in self-important House of Commons style, the Council chamber sits nationalists facing their unionist counterparts. I took a pew in the front row, separated from the

DUP's Sammy Wilson by a row of journalists who filled the role of scribbling sandbags, soaking up the abuse and vitriol hurled across the chamber from the unionist benches.

Towering above the proceedings was the Official Unionist Lord Mayor Dixie Gilmore. If the portly South Belfast councillor's legendary girth and size – he stood at well over six feet – didn't betray his background with the Palestinian police force, his intellect certainly did. He and I both knew we had a job to do as the temperature soared on the Council shop floor and the meeting descended into a series of by-now predictable unionist protests at Sinn Féin efforts to speak. I intended to make what I would rather pompously term my inaugural speech; he intended to stop me.

I had run on a ticket of winning recognition for the nationalist ethos in Belfast City Council and was determined to speak in Irish – if given the chance. For new unionist councillors, the Lord Mayor would be expected to make a formal statement of welcome, but when I rose to speak – under the patently ridiculous guise of wishing to make a statement on the funding of the Ulster Orchestra – Dixie was out of the blocks like the winner of the 7.30 at Dunmore. 'Ba mhaith liom buíochas a thabhairt do na daoine a thug vóta…' was as far as my personalised Gettysburg Address went before Sammy Wilson was on his feet demanding I be formally censured by the Lord Mayor for speaking Irish.

That involved a lightning show of unionist hands to demand that I 'be not heard', the equivalent of giving the Lord Mayor the right to ignore my contribution and tell me to sit down. With the blood up and unversed in Council protocol, I launched into my second sentence which, given the baying of the unionist pack, couldn't be heard by the Sinn Féin contingent never mind the rest of the Council. That was the signal for Dixie to bring the shutter down. At the request of Sammy Wilson, who coined on the spot the phrase 'leprechaun language', the Lord Mayor called a vote to have me removed from the chamber as punishment for my 'disruptive behaviour'. Almost to script, the RUC appeared at the entrance to the Council chamber and I was frog-marched out of the hall. It may not have been seven minutes that shook the world but it certainly shook this political neophyte. Twenty seven years of relative separate development in the heart of West Belfast had meant that until that night I had never come face to face with unionism's almost pathological loathing of Catholicism. This is a hatred which can only be appreciated when experienced in-close and dangerous; a Pavlovian outburst of bitter bigotry so intense it was as if a Lambeg drum-strength alarm clock had gone off inside the head of every unionist councillor who saw me rise to speak. It was a political premiere which earned me two column inches in the *Irish Times* – and cost me a night's sleep.

The Belfast City Council I entered was still coming to terms with the dramatic growth of Sinn Féin and the presence in the Council chamber of what the razor-tongued and quick-witted Sammy Wilson dubbed 'a battalion of Sinn Féiners'. While unionists maintained a sizable majority in City Hall (in the 1985 local government elections, Sinn Féin and the SDLP between them had captured just 13 of the Council's 51 seats), there was an uneasiness and lack of self-confidence in their ranks which were to become the hallmarks of the unionist regime over the next ten years. Ulster Unionist councillors spurned opportunities to find common ground with the emerging republican party – hardly surprisingly given the ferocity of the IRA campaign – in favour of the DUP's knee-jerk reaction to any move by Sinn Féin or the SDLP to democratise the Council. It was a policy which – by exposing the Council's own sectarianism and narrow mindedness – contained within it the seeds of unionism's own defeat. But coming to terms with the changing times was never the forté of the unionist City Fathers.

2.
Turning the Tables

The harbingers of change in Belfast City Hall were to be found in an unlikely quarter: the H-Blocks of Long Kesh. The pro-republican prison campaigners elected during the traumatic 1981 hunger strike (ironically at a time when Sinn Féin – the official spokespersons for the prisoners – was pursuing an ostrich-like abstentionist policy), were the first mainstream republican councillors elected to local government positions since 1921. Despite the huge groundswell of support for hunger striker Bobby Sands, which resulted in his election as MP for Fermanagh-South Tyrone in April 1981, republican strategists decided not to field Sinn Féin candidates in the Council elections the following month. It was a decision made at the 1980 Sinn Féin ard-fheis which confounded supporters of the hunger strikers and owed more to outdated republican dogma than to realpolitik. Even though senior Sinn Féin spokesperson Joe Austin was to acknowledge that the omens could hardly have been more fortuitous for the party – 'the timing was exactly right, something which doesn't happen very often in politics' – the party left the field to the nascent Irish Independence Party, the Irish Republican Socialist Party, assorted independents and, in Belfast, People's Democracy. Sinn Féin's rain check may have been good news for the SDLP, which maintained its dominant position in the nationalist community, but there were other casualties of the intervention by the prisoners' supporters. In North Belfast, the fiercely anti-republican West Belfast MP Gerry Fitt lost his seat to unknown PD candidate Fergus O'Hare, who stood on an anti-H-Block and Armagh Prison ticket. O'Hare later recalled how his novice team had to go to the Linenhall Library to enquire as to how a candidate stood in an election and where the electoral boundaries for Fitt's ward actually were. Across Belfast, the IRSP took two seats and the PD two, while independent nationalist Larry Kennedy – also a strong advocate for the prisoners – romped home in Ardoyne.

Riding to success on the back of Sinn Féin's no-show policy, the Irish Independence Party picked up a respectable 21 seats across the North. Despite the heightened support for the hunger strikers, the SDLP lost only 10 seats overall. On the unionist side, Ian Paisley's Democratic Unionist Party polled strongly, picking up an additional 68 seats to put them on a level pegging with the Ulster Unionist Party.

The awful human toll of the H-Block hunger strike was already leaving its mark on the body politic. As Fr Des Wilson, community priest in Belfast's Springhill estate observed:

> The tens of thousands who attended Bobby Sands' funeral were an indication that a new understanding was blooming among the community in West Belfast. There were some of us here who said, 'if a hunger striker dies, that's the end of British rule in Ireland'. I believe that is true, no matter how long it takes. I believe that history will look back on this hunger strike in which men died as the beginning of the end of Westminster's oppression of Ireland.

Following the 1981 Council elections, the much-vaunted unionist hospitality didn't exactly amount to the red carpet treatment – inside or outside the chamber – for the new nationalist councillors setting awkwardly about the task of transforming City Hall from a glorified Orange hall into a modern, forward-thinking local government forum. In fact, when the newly-elected nationalist councillors held a rally outside the City Hall, 30 of their supporters were arrested.

In the committee rooms and corridors of power, plans were also being hatched to use the new pro-prisoners' team as a unionist punch bag. The Council's powerful General Purposes and Finance Committee – which controlled the City Hall purse strings – ruled that the five republican councillors couldn't sit on any of its myriad sub-committees (including one with the weighty civic task of selecting menus for City Hall functions). For good measure, the new boys were also barred from participation in any official Council delegations to meet Stormont ministers. Not a peep was heard from the SDLP in response to this à la carte approach to Council standing orders but then the Council hadn't yet descended completely into its ein reich, ein volk... mode: the new mayor was liberal unionist Grace Bannister and members of the SLDP and Alliance Party were elected to the positions of chair and deputy chair of committees. But the DUP, with 14 seats on an equal footing with the UUP, was determined to set the sectarian pot boiling.

When a Tricolour was hoisted on the roof of the Whiterock Leisure Centre in West Belfast, George Seawright, a newly-elected DUP councillor (set for higher things as it turned out) proposed the building be closed down. At a series of meetings, he failed to win majority Council support for his shutdown motion. However, the DUP were to have more luck with a proposal that the new councillors be prevented from sitting on the management committees of Council community centres in their own areas. In September 1981, when the Community Services Committee appointed Sean Flynn of the IRSP to the board of the Markets' Community Centre in his own constituency, the DUP successfully proposed at a full meeting of Council that the decision be rescinded.

On 8 October, independent councillor Larry Kennedy was shot dead in a loyalist gun attack on a social club in Ardoyne. His death came just days after the end of the protracted hunger strike in Long Kesh which resulted in the deaths of ten prisoners, including MP Bobby Sands and TD Kieran Doherty. It was only after the hunger strike ended that the new nationalist councillors consented to take their seats. As a result, Larry

Kennedy had played no part in the formal Council proceedings. The DUP blocked a bid to nominate a colleague of the late councillor to fill his vacant seat, pushing instead for a by-election which the unionists won. That clear unity of purpose between the DUP and the loyalist killer gangs proved too much for even the Alliance Party whose spokesman, Will Glendenning, warned: 'This refusal by the DUP, backed by the leader of the Official Unionist grouping, to allow Mr Weir (who had been nominated by Larry Kennedy's election team) to be co-opted means that gunmen have succeeded in altering the make-up of Belfast City Council by murdering Councillor Kennedy'.

But not all the DUP's guns were trained on Republicans. In November, when the Lord Mayor took part in an official visit to Dublin, the Paisleyites successfully proposed a motion condemning her action and putting on ice any further cross-border contacts. Ironically, the DUP engaged in quite a lot of cross-border travelling themselves in the same period as Sammy Wilson and Rhonda Paisley, daughter of party founder Ian, engaged in a round of chat show engagements, courtesy of RTÉ. Unionist antipathy towards the Republic was to peak after the 1985 signing of the Anglo-Irish Agreement when the two large unionist parties united to ban any cross-border contacts.

In January 1982, Sean Flynn and Gerry Kelly of the IRSP issued a joint statement with Fergus O'Hare and John McAnulty of the People's Democracy announcing an end to their boycott of Council business. As it happened, Sean Flynn's participation in the affairs of the Council was as brief as it was sensational. He was shot and injured in an INLA feud just weeks later and, while still recuperating, was arrested on the word of an INLA member who had been 'turned' by the RUC. Once released on bail, Flynn fled to the South.

The DUP's poisonous campaign continued unabated throughout 1982 with their proposals – rejected by the Council – to halt the building of a leisure centre in the nationalist Lower Ormeau in South Belfast and to ban the development of co-operative links with Dublin Corporation.

In June 1983, Andersonstown republican Alex Maskey became the first Sinn Féin councillor to take a seat in Belfast City Council since 1920 when he was returned in a West Belfast by-election caused by the resignation of the sole remaining IRSP councillor Gerry Kelly, who found the bloody feuds ripping apart the tiny grouping inimical to a career in politics. A small but formidable figure, Maskey, as an ex-prisoner, former docker and one-time boxer, had an enviable c.v. He wasted no time leaving his mark on City Hall (quite literally, DUP Lord Mayor Eric Smyth later claimed). 'For too long, City Hall has operated as a bastion of unionism with a cosy arrangement which suits the SDLP, Alliance and Unionists', he told *The Irish News*. Most pundits agreed with unionist councillors who predicted the newly-elected Sinn Féin man would make a no-show at his first Council meeting. They were to be sorely disappointed when he turned up at his first meeting in July 1983 and proceeded to deliver a speech above the catcalls of the unionist councillors. However, after the histrionics for the press, Alex Maskey found that the unionists proceeded to work with him in the Council committees. 'The committees worked fairly well', he said, 'without much interference'.

But not for long, as the bar room ballad has it. At the end of 1983 when the Community Services Committee appointed Councillor Maskey as the Council's representative on the board of the community advice organisation, Community Technical Aid, and John McAnulty as its representative on the Steering Committee of the Citizens Advice Bureau, the DUP proposed that both nominations be rejected by the full Council. With the support of the Alliance Party, a motion from the DUP giving both the elbow was passed by the Council. Alliance members filled both vacancies. Said Maskey: 'These activities show that the unionists feel democracy is okay as long as the correct people are elected.'

In March 1984, Sean McKnight became the second Sinn Féin councillor to be elected to City Hall when he won a by-election caused by the failure of Sean Flynn – by now ensconced in

Dublin – to attend Council meetings. A canny Markets' social club manager with an impeccable republican pedigree, he arrived in the Council as the anti-Sinn Féin drive was heating up, courtesy of the colourful Scottish-born Shankill councillor George Seawright. At the February meeting of Council, DUP man Seawright announced that PD councillor John McAnulty didn't have the right to draw breath and – never one for half-measures – revealed that he had 'a soft spot for him in Milltown Cemetery'. Just weeks after his arrival, the full Council turned down a request by the Community Services Committee that Sean McKnight sit on the committee of the Markets' Community Centre, just yards from his own home.

In May 1984, Seawright's bitter sectarianism landed him in hot water with his party hierarchy when his comments at a meeting of the Belfast Education and Library Board were reported by the press. Speaking during a debate on Catholics who refused to stand for the British National Anthem during the BELB annual schools' concert, he proposed a novel way to stifle nationalist protest:

> Taxpayers' money would be better spent on an incinerator and burning the whole lot of them...The priests should be thrown in and burnt as well.

Two days later, Seawright was out canvassing on the Shankill Road in the company of party leader Ian Paisley who was standing for re-election to the European Parliament.

A special meeting of the Council was convened to consider Seawright's comments and to demand that the relevant Stormont Minister remove him from the Belfast Education and Library Board. Despite DUP attempts to amend a motion of censure and a bloodcurdling defence of his words by George Seawright, the proposal was carried. Seawright was dumped by the DUP in December 1984 but maintained a fiery presence in local politics until October 1986 when he was sentenced to nine months imprisonment for attacking Secretary of State Tom King as he visited City Hall. There was also an enigmatic side to George Seawright – he was one of the very few unionists who spoke to his republican counterparts, once joking to Fergus O'Hare, after both had been ordered out of a meeting, that they set up a club for expelled councillors. While his wife picked up the vacant seat in the Shankill by-election caused by his detention, Seawright's own chapter in the murky sectarian underbelly of political life in the North ended in December 1987 when he was shot dead by gunmen associated with the tiny INLA splinter group, the IPLO.

A welcome diversion from the increasingly belligerent exchanges between unionists and nationalists on the Council came in September 1984 when SDLP councillor Cormac Boomer landed a haymaker on the PD's Fergus O'Hare. The melée broke out when O'Hare approached the SDLP benches to ask the volatile Andersonstown SDLP man to sign a   petition condemning the plastic bullet killing in Belfast the previous month of John Downes. Boomer manhandled O'Hare over the benches before lashing out at colleague Pascal O'Hare when he tried to intervene. Unionist Good Samaritan John Carson rushed forward to separate the warring parties only to slip and land on his back. 'Unionists thought I had hit Carson and the whole place nearly erupted', O'Hare later recalled.

SDLP councillor Mary Muldoon railed against the 'horrible' behaviour of Boomer but when PD man John McAnulty rose to pass a motion censuring the SDLP representative, he was shouted down and a motion passed instead to eject O'Hare from the meeting. The RUC was duly called and escorted the PD representative from the chamber once again.

As 1984 rumbled to a close, it was a Tricolour above a leisure centre which again lit the blue touchpaper of explosive outrage among Belfast's unionists. When Whiterock Leisure Centre was to open officially in September 1984, the unionists refused to invite the West Belfast MP Gerry Adams – who had unseated Gerry Fitt of the SDLP the previous year – to the ceremony. In response, locals organised their own 'people's opening'. Gerry Adams was asked to cut the ribbon, an Irish language plaque marking the occasion was erected and the Tricolour hoisted, before a slap-up party for local children. Gerry Adams told reporters, 'In our view this community opening is the official opening.' Backing the event was community cleric Fr Des Wilson. 'Once the people speak', he declared, 'the churches and the politicians must accept their choice, even if they don't agree with that person'.

That was hardly a fashionable opinion in City Hall. Apoplectic unionists threatened to bring the shutters down on the new sports complex if the flag wasn't hauled down. 'I would like to see Whiterock Leisure Centre closed down or burnt down', said that soul of moderation, George Seawright. But at a specially-convened meeting of the Council, Seawright failed to get a seconder for his proposal to close the building if the flag and Gaeilge plaque weren't removed. Not one to take defeat lying down, Seawright led a UVF gang to the centre to remove the flag and was pictured by an invited photographer carrying the flag from the roof of the building while brandishing his legally-held pistol. Seawright brought the flag to the steps of Stormont, much to the amusement of West Belfast nationalists who thought that was the appropriate place for the national colours. Later, one of those involved in the dawn raid with Seawright, UVF leader William 'Frenchie' Merchant, was shot dead on the Shankill by the IRA.

On 1 December, a speculative motion by the DUP's Sammy Wilson to the effect that no fire safety maintenance work be carried out at the Whiterock centre until the offending flags – three were swiftly erected to replace the one spirited away by Seawright – were removed was also voted down. Earlier the same year, six people had died in a blaze at the Maysfield Leisure Centre in East Belfast. However, later the same month, a proposal that the centre be closed down in one month's time if the flags were still flying was passed. Stormont Education Minister Nicholas Scott intervened to remind councillors that they didn't have the power to close the complex down and that if they did the Council would have to repay a £1.5 government grant towards the building of the centre. Unionists might also find themselves personally responsible for £600,000 of ratepayers' money which had been spent on the centre if it were shut down, he added. Eventually, the dispute over the flag drifted off the front pages of the Belfast newspapers, but for a while the issue was considered so important that the *Sunday Tribune* advised its readers, 'If you wish to follow the development of the relationship between

Dublin and London, keep an eye on the flags over the Whiterock Leisure Centre.'

But the Tricolour wasn't the only flag exciting the attentions of Belfast councillors. In December 1984, John McAnulty was once again bundled out of a meeting, this time for branding the Union Jack 'a butcher's apron'. Tracing the historical antecedents of his metaphor back as far as the the Battle of Culloden in 1745, a resolute McAnulty refused to withdraw his statement or apologise to wounded unionists. In response, outraged City Fathers banned him from any further participation in civic affairs until he had recanted. Undeterred, McAnulty, setting down a marker for others to follow, slapped a court injunction on the unionists for 'de-electing' him. 'The way the Standing Orders are being used at the moment, the unionists can say what language is permissible. Insulting references to Catholics or nationalists are ignored or defended', he protested. 'Every opportunity is availed of to belittle nationalists and to hammer home the message that they have no role to play.'

Justice Hamilton ruled that the ban on McAnulty was illegal and ordered the Council to pay costs of £5,000. When the vindicated PD man returned to the chamber, unionists were unrepentant: the Reverend Eric Smyth of the DUP announced angrily that McAnulty should return to the 'Banana Republic', before launching into a litany of loud insults which eventually led to his dismissal on the votes of his colleagues.

With election fever starting to bite as the May 1985 poll neared, unionists stepped up their campaign of attrition and the SDLP, with one eye on the forthcoming polls, endorsed a rare display of nationalist unity to join with their PD and Sinn Féin counterparts to call a special meeting of council on the issue of the dilapidated Divis Flats in West Belfast. (Though eleven councillors can call a special meeting of Council on any issue, SDLP and Sinn Féin were so often at daggers drawn that the prerogative was rarely exercised.)

Unionists had other ways of whipping up sectarian emotions. Groups which were viewed as being 'too nationalist' were picked off like Taigs at a shipyard soirée. In September 1994, the Council stopped the annual grant to the Springhill Community House because it was led by Fr Des Wilson. New rules were introduced which restricted the rights of Sinn Féin members. The republican councillors were denied participation in outside delegations after Economy Minister Rhodes Boyson turned back Alex Maskey and Sean McKnight at the doors of Stormont Castle. Eager Alliance councillors backed the ban move even though SDLP members trenchantly opposed the proposal; in fact SDLP councillors stormed out of the meeting with Boyson when it became clear he wasn't willing to meet with the Sinn Féin members of the delegation.

The Council went on to pass motions demanding that the British introduce an oath of allegiance to the British monarch and an anti-violence declaration for councillors in an attempt to pave the way for a new Council resolution which would ban the Sinn Féin duo from all City Hall committees. However, the Council's own brief advised them any such move would be ultra vires – beyond the powers of the Council – and it was quickly dropped, for the time being. A motion in similar vein from Sammy Wilson to the effect that Council officials deny all assistance to Sinn Féin councillors met a similar fate. When the British did introduce the anti-violence declaration before the 1989 election, Sinn Féin candidates queued up to sign their names on the dotted line. After all, as Danny Morrison pointed out, if they had to sign an anti-violence declaration in Britain, the benches at Westminster would be empty.

As Sinn Féin prepared to triple its representation at the May '85 Council elections in the city, the unionists maintained their King Canute-style defiance in a building which they viewed as their personal fiefdom. Even Alliance Party members complained to the current affairs magazine Fortnight that the unionists behaved like 'swaggering bullies' who regarded City Hall as 'their personal property'. Unionism's final fling of the 1981-85 term came with a motion disassociating the Council from elected representatives who supported the IRA. Alex Maskey riposted that he had no desire to be associated with a Council which was 'bureaucratic, inefficient, conservative, hypocritical, right-wing, sectarian and anti-democratic'.

Both sides were braced for the new term.

3.

Belfast Says Ho-Ho

Sinn Féin's electoral bandwagon moved up a gear for the
Assembly elections of 1982, where the party garnered
ten per cent of the vote, but its first foray into council
elections had come in March 1983 when 21-year-old Séamus
Kerr won a spectacular by-election victory to capture a seat in
Omagh Council. The Carrickmore man, who got 2,289 votes to
the SDLP's 654, became the first Sinn Féin representative to
take a seat on a local council since the 1920s. At the
Westminster elections in June, the Sinn Féin percentage of the
vote jumped to 13.4 per cent and Gerry Adams relieved Gerry
Fitt of the West Belfast seat.

Despite a more modest showing in the European elections in
1984, the Sinn Féin sights were now firmly set on the local
government elections of May 1985. Other loins were also being
girded.

Ian Paisley launched his party's manifesto for the councils,
whose powers were limited to 'bogs, bins and bodies', with a
sledgehammer and vowed to spearhead a 'crusade' against Sinn
Féin. The DUP election slogan was 'Smash Sinn Féin;
Annihilate the IRA' while the UUP pledged that they would put
Sinn Féin 'out of business'. The party published an election
poster showing an armed IRA man standing over Danny
Morrison and Gerry Adams with the message 'IRA Army
Council on your next district council'. In some unionist areas,
the posters were mistaken for Sinn Féin election flyers and torn
down. Sammy Wilson warned of more strife on the already
troubled Belfast City Council if, as he feared, 'half a battalion

14

of IRA men' were returned for Sinn Féin in the May poll. Meanwhile, the DUP deputy leader Peter Robinson was threatening a party pull-out from the councils if Sinn Féin candidates weren't prevented by the British government from taking any seats they might win. To push home his point, he tried to pass a motion at Westminster banning Sinn Féin councillors from councils with a unionist majority.

Sinn Féin fielded 90 candidates for the May elections – just over half the number standing for the SDLP – including three sitting councillors, Alex Maskey and Sean McKnight in Belfast and Séamus Kerr. One quarter of the candidates were under 30. The party won 59 seats – 29 more than the deliberately low target of 30 it had set itself – and took 11.8 per cent of the vote. In the process, it effectively wiped out the Irish Independence Party and the independents elected on the back of their support of the republican prison protest. The SDLP weathered the storm of Sinn Féin's enthusiastic entry into council politics, dropping just two seats from its 104 total in 1981.What an indignant *Irish Independent* dubbed 'Sinn Féin's surprisingly strong showing which took both Dublin and London by surprise' left the party with representatives on 17 of the North's 26 Councils and made it the majority nationalist party in Fermanagh, Belfast, Omagh and Cookstown. In Omagh, Séamus Kerr was appointed to the chair but his acceptance speech in Irish was drowned out by DUP supporters in the public gallery with shouts of 'No Pope here' and 'Speak English'.

At the first gathering of his party's newly-elected Sinn Féin councillors in the Conway Mill, Gerry Adams spelt out their priorities in local government:

> We will defend the rights of nationalists but on those Councils on which Sinn Féin has strong influence we will also ensure fair play for unionists. Despite the efforts of unionists east of the Bann to disenfranchise our voters, we will do our utmost to ensure that the unionists have an opportunity to play a full part in the council.

Unionist leaders Ian Paisley and James Molyneaux had their own post-election agenda. On the day of the election count, they joined forces in Belfast City Hall to sign a new treaty against Sinn Féin, pledging their parties to boycott the republican representatives. Effectively, this committed the unionists to opposing all motions from Sinn Féin, barring the party from holding the chairs of council committees, and walking out from council chambers when Sinn Féin representatives were speaking in order to leave meetings without a quorum. The Belfast weekly, *Andersonstown News*, predicted that it would not be the presence of Sinn Féin but the unionists' obstructionist tactics which would make the councils unworkable, adding: 'The Sinn Féin terrier will be forever snapping at unionist heels and highlighting much of the bunkum attached to our form of representative democracy.'

A political new kid on the block who had enlisted in the republican movement along with a band of like-minded Irish language activists in the wake of the hunger strike, I was a reluctant candidate in the 1985 Council elections, allowing my name to go forward on the understanding that I didn't have a snowball's chance in hell of being elected. Of course, announcing that you didn't want to be elected was a mental safe-house for republicans, allowing falsely modest wannabe politicians like myself to hide their electoral hunger under a skin-deep I-couldn't-care-less-if-I-lose veneer. It also became a well-established ruse of wily election strategists to assure prospective candidates that they could afford to let their names go forward as they faced certain defeat, even when their own internal party tallies told them otherwise.

By mid-1985, I was a three-year veteran of the republican movement, having known a few of the supergrasses but thankfully, none having known me (or, as was more likely, not considering me of any import in the lists of 'players' they dutifully coughed up for their Branch handlers). The years following the hunger strike were a time of great optimism in republican Ireland, even if delight at electoral successes was serving to smother the much-needed debate on the IRA campaign. As well as juggling the responsibilities of my unspectacular journalistic career, I was   promoting the Irish language via the Sinn Féin Cultural Department – which sounds like a cross between a New Romantic band and a Calvin Klein deodorant but which was in fact a fairly effective group of battlers who put the question of Gaeilge rights on the map. Putting the arán on the table was the *Andersonstown News*, where I effectively worked five days a week even though I dutifully described myself as a freelance journalist and wrote under a string of prosaic pen-names to keep some distance between my newsroom haven and the attentions of loyalists in and out of uniform. Somewhere in there, I had tied the knot with Helen O'Hare, and moved into a home-cum-bunker in Beechmount off the Falls Road but until the first bambino came along, political work was the number one priority.

When the elections came around, I was considered to have a high enough profile due to my language campaigning to be allowed to make up the numbers in the Upper Falls electoral area where Sinn Féin entertained hopes of having former Armagh prisoner Tish Holland join Alex Maskey in City Hall. The middle-class area of the ward was carved off – middle-class equating roughly in West Belfast to employed – and I set to work drumming up support. Most householders thought Máirtín was a girl's name and even the 'green' voters – those expected to vote for Sinn Féin – fought hard to conceal their disappointment when I arrived on their doorstep. Tish and Alex were dutifully returned with an increased majority and I cruised in sixth – a position for which there were no medals. Though facing an uphill challenge in the five-seater, it was still a disappointment to be pipped at the post – pun intended by newspaper columnists at the time – by the Alliance Party's Pip Glendenning. A former neighbour of mine from Ramoan Gardens in Andersonstown (and since deceased), Pip and councillor husband Will were to be the last standard bearers for the middle-class Alliance Party in West Belfast. Two thirds of the votes from the last SDLP candidate to be excluded in the Upper Falls contest transferred to the Alliance Party to give the party one seat alongside a brace apiece for the SDLP and Sinn Féin. I unclipped my rosette and settled back for a four-year wait in the stands until the next local government elections rolled along. In my humble absence, there was plenty to keep all eyes on the City Hall arena.

When the new Council convened in June 1985, the Shinners had for the first time in three generations a strong team of councillors. With seven members to the SLDP's six, they were the largest nationalist party even if, in a 51-seat chamber, their ability to affect change was severely limited. Among the republicans were the aforementioned Tish Holland, a woman only a few years my senior but who was accused by the British of once being part of a chic early-seventies Upper Andersonstown IRA unit which sported knee-length kaftan coats and carbine rifles, and Turf Lodge stalwart Lily Fitzsimmons who had come to politics via the mothers' protest over the conditions endured by H-Block prisoners, including her son Sean. In a hysterical speech, Sammy Wilson 'welcomed' the newcomers to City Hall. 'It's obnoxious for unionists to have to sit across the chamber from evil gunmen who have crawled out of West Belfast, evil human pus who are part of the Republic's poison in this city', he told the inaugural meeting of the new term.

It's not known whether Wilson, who kept up this bitter barrage for the following 14 years – and counting – ever asked himself why Catholics found his behaviour appallingly sectarian. In his defence, party colleagues would insist that he was quite a fun guy to be with who liked nothing better than to bare his soul and let it all hang out. The naked truth, of course, is that he is as funny as vomit.

The vicious unionist counter-charge on Sinn Féin began immediately. All appointments on outside boards – among them the powerful Belfast Education and Library Board and the Health Councils – were denied Sinn Féin members. In fact, every one of the 48 external appointments made by the Council at the first meeting of the new term went to unionists – fortunately for some of those chosen, basic numeracy and literacy were not prerequisites for positions on the governing body of the Education and Library Board. But some key positions on the new committees which were formed throughout the month of June were given to the SDLP and Alliance by the unionist brüderbond.

For the first official Council meeting of the new term, Rhonda Paisley brought along a toy trumpet which she blew every time a Sinn Féin councillor tried to speak. Soul-mate Sammy Wilson proposed that the Sinn Féin members be barred from the Members' Room and the City Hall car park. Town Clerk Cecil Ward, an urbane figure who always gave the impression that he would rather be off listening to his beloved Ulster Orchestra than refereeing the Council dog-fights, ruled that both proposals would be illegal. Sinn Féin was denied any positions on the Council's most powerful body, the General Purposes and Finance Committee, while the legal minimum of places – two – were allocated the party on the Council's other standing committees. A succession of determined efforts by Sinn Féin councillors to speak were drowned out by a cacophony of howls from the unionist benches which reached a rousing crescendo at night's end when the unionists, complete with anti-Sinn Féin posters and accompanied by Paisley mère, Eileen, and Peter Robinson who had come along for the show, rose to sing 'The Queen'. Robinson told reporters that 'hygiene inspectors' would now be needed at City Hall.

Incoming Lord Mayor, liberal unionist John Carson, urged his colleagues to resume normal business at future meetings, even while maintaining their resolute opposition to Sinn Féin. It was an appeal which fell on deaf ears. When the First Citizen invited Catholic Primate Cardinal Tomás Ó Fiaich to his inauguration dinner, George Seawright (who had been re-elected on a Protestant Unionist ticket) taunted him across the Council chamber, 'Go away and play with your Rosary Beads'.

The anti-Sinn Féin crusade sharpened in November with the adoption of a Council motion suspending all Council meetings as a protest against the presence of the republicans. But Unionists had not been idle in the meetings leading up to the suspension of business. Sean McKnight was expelled from the management committee of the Markets Community Centre and a unionist appointed in his place, while at the monthly meetings of council, unionists thumped their bench desks with their fists and hammered the floor with their feet to prevent the Sinn Féin members being heard. At one meeting, the seven Sinn Féin councillors rose from their benches and sat down beside the cat-calling DUP members – leading to the adjournment of business.

The public opening of a new community centre in the nationalist Ardoyne district of North Belfast also proved a bone of contention with unionists when it was revealed the ribbon-cutting event had included the erection of the Tricolour and the unveiling of a plaque in Irish. At an emergency meeting of Council in October, unionists hit back by postponing the official Council opening of the centre and demanding a meeting with the Stormont Minister responsible for funding the project. Unimpressed, the Minister let it be known that the Council would have to repay the £310,000 grant it obtained towards the cost of the centre were the premises to be closed. The Local Government Auditor warned that he could also individually surcharge councillors who voted for closure, effectively making the unionists put their money where their mouth is, traditionally an effective threat in northern politics. Despite that uncompromising message, the Council's Community Services Committee ordered the closure of the facility – a proposal which fell when unionists backed down at the next full meeting of Council.

Disruption of Council business moved up a gear in November 1985 in protest at the signing of the Anglo-Irish Agreement. Tactics used to protest the presence of Sinn Féin in the council chambers were now deployed against the 'Anglo-Irish Diktat': meetings were adjourned indefinitely; repetitive motions condemning the Hillsborough Treaty were passed at countless Council meetings; and government bodies were boycotted.

A formal Belfast City Council motion cut off all contact with Stormont Ministers. Along with their Irish government counterparts, they were barred from entering any Council property and struck off official invitation lists to civic events. That particular edict was later extended to cover all civil servants from the Republic as well as officials at the Irish Secretariat at Maryfield – focus for unionist fury. Ironically, the most immediate result of the 'no-go' policy was a dramatic fall-off in business at the Council-owned Belfast Castle – recently renovated at a cost of £2m – as prestigious organisations switched venue for their annual conferences rather than snub British and Irish government officials. Cross-border activity, already virtually non-existent, was axed by the Council and all council powers delegated to the Town Clerk during the suspension of Council meetings. The icing on the cake for irate unionists was the draping (without planning permission) of a forty-foot banner, bearing the legend 'Belfast Says No', across the dome of City Hall.

With nationalists unable to agree a joint response to the unionist tactics, the Alliance Party launched a court challenge to the no-business policy.

In early February 1996, the High Court ruled in favour of the Alliance Party, stating that the policy of indefinitely adjourning Council meetings was ultra vires. The Council was instructed to remove the 'Belfast Says No' banner from City Hall, reconvene meetings of standing committees and strike a rate for the incoming financial year before 15 February. Unionists dismissed the court ruling and initiated an appeal. 'There's only a chance in a million that we will lose this court case', declared Sammy Wilson. Despite Wilson's optimism, the appeal was swiftly thrown out and costs awarded against the Council. In their judgment, the Appeal Court judges again insisted that the Council immediately strike the rate. Undeterred, the unionists continued their policy of adjourning the monthly meetings of Council. According to Sammy Wilson, the 'Alliance Party poison' had killed the Council.

More likely to face their demise were the many community groups in the city who had been operating without their regular Council grants as a consequence of the adjournment policy. As the Council's fuel supplies dwindled and it appeared that the weekly refuse collection would have to be abandoned due to a lack of petrol, the unionists remained unmoved. An 8 March deadline for setting the rate came and went as the Belfast unionists joined forces with 17 other councils to refuse to strike the rate, eventually forcing the British to send in a Commissioner for two days to strike the rate, greenlight urgent Council business and release funds.

It was only when five Ulster Unionists broke ranks on 6 May to vote with the opposition parties to resume normal business that the adjournment policy finally ran into the sand. For their troubles, all five had the whip removed.

But whatever uncertainty there was in Ulster Unionist circles about the benefits of the adjournment policy, there were no such doubts in the minds of the DUP zealots. The election of Sammy Wilson as Lord Mayor on 3 June 1986 and the appointment of Rhonda Paisley as Lady Mayoress was a shot in the arm for the adjournment campaign. Though, in accordance with court rulings, meetings of the standing committees were once again convened, the unionists continued to adjourn all business.

At the annual general meeting of Council on 17 June, independent unionist and self-styled 'Super Prod' Frank Millar proposed that Sinn Féin be barred from sitting on the incoming Parks Department Committee. Though such a suggestion was ruled illegal, unionists decided not to reconvene the seven standing committees until the republican-free General Purposes and Finance Committee (the only committee re-established) had re-visited the tickly issue of committee membership. This was not a particularly complex Council code for finding means of barring Sinn Féin from participation in the committees.

In the meantime, there was some ducking and weaving by unionists in a bid to stay one step ahead of the courts. The illegal 'Belfast Says No' banner was moved from the dome and re-erected in the Council car park where it was rarely seen by the public but still served the purpose of marking out the City Hall as unionist territory. The Fair Employment Commission refused to act to have the banner removed on the grounds that it was contrary to all fair employment legislation and obviously discriminatory to Catholic staff. The banner, though, did spark a rare comic crack in the unionist armour when it was changed at Christmas time to read, Belfast Says Ho-Ho!

By the first anniversary of the Anglo-Irish Agreement in November 1986, the unionists had good reason to be pleased with the success of their campaign to block normal Council business. There hadn't been a committee meeting worthy of the name since Thatcher and FitzGerald had signed the Hillsborough treaty while the monthly full meetings of Council were being used to piss on the Agreement parade. In June, the Council's monthly session completed only one major piece of business – inviting the Stormont Assembly, disbanded by Secretary of State Tom King, to gather in City Hall. Likewise, at its October meeting the Council established a sub-committee to co-ordinate its anti-Agreement campaign but adjourned all other business.

4.

Docking with the Mothership

Unionists ushered in 1987 in bullish form, setting up a new committee – similar to those already existing in those liberal heartlands of Larne, Cookstown and Lisburn – to oppose the Anglo-Irish Agreement. The new body's first bold step was to buy expensive advertisements in the London *Times* and *Daily Telegraph* to plead the anti-Agreement case. Publicity trips to the 'mainland' followed shortly after. The five member, all-unionist committee immediately slapped a quarter penny hike on the rates bill to bring in the £90,000 it needed for its campaign. Easy come, easy go: £9,000 alone was spent on 'Ulster Says No' bonfires on New Year's Day 1997. Heavy fogs meant even the gang of five on the anti-agreement committee had trouble seeing the Council's handiwork. Warnings from Town Clerk Cecil Ward that the expenditure on 'wholly political' activities could be illegal under the 1972 Local Government Act went unheeded by the unionists who claimed, tongue firmly in cheek, that their campaign was in the public interest. SDLP councillor Brian Feeney bust a blood vessel at the antics of the new committee. 'No important powers will ever be given back to these people as long as their bigotry and malice remains unchanged', he told reporters.

The prospect of another High Court case served to cool the heels of Ulster Unionist councillors who feared the anti-Agreement campaign was proving counter-productive. In January 1997, they refused to vote through another motion continuing the adjournment policy. Satisfying themselves with having blocked an effort to re-establish the Council's standing committees, they then walked out. Their deserted DUP colleagues, fearing the opposition councillors would use their majority to restore normality to the Council, succeeded in forcing the adjournment of the meeting.

Sensing a weakening in Ulster Unionist support for the campaign to paralyse Council business, the Alliance Party moved to suspend the threat of legal action hanging over the Council. On 15 January, they petitioned the High Court to freeze a case they had taken against the Official Unionist councillors for failing to comply with the court's judgment of the previous February which declared the adjournment policy illegal. 'The Official Unionists are afraid of a court action', said Alliance North Belfast councillor Tom Campbell. 'There's no doubt about that.' Although the court responded by allowing the Council until 2 February to strike a rate, the DUP was not impressed. Alliance Party leader on the Council David Cooke accused the DUP hardliners of using 'threats, insults and intimidation' against his councillors. Lord Mayor Sammy Wilson hit back, branding the Alliance Party councillors 'the boot-boys of the NIO' and 'pin-striped Alliance thugs'.

Ulster Unionists stayed away from the full meeting of Council in February but in an unexpected twist, the opposition councillors failed to strike a rate when Sinn Féin refused to join the Alliance and SDLP members in outvoting the DUP irredentists. The republicans insisted they needed more time to study the rate estimates, which in real-speak meant they were flexing their political muscle. A fortnight later, and with pride satisfied, Sinn Féin joined forces with the other parties at a special meeting of Council to strike a new rate, with 21 votes against the DUP's 14. But the unionists repaired damaged bridges between their warring factions to stymie opposition efforts to reappoint standing committees until, said Sammy Wilson, they had an opportunity to study ways of ensuring the reborn committees would deliver 'unionist-loyalist dominance'. But the belated unionist about-turn didn't shield them from the wrath of the High Court over the continued boycott of normal business: the Council was fined £25,000 for its refusal to observe the court's rulings. A later ruling by the Local Government Auditor that protesting councillors were responsible for clearing that fine meant each unionist had to stump up almost £1,000. For the next ten years, irate unionists would hold that penalty against their Alliance adversaries and refer to it frequently at Council meetings. Reports that some unionists never divvied up their share of the fine, leaving colleagues to pay over the odds, were never confirmed.

The unionist campaign against the Anglo-Irish Agreement continued apace with a series of moves which served only to strip unionism of the little power it exercised. In February 1997, the unionists resigned *en masse* from the health and education boards which they monopolised. The NIO side-stepped a mischievous SDLP suggestion that the vacant seats be handed over to councillors willing to take their places.

The committees' master-plan was revealed in mid-March when a special meeting of Council endorsed what Councillor Alban Maginness of the SDLP slammed in *The Irish News* as 'an elected dictatorship' in City Hall. The complex new system had been drawn up with the help of deft and skilful legal minds – fuelling (unproven) suspicions that unionists who basked in their academic under-achievement had received assistance from senior Council officials. Under the new system, the standing committees were re-established but now there were 17 members rather than 13 – all the extra places went to unionists. The quorum for a committee meeting was raised from three to eight but – in an admirable stroke of Machiavellian genius – opposition members were never allowed more than seven members on a committee. If frightened unionists ever feared that, because friends were absent, they were about to be out-voted on any issue they could simply leave the room and proceedings would have to be aborted. From now on, unionists would sit on three, four or even five standing committees – which ranged from the powerful, purse-string controlling General Purposes and Finance Committee to the Town

Planning Committee and Leisure Services Committee – while Alliance, SDLP and Sinn Féin members could have representation on a maximum of two committees. That was effectively the minimum representation allowable under the law. For good measure, Sinn Féin councillors were barred from the General Purposes Committee while the Alliance and SDLP groupings were allowed just one seat apiece. On committees where Sinn Féin was represented, unionists would pointedly leave an empty seat between themselves and any Sinn Féin representative, for fear, presumably, of contamination from republicans who kept pigs in the bath and coal in the kitchen. To unionists who had seen vote-rigging disappear with their beloved Stormont, this was a gerrymandering wet dream. It was also totally unnecessary and ultimately counter-productive for unionists who under normal democratic rules enjoyed a clear majority in the Council and in all committees. Nevertheless, in June 1987 the annual general meeting of Council reaffirmed the new structure as Council policy.

But normal business was still a long way off. Meetings in April and May were adjourned – the latter as a protest against the presence of Sinn Féin in the chamber. Between June and November, Council meetings were conducted without any discussion while nationalist councillors were regularly ejected from meetings for daring to speak out against this policy.

It was also a case of back to the future in the reconvened committees. Some meetings lasted only 90 seconds; exactly long enough to allow the unionists to adopt the report of the Department Director. But delay was tolerated if it meant rubbing nationalist noses in the proverbial. Grants to community groups in the Short Strand and Divis Flats were halted. To the delight of unionists, backing for their McCarthyite witch-hunt came from an unusual source – SDLP councillor Brian Feeney. In an interview, subsequently recorded in Council minutes of 19 June 1987, he claimed that 'certain so-called community centres in West Belfast were receiving government assistance even though they were in fact only Provo fronts'. Using Councillor Feeney's alleged comments as justification for their action, unionists ordered the Director of Community Services (a Catholic who had survived an assassination attempt) to immediately launch an enquiry to determine the truth of the SDLP man's claims. When well-known community activists in the city raised a question mark over the political vetting of nationalist community groups – and the implications to funding of the ongoing adjournment policy – they were targeted by angry unionists. Sammy Wilson warned his critics in the community sector, 'They ought to keep their tongues in their mouths before using adjectives which unionists will remember once the boycott is over'.

But with the Council now functioning – albeit fitfully – the media had a field day reporting the unionist ban on a naturist society from using a Council swimming pool. The DUP, including the later infamous streaker Sammy Wilson, led the charge. Nigel Dodds, a secretary to Ian Paisley, reminded councillors that 'cavorting in such a manner was contrary to God's law' – a position endorsed by party colleague Ted Ashby who revealed to Council that he had never seen his wife naked in their 50 years of marriage.

In October 1987, Sinn Féin's Council campaign received a fillip when myself and former blanket man Fra McCann – a driving force in the fight to demolish Divis Flats and fully deserving of his nickname, Cuddles – were elected to the Council in West Belfast by-elections. The double poll had been called following the shock resignation of sitting Alliance Party members Will and Pip Glendenning who decided to put the business of rearing a family before the headache of City Hall. Their departure from politics was to mark the exit in perpetuity of the Alliance Party from West Belfast. A half-hearted unionist attempt to fill one of the vacancies by the co-option of one Brian 'Oliver Cromwell' Miskimmon failed when nationalists objected (co-options were only permissible with the backing of all 51 elected members). In Lower Falls, Fra McCann was a shoo-in. He garnered 5,425 votes (a majority of 3,507 over the SDLP) while in Upper Falls, Sinn Féin outpolled the SDLP by over 700 votes. (In Lower Falls, the Alliance Party vote fell from 1,200 in 1985 to just 173.) Sinn Féin representation on the Council had risen overnight from seven to nine seats. Coming just a few months after the attempted assassination at his Andersonstown home of Council leader Alex Maskey, the result was seen as a public endorsement of the Sinn Féin Council team. Seriously injured in the shotgun attack, Alex Maskey retained his seat on the Council though he never recovered full health until some years afterwards.

Sinn Féin now had nine representatives on the Council as opposed to six apiece for the SDLP and Alliance but the combined total of the three parties was still five short of the magic 26 which would give them an overall majority. I entered City Hall six years into a concerted unionist blitzkrieg designed to reduce republicans to invisible public representatives. Needless to say, those same unionists were distinctly unimpressed by Sinn Féin's double electoral whammy. When I tried to speak a few words of Irish in my first contribution to Council on 3 November, I was unceremoniously shown the door by the Lord Mayor for daring to speak through my Erse.

The IRA's calamitous Remembrance Day bombing in Enniskillen inflamed unionist passions on the Council and, in the nationalist community, put the brakes on Sinn Féin's electoral march. Accidental deaths caused by IRA activities were to be a recurring theme of the next several years, culminating in the disastrous Shankill Road fish shop bombing of October 1993. In response to the Enniskillen bombing, unionists revived their adjournment policy and set about new strategies to block Sinn Féin. In November and December, unionist councillors locked committee room doors to deny Sinn Féin members access. The party hit back by initiating a court action accusing the unionists of preventing them from discharging their responsibilities as elected representatives. At the full monthly meetings of Council, frenzied unionists erupted in anger every time a Sinn Féin councillor rose to speak. Minutes from the standing committees were rubber-stamped without discussion and DUP hardliners proposed the relocation of Council meetings to a community centre in the loyalist Highfield area in West Belfast.

Given new vigour by the Enniskillen tragedy, the unionist boycott was as staunch – and as absurd – as ever at the beginning of 1988. Meetings were aborted, committees refused to carry out normal business, and Sinn Féin members were gagged at Council meetings. Only the General Purposes and Finance Committee – a Sinn Féin-free zone – was operating with any degree of normality but even then the bulk of its time was taken up plotting the fightback against Sinn Féin and the Anglo-Irish Agreement. However, among the less urgent items of business the Committee managed to sanction was the expenditure of £17,000 on sparkling ermine robes for councillors (this was a particular bargain in unionist eyes as Sinn Féin councillors in Belfast refused to wear the official robes of office). A Dublin bid to build bridges with their Belfast counterparts also got short shrift from the General Purposes and Finance Committee when unionists turned down the offer of a commemorative Viking ring to mark the capital's millennium celebrations. (I wrote to Dublin First Citizen Carmencita Herdeman to apologise for the boorish behaviour of the unionists and received a letter in return assuring me the ring could be picked up at any time in the future. Present-day councillors seeking a gesture of reconciliation for the millennium, please note!) The Committee also gave its blessing to a plan to repair a statue of the Reverend Hugh 'Roaring' Hanna – a 19th century Ian Paisley responsible for inciting sectarian violence – and re-site it in the grounds of City Hall.

A rate was struck at the full Council meeting in February 1988 – though Sinn Féin was prevented from voicing its tuppence worth on the issue – but a rider condemning 'fascist murdering republicans' was added for fear that the loyalist public would feel the Council was going soft.

At meetings of the standing committees, motions were passed endorsing the reports from officials before the unionists would scurry from the room, leaving the meetings without a quorum. While there may have been little opportunity for reasoned

debate, there were heated exchanges over a whole raft of
unionist decisions. These included a move to ban funding to
the Short Strand Festival – a community event in the
beleaguered East Belfast nationalist district – the green-light for
an Ulster Covenant exhibition in a Council leisure centre (in an
attack of hyperbole, I branded this as akin to a Nazi exhibition
in a synagogue); and a refusal to open a pedestrian gate from
the City Cemetery in West Belfast onto the neighbouring
Whiterock Road until the Council received a full report on the
cost to the ratepayer of IRA attacks on civic property! No
niggling restriction on nationalists was too petty for the City
Fathers.

In March 1988, the unionists were forced to abandon their
revamped adjournment policy when Sinn Féin threatened to
follow the Alliance Party into court if business wasn't carried
out normally. 'It's wonderful the effect the whiff of a court case
in the air can have', commented the SDLP's Alban Maginness.
But the abrasive anti-republican campaign continued unabated.
Sammy Wilson and Rhonda Paisley became the self-appointed
cheerleaders of the unionist mob, whipping their colleagues
into a frenzy every time a Sinn Féin member tried to address the
Council. A republican councillor rising to his or her feet was the
signal for a chorus of insults, feet-thumping and bench-bashing
from the unionist ranks.

But there was still room to fine-tune the Council's already
gerrymandered committee system. In April, the Leisure
Services Committee – on which I dutifully served – decided to
set up a sub-committee which included all its unionist members
but excluded Sinn Féin and the SDLP's troublesome Brian
Feeney. The SDLP man's exclusion was hardly unexpected;
Committee Chair Tommy Patton, a doddering dinosaur,
regularly interrupted contributions from Councillor Feeney to
accuse him of trying to close down aircraft manufacturers
Shorts by spotlighting their atrocious fair employment record.
Despite the fact that there were five leisure centres in West
Belfast, the exclusion of myself and Fra McCann meant the
area went unrepresented on the sub-committee. That was one

worry Brian Feeney didn't have; despite generous offers of government grants, City Hall unionists had always refused to site a leisure centre in his nationalist North Belfast ward.

A month later the Community Services Committee set up its own sub-committee, purportedly to examine its workload. Three Sinn Féin members of the main committee were excluded from the new body which concentrated its energies on pruning the Departmental budget – despite on some occasions only attracting three members to its meetings. When the Parks Committee – which boasted four Sinn Féin councillors, made up of our original two plus the by-election pair – established a sub-committee to take responsibility for a wide range of issues, the republicans were once again persona non grata. The SDLP hardly did much better. One of their members was permitted to serve on the Leisure sub-committee but they endured a blanket ban from the Parks and Community Services sub-committees. In essence, the sub-committees became the main decision-making bodies, usurping the role of the larger body. Every decision, in theory, had to be ratified by the principal committee but this amounted simply to a unionist rubber-stamp once a month.

When opposition members tried to raise issues relevant to their own constituents at main committee meetings, unionists would storm out – leaving proceedings without a quorum – or shunt the matter into a sub-committee limbo where it could be ignored. Thus when I, in a rush of Utopian blood to the head, proposed that the Parks Committee organise a development plan for Gaelic sports, unionists voted to dispatch the issue to their sub-committee – a no-go area for nationalists. Once there, the unionists conveniently forgot to discuss the proposal.

Though the unionists considered it legal to bar Sinn Féin members from the rash of new sub-committees – an erroneous view as it emerged but one which was supported by some Council officials who should have known better – they balked at changing Standing Orders to bar the party from actually attending the sub-committee proceedings. However, under

Standing Orders, non-members of a sub-committee could only speak on the invitation of the Chairman.

On cue, Sinn Féin councillors trooped along to the sub-committee meetings (though they drew the line at ringing bells and crying 'unclean' as they went). In response to this invasion by the proles, unionists introduced a ruling that non-members couldn't sit at the committee table. Again this apartheid policy was given the nod by some blinkered officials who were clearly allowing their personal political preferences to affect their normally officious approach to Council business. It was a restriction too far for even the meekest Sinn Féiner and when, in October 1988, an irate Fra McCann ignored the cordon sanitaire around the sub-committee members and threw his size 14s up on the mahogany veneer, the unionists abandoned their meeting in horror. From that date on, the unionists gave up efforts to try and force Sinn Féin councillors to sit in seats set aside for their use at the back of the committee room.

Throughout, unionists continued to give the two fingers to Council protocol. Opposition members were effectively deprived of any input into the business of Council, whether at full Council or committee level. 'Pre-meeting meetings' were organised for unionist members before each committee and Council meeting to agree a united approach to the items on the agenda. This kitchen cabinet would select members to propose and second reports from officials so that business could be rushed through without discussion.

Monthly meetings were mini skirmishes between the Sinn Féin contingent and unionists determined to prevent them speaking. There was uproar on the unionist benches when Sinn Féin members tried to speak and republicans who ignored the Lord Mayor's predictable instructions to sit down were dumped out on their arse. In a party which normally left its women-folk at home, Rhonda Paisley was determined not to be outdone by soul-mate Sammy Wilson. When Alex Maskey hobbled into his first Council meeting after the shotgun attempt on his life which cost him large tracts of his bowel, she shouted 'leadbelly' across the chamber at him, much to the delight of her guffawing colleagues. The odd thinking unionist argued that the cat-calling and abuse wasn't projecting a positive image of unionism – and that Sinn Féin's standing in its own community was, if anything, enhanced by the treatment meted out to its members. But such sophisticated logic smacked of Lundyism to Paisley and co. At the May meeting, Alex Maskey was ejected when he insisted on speaking on a Council decision to deny CND the use of a public park for an anti-nuclear festival. Things went downhill in June even though, in a preliminary finding, the courts warned the unionists that they had to permit all councillors to participate in Council business. The only concession by unionists to the threat of court action was to leave their seats at the June meeting when Sinn Féin members rose to speak. Cat-calling would then continue from the door of the chamber where the unionists gathered. Three Sinn Féin councillors were 'silenced' by the unionists, as David McKitterick reported in his book of 'Troubles' reportage, *Despatches*:

> 'I would like', the Sinn Féin councillor said, 'to raise item B572 of the minutes'. All 30 unionists councillors immediately rose to their feet and headed for the door. 'We object to the proposed closure of St George's Market', the Sinn Féin man said. One of the unionists, Alderman Sammy Wilson, turned and shouted, 'Gunman, gunman, that's what he is'. His colleagues joined in: 'Gangsters, IRA men get them out'. Some banged desks... After some minutes of bedlam, Alderman Wilson could be heard proposing that the Sinn Féin councillor 'be no longer heard'. A quick show of hands and the Sinn Féin microphone was cut off and business moved on.
>
> After a few minutes, Sinn Féin councillor Sean McKnight stood up. The Lord Mayor, Nigel Dodds, called everyone else who wanted to speak, then finally pointed to him and said: 'You. What's my name?' Mr McKnight demanded. 'The Lord Mayor repeated: 'You'.
>
> Throughout the evening, Mr Dodds, a young solicitor who is one of the Rev Ian Paisley's closest aides, would not name him or any of the Sinn Féin councillors. When a Sinn

Féin man called for more recognition of the Irish language and spoke a few words in Irish, the Lord Mayor called him to order: 'It's not in order to speak a foreign language in this chamber. You'll not be allowed to say that as long as I'm in the chair.'

Unionist councillors, who had left their seats and were chatting over at the door, quickly resumed their seats, proposed that the Sinn Féin man not be heard, and voted him down. Rhonda Paisley, her father's daughter in every way, said Sinn Féin used the Irish language as a political weapon. 'It drips with their bloodthirsty saliva', she said. 'For heaven's sake, grow up', an SDLP man told Alderman Wilson. 'Show a bit of political maturity.' The said Alderman, undaunted, continued to deliver taunts about what he termed 'leprechaun language'.

Republicans found themselves impaled on the horns of a dilemma. Members of the press – positioned between the rival political factions – couldn't hear the Sinn Féin members speaking due to the uproar caused by the empty unionist vessels. What chance then that they could make any meaningful points during debate? While the unionist tactic certainly didn't enhance their own troglodyte image, it was fairly effective in neutering Sinn Féin. Under the leadership of Sammy Wilson, the unionists were boasting that their disruptive behaviour was preventing Sinn Féin councillors from speaking. There was a feeling in nationalist areas that Sinn Féin, while exposing the bigotry of the DUP and UUP, was unable to provide adequate representation for its constituents within the Council proper. Meetings of the Sinn Féin group considered a number of methods to tackle the unionist white noise tactic. The suggestion, in jest, that the ringleaders be given a tanking in the loos and told to watch their manners was discarded in favour of an in-your-face ploy designed to flush out the unionist old guard who had no stomach for the confrontational tactics of Wilson and co.

At the full meeting of Council in July 1988, unionists took up where they had left off. When a Sinn Féin member rose to speak, the majority of the OUP and DUP councillors came off their benches to stand at the door into the chamber. From that vantage point, they created a dreadful racket so that the republicans couldn't be heard. Sinn Féin dispatched those members not speaking to the door to confront the Orange mob. The tension was ratcheted up a notch or two when the inimitable Elizabeth Seawright responded to this challenge by spraying the Sinn Féin members with deodorant. Andersonstown councillor Tish Holland was maintaining a lonely vigil on the Sinn Féin benches by addressing an issue in the minutes when a number of unionist heavies crossed the chamber to the Sinn Féin benches and started to push her. At the door meanwhile, two prominent DUP politicians launched into the delightful ditty, 'No Pope and no priests, no Rosary Beads, every day is the Twelfth of July'.

With both sides eye-balling each other, schoolyard-style, Lord Mayor Nigel Dodds twice called for an adjournment to allow passions to cool. After each time-out, however, hostilities resumed. Sammy Wilson poked at my sweat-shirt with a sharp Council-issue pencil while we exchanged banter about whose head would be put through the wall quickest if a row broke out.

Eventually, the vulnerable positioning of Wilson proved too much and I brought my knee up sharpish into the area where, as Sunday newspaper pictures would later confirm, his manhood rested. (Pathetic and undoubtedly childish, to be sure, but it was certainly one of the sweetest moments of my Council experience and well worth the years of abuse from the same quarter which were suffered in silence.) All hell broke loose. Fortunately, Sean McKnight and Fra McCann proved more than a match for the assortment of pensioners and misfits making up the unionist ranks. DUP councillor Peter Lunn, having been introduced to the Divis Flats kiss by Councillor McCann, ran from the chamber with his hands up. Thankfully, peace was restored just moments before Ardoyne councillor Gerard McGuigan had to make good a threat to bring a Council clerk's ornate chair he was brandishing down on the heads of the advancing unionist hordes. Sadly, Shankill scrapper

Elizabeth Seawright, fighting her way into the thick of the action, slipped on a loose Council carpet and went down like the proverbial ton of bricks.

Untypically, Alex Maskey was far from the heat of battle; recovering from his bullet wounds, he enjoyed a ringside seat on the Sinn Féin benches during the free-for-all. Two unionists required hospital treatment after the melée for unspecified injuries while, anticipating RUC charges, I trooped along to the Royal Victoria Hospital to seek treatment for an imaginary neck strain. In Westminster, Ian Paisley claimed that Seawright had been thumped to the ground in a 'barbaric attack'. Both sides blamed each other while Sinn Féin also had a pop at Lord Mayor Dodds for allowing unionists to gather at the chamber door and hurl abuse. The *Belfast Telegraph* report on the meeting noted that the Lord Mayor was reading a newspaper when Sinn Féin members were speaking as his own studied insult to the republicans. Cormac Boomer of the SDLP left the blame for the ruckus at the Lord Mayor's door. 'If it was possible, I would have him charged for what happened', he said. 'But of course, he was only following the traditional approach bequeathed him by previous Lord Mayors. He should do the people of Belfast a big favour by resigning now. He sat there reading the *Telegraph* when Sinn Féin was trying to speak.'

Secretary of State Tom King was moved to condemn the brawl while some senior and more erudite Sinn Féin people (most notably Mitchel McLaughlin) thought we had overstepped the mark and presented ourselves as corner boys rather than politicians. All of which was probably true but, interestingly, the fisticuffs brought to an end the intense loyalist barracking of Sinn Féin.

The RUC were called in to investigate the fracas and drew up a list of complaints – which I still have framed at home – from the battered unionists. Surprisingly, since I am the original wimp, there were more allegations of skullduggery made against me than against any other Sinn Féin councillor. A string of unionists had spotted my knee to what Rhonda Paisley, one-time paramour of Sammy Wilson, referred to as 'the groin area'; but the DUP man himself, in his statement, claimed I had failed to dock with the mothership – a case of pride over prejudice. Our solicitor Pat Finucane, who was to be gunned down by loyalists working hand-in-glove with British Intelligence, briefed us all on the allegations against us and then permitted us to give equally colourful defence testimony to the investigating RUC officer. Pat predicted that we would all be bound over to keep the peace given that Council officials had been struck with myopia during the bun fight and were refusing to make statements indicting any councillor. As a result the only statements were from the opposing sides – hardly unpartisan. In the event, there were no charges on either side.

Following the Battle of the Burghers – as one newspaper cheekily branded the bust-up – an unusual calm descended on Belfast City Council as shame-faced unionists scaled down the campaign against Sinn Féin. However, the nationalist electorate wasn't to benefit from the Council ceasefire. Under the chairmanship of the bigot's bigot, Frank Millar, the Parks Committee resolved to omit a children's play park in the republican Whiterock from a list of five playgrounds which were to receive new equipment. This was despite the recommendation of the Parks Department Director that the equipment – part-financed by the Department of Education – be allocated equally to all five parks and in face of opposition from Sinn Féin members whose efforts to speak were overruled. Not content with creating the ultimate park with no swings in the Whiterock – even though the Department of Education had specified it by name when awarding grant-aid – the unionist-controlled committee proceeded to share out the £4,280 worth of play equipment between four parks in middle-class areas of the city.

That unique unionist mixture of ignorance and arrogance – more the former than the latter in the case of Frank Millar – was to put the Parks Committee on a collision course with the courts.

After consulting with our lawyers, Sinn Féin was confident that the decision could be challenged in the courts. Whiterock community activist and mother-of-three Josie Quigley agreed to put her name to a court challenge to the decision. Counsel for Josie Quigley argued that the decision was discriminatory and thus illegal. With Frank Millar as their star defence witness, the Council scored a classic own goal when the case eventually came to court two years later. Memorably, when asked in the High Court if he knew what discrimination was, Frank Millar replied that it was what Protestant workers in Newry experienced. Even mining the very depths of his memory banks, he was unable to remember ever encountering a single experience of discrimination against Catholics.

But Millar's bigoted bluster was hardly surprising from a man who gloried in the title of Belfast's most hateful councillor. Among his vituperative soundbites were: 'The Gaelic League is oozing poison.' (*Sunday World*, 21 August 1988) 'Nelson Mandela is a black Provo.' (*Sunday World*, 11 March 1990) and 'Cliftonville supporters are black bastards.' (*Sunday World*, 13 November 1988)

In his Richter scale of opprobrium, republicans ranked only slightly lower than the Travelling community. 'Itinerants are rubbish', he once declared. 'The only place for rubbish is the incinerator. The Council's Duncrue Street plant (the city waste incinerator) is badly underused.' (*Sunday World* 21 February 1988) On another occasion, he blasted a group of councillors who called a special peace meeting at Christmas, to condemn violence, as 'a pile of shite' (*Sunday World* 18 Christmas 1988). When a member of the Alliance Party raised a question about free trips abroad taken by the independent unionist, he fired back, 'He is a know-all who knows fuck-all.' (*Irish News*, 31 October 1989) But he wasn't a total reprobate; in November 1989, he was fined £50 for punching Sammy Wilson in the mouth during a committee meeting.

Despite his colourful background, Frank Millar was to enjoy some of the most powerful positions in the Council, courtesy of the unionist bloc-vote. Son Frank, now London correspondent of the *Irish Times* but in another life UUP Westminster candidate in West Belfast, describes Millar père as a 'hard character who says straight out whatever he thinks'. Like a circus seal, he rose to every propaganda ball thrown to him by Sinn Féin, emerging with ever more crazed denunciations of the republican cause. For my sins, I goaded the old bugger into a series of increasingly wild comments in order to portray him as unionism's bigoted point man. Even my own colleagues thought I went too far when I suggested Suzy the chimpanzee, much-loved resident of Belfast Zoo, should be sent on a Council junket to Barcelona instead of Alderman Millar on the basis that she outshone him intellectually. In truth, Frank was a likable old dinosaur and, as his health failed during his twilight years on the Council, it was hard not to feel sorry for him as he saw the sun set on the Orange empire. Given that my name, before deed-poll, was Martin Millar, there's every possibility that he might have been a long-lost relation, though one felt that somehow he mightn't have been overjoyed at such a discovery.

The assault on nationalist community groups continued unabated despite the court action hovering over the Parks Committee playgroup decision. West Belfast-based community photography group Belfast Exposed had its Council funding stopped at the instigation of the DUP thought police. Shortly afterwards, the group, which operated two offices and employed 12 people under a government scheme, was banned from every Council building. In response, the group organised photo exhibitions of its work – admittedly cutting-edge stuff which gave a warts-and-all view of working class Belfast, but which was hardly anti-unionist – outside Council leisure centres. At the end of the year, the vetting guns were turned on the MacAirt Centre in the Short Strand – a nationalist enclave in Sammy Wilson's own backyard. The Department of Community Services refused to take responsibility for the building, even though it had been a Council-built and backed centre. And Community Services Department official Roisin McDonough found that even expressing a personal political opinion contrary to that of the unionist hegemony was not permissible. In an article for the *Irish Times* following the killing of two British Army corporals who drove into a republican funeral in Andersonstown, she criticised 'the moral zealots' who castigated the entire community of West Belfast. At the request of senior unionists, she was immediately suspended and an investigation into her article begun. Ms McDonough was eventually reinstated and subsequently successfully sued the Council for damages.

The preparations for the celebration of the Council's centenary in 1988 also sparked outrage in nationalist areas and cast a welcome cloud over the Orange-fest. On 9 October 1888 the Marquis of Londonderry presented the city charter to Belfast. In 1987, an all-unionist sub-committee of the Council was established to plan a programme of centenary celebrations. When the deliberations of the sub-committee were unveiled in the spring of 1988, Sinn Féin wrote to Town Clerk Cecil Ward making clear its displeasure with the unionist bias in the programme. Gaelic games and the Irish language were excluded from the celebrations while Windsor Park, home to the notoriously bigoted Linfield Football Club (who at that time boasted that they had never fielded an Irish Catholic), was the venue for a civic fireworks show. Any Catholic brave enough to venture into the loyalist Village area for the pyrotechnics would have been likely to end up on a bonfire. Stressing progress in the 'Province' under the twin blessings of Belfast City Council and Stormont was the underlying theme of the commemorative events. Going through the motions, Sinn Féin proposed its own additions to the itinerary: an exhibition of books in Irish about the city's history, a seven-day feis in the Falls Park, and a Gaelic sports gala in West Belfast. All were 'exoceted' by the commemoration sub-committee. At the same time, efforts to involve the Council in the bicentennial celebrations of the French Revolution were rebuffed.

The Orangemen fared somewhat better: another sub-committee was set up to draw up plans for a massive civic bash to mark the tercentenary of the Battle of the Boyne. Sinn Féin boycotted the lot, damning them as 'anti-nationalist and anti-working class celebrations of bigotry'.

Oblivious to the negative media response to their Council antics, unionists trenchantly defended their centenary bash. But their intransigence sparked more criticism. SDLP councillor Brian Feeney, never one to suffer fools gladly, sabotaged plans to host a gathering of mayors from the 'mainland' in City Hall during centenary year by writing to the targeted first citizens and warning them that their presence would be seen as rubber-stamping a carnival of intolerance. He appealed to them to boycott 'a celebration of one hundred years of oppression and bigotry being organised by one side of the community'. As a result of his letter, six cities withdrew from Lord Mayor Dodds' commemorative function on 16 October. Astonished at the news that both the Northern Ireland Office and Irish Government officials were to be barred from the celebrations, David Knowles, Labour Leader of Birmingham City Council, contacted Brian Feeney to assure him that neither he nor the city's Tory Mayor would attend. 'This is a humiliating blow to the unionists on Belfast City Council who believe they have a special relationship with Birmingham', crowed the North Belfast councillor. Councillor Feeney also roasted unionists for refusing to grant-aid a cross-community concert in the Ulster Hall which would mark Belfast's hundredth birthday and Dublin's millennium celebrations. Belfast's centenary party was, he fumed, 'sectarian and divisive', without any trace of the nationalist tradition. One-time councillor Paddy Devlin, a former republican prisoner with, ironically, impeccable anti-Sinn Féin credentials (he eventually lost his Council seat in 1985, mainly as a result of having opposed the demands of the H-Block prisoners), launched a blistering attack on the celebrations as a 'false commemoration'.

Dour-faced DUP stalwart Nigel Dodds, nick-named the Family Glum by City Hall staff, probably lost no sleep about the nationalist decision to stay away from the centenary celebrations. Certainly he didn't go out of his way to win friends in the nationalist community. In November, he accused 13 workers from the Andersonstown Leisure Centre of insulting him during a BBC Children In Need event. The workers had just taken part in a marathon bed-push from Andersonstown Leisure Centre in the west of the city to City Hall to raise money for the top charity when they encountered the Lord

Mayor in his chauffeur-driven Bentley. In order to get by the charity volunteers, the driver sounded his horn angrily – earning a few sharp remarks from the bighearted bed-pushers in response. The whole affair, fumed Dodds, was a personal insult. The unlucky 13 were suspended while an internal investigation was set in motion. When the Lord Mayor failed to substantiate his claims, the workers were reinstated.

For most of the city's Catholics, the centenary commemoration was a non-event. Local historian Fred Heatley, himself an early civil rights activist, best captured nationalist disdain for the pomp and ceremony which marked Belfast's one hundred years a-growin' in an article in the *Andersonstown News* which noted that only one non-Protestant had ever held the post of Lord Mayor in Belfast: Otto Jaffe, a Jew.

> It may be that people do get the government that they deserve. But the people of Belfast deserve much, much better than that which has been theirs. Strangers, who have mixed with the ordinary folk of Belfast, even during the worst of the bitterness of the past 20 years, have often commented on the friendliness and goodwill shown to them. They simply cannot understand why these Belfast folk chose such abominable leaders. They cannot understand the pettiness and sectarianism which parades as politics in Belfast. They cannot understand why we will not accept this 20th Century. They are not alone in their confusion. Many of us who were born and reared in this city, with roots going back four or five generations, now have ambivalent feelings towards it. Here we are at the closing days of 1988, a hundred years of Belfast City, with a corporation celebrating that centennial and the question must be Why? What has been achieved? Our industrial base lies on quicksand with the older traditional manufacturers but a memory; linen is now a luxury, the ropeworks have closed, the tobacco industry is dying after itself having killed millions, and shipbuilding is grasping at straws to stay afloat. Our corporate record has often proven questionable and, at times, lethal. Our inhabitants, with due cause, are wary of each other. Our violent deaths are increasing. There is nothing in that list to have celebrations about. It is Hamlet without the ghost.

5.

Save Our Souls

As 1988 came to a close, unionists switched tactics at full Council meetings, walking out when Sinn Féin members rose to speak and then trooping back in to vote down any proposal put forward by the representatives from the badlands. Still, it was a pleasant change to get talking without Rhonda Paisley playing a toy trumpet (out of tune; her musical ability mirrored her artistic ability) or Sammy Wilson tapping out Lilli-burlero with his Oxfords on the wooden floor. Sinn Féin took advantage of the improved climate to table a raft of motions on issues crucial to our electorate but certain to be torpedoed by the unionists. Motions about the lack of recognition for the Irish language in the proposed Belfast Urban Area Plan and the appalling unemployment rate in nationalist areas of the city sent the unionists into fits of apoplexy. They rushed to the barricades to vote down a Sinn Féin proposal to develop hill walking paths on the Black Mountain (shades of the Ho Chi Mihn trail when viewed from the Martyrs Memorial, no doubt). With similar distaste, the red, white and blue brigade blocked a proposal I put forward, after being approached by a constituent with severe walking difficulties, to erect a handrail for the disabled beside the swimming pool in Andersonstown Leisure Centre and similarly scuttled a proposal to open a fitness suite in the Falls Swim Centre. The response of officials to the latter proposals gave a revealing insight into how the Council worked despite the mad machinations of the unionists. The hand rail was placed in the ALC within two months (without as much as a by-your-leave to unionist councillors) and the fitness facility was opened in the Falls centre. Leisure Services Director, Mervyn Elder, one of the fairest officials in City Hall, simply by-passed the committee by moving old equipment which was being replaced in unionist centres to the Falls.

1989 found DUP Obergruppenführer Sammy Wilson in fine form. At the first meeting of the New Year, he set off a high-pitched personal alarm when Alex Maskey rose to speak. But his antics didn't find favour with unionists chastened by the media drubbing their behaviour had earned them in 1988 and determined to show a serious face to the electorate in an election year. Red-faced Official Unionists started to distance themselves from the Waldorf and Stadler buffoonery of Rhonda and Sammy. Rather than fulfilling the role of cheerleaders to the DUP assault troops, the UUP members left the chamber when Sinn Féin councillors were speaking. The penny had finally dropped at party headquarters in Glengall Street where unionist leaders were now determined to put clear blue water between themselves and the DUP 'ruffians'.

Without UUP support, the DUP protests were doomed to failure. Before the February full meeting of Council, Sinn Féin warned that it had instructed solicitors to take court action against City Hall if the Lord Mayor Nigel Dodds didn't censure the DUP protesters. Indeed, prominent Belfast solicitor Peter Madden, with practice partner Pat Finucane one of the most prominent civil liberties' lawyers in Belfast, came along to the February meeting and from the visitors' gallery witnessed a rare treat: a DUP member being ejected from the Chamber. When Paisley and Wilson tried to shout down Sinn Féin speakers, the party proposed a motion that they be removed from the chamber. With the UUP members out of the chamber, the Sinn Féin proposal was, to the great surprise of the proposers, never mind the DUP, carried. RUC officers were called to the chamber to escort the terrible two out. That led to much predictable outrage and allegations of Lundyism from the DUP ranks, but no matter how strident the insults, the UUP was not for returning to the failed disruption strategy. They would maintain their own protest – filing out silently when Sinn Féin rose to speak and returning for the vital votes – but generating votes for Sinn Féin through Council dog-fights was no longer on. Gradually, all hope of using the structures of local government to defeat the 'twin evils' of Sinn Féin and the Anglo-Irish Agreement was being extinguished. Before long, the counterproductive policies of refusing to meet government ministers would also be ditched and the DUP left to man its lonely outpost of protest against the 'Hillsborough Diktat'. But there would be other ways to try to stymie Sinn Féin's push for full recognition of its mandate. A fortnight after the February meeting and Sinn Féin's threat of legal action, solicitor Pat Finucane was shot dead by loyalists.

But the Ulster Unionist arm's length approach to the DUP didn't extend to committees and sub-committees of the Council where the parties were willing partners in a series of schemes designed to debilitate Sinn Féin. In February, at the instigation of Sammy Wilson, the General Purposes and Finance Committee wrote to Richard Needham, the egotistical minister for local government at Stormont, pleading for new legislation which would allow unionists to bar 'minority parties' from standing committees and green-light the expulsion of Sinn Féin from councils. Though he ran his own private vendetta against Sinn Féin for many years – overseeing a sordid policy of political vetting which saw money pumped into West and North Belfast through the 'safe hands' of the Catholic church – even Needham balked at the draconian nature of the legislation requested by the unionists. Undeterred, unionists continued to block any proposals which would bring benefits to West Belfast, plumbing the depths of petulance by refusing to ratify moves to save an ancient hill fort on the Black Mountain overlooking West Belfast.

As the May elections drew ever-closer, opposing sides in the Council jockeyed for positions of political advantage. Even the usually well-mannered members of the SDLP were moved to histrionics in the Council in a (successful) bid to be ejected from the chamber on the election eve. Such protests were, of course, the meat and potatoes of the Sinn Féin contingent and they were confident that their performance over the Council term would pay its own dividends on polling day. Indeed, commentators agreed that there was strong support in nationalist areas for Sinn Féin's performance within a forum long-regarded by Catholics as a 'Protestant Council for a Protestant people'. Even with the introduction of the broadcasting ban by the British in October 1988, the party's defiant message was pressing all the right buttons on the streets of North and West Belfast.

Coupled with a constituency service the envy of its political opponents – Sinn Féin ran five advice centres across Belfast – the party was well-placed to fight the May election. Sinn Féin activists were dug in at grassroots level; there was no community campaign in West and North Belfast which didn't involve local members of Sinn Féin. In the Council Sinn Féin had highlighted abuses of power while fighting cutbacks in the already embattled Department of Community Services and Department of Leisure Services – two major employers in the working class districts of the city.

In a polemical flourish, the party's candidates called for an increased vote with their own pledge, if elected, to investigate the feasibility of a separate nationalist council in the city. 'Sinn Féin stands unapologetically for the demands of the nationalist community', read the election manifesto. 'We pledge to continue exposing injustice, resisting the privatisation of Council services, providing a full-time constituency service, and examining the feasibility of a nationalist council which would give representation to every nationalist from Poleglass (in West Belfast) to Bawnmore (on the outskirts of North Belfast).'

As the election results were to show, that strident tone certainly caught the zeitgeist; Sinn Féin scored its highest-ever local government vote in the city to return eight councillors – a feat equalled by the SDLP. Nevertheless, despite boasting 35,000 votes between them, both the SDLP and Sinn Féin were still restricted to the seats at the back of the bus. Sinn Féin had lost one of the two seats it gained in the 1987 by-elections (after which it had held nine seats) but in percentage terms, the party continued to hold around 20 per cent of the first preference votes in the city and eight seats was one more than the party won in 1985.

In Upper Falls, I found that doing the odd bit of constituency work and having your name in the paper brought its own reward in the shape of more votes. My victory was particularly sweet as Shankill PUP councillor Hugh Smyth, a diminutive figure who likes to wear suits as sharp as his wit, had bid me farewell from the last term with the prediction that 'at least you won't be back'. I lost no time in letting him know that the boys were back in town at the first heated meeting of the new term in June 1989, when a Sinn Féin councillor was dumped out of the chamber for protesting unionist efforts to appoint the membership of the standing committees without consulting with the other parties. The SDLP rapped the plan as 'an insult to the intellect of the people of Belfast' but unionists used their comfortable 28-23 (8 SDLP, 8 SF, 6 Alliance and 1 WP) majority to push the measure through.

Though suffering a setback in the May '89 poll – shedding three of their 11 seats to the UUP – the DUP, à la the Bourbons, had learnt nothing and forgotten nothing. When Sinn Féin members rose to speak, the DUP cranked up their barracking – but without Official Unionist support. While unable to hermetically seal themselves off from the musings of Sinn Féin members on weighty matters of civic interest, such as the price of a game of squash in Andersonstown Leisure Centre, and lacking the ingenuity to purchase ear-plugs, the UUs nevertheless maintained their distance from the dreaded foe by walking out once a republican rose to speak. On occasions, mischievous Sinn Féiners would rise to speak, provoking a unionist stampede, and then apologise to the chair for referring to the wrong minute. Unionists would halt in their tracks and – silent movie style – troop back to their pews only for another Shinner to rise to his or her feet.

Sammy Wilson preferred the primal scream. He would continue to take a stand against the 'scummy cowards', he insisted. 'Our message to the perverts who voted for Sinn Féin councillors is that they will get nothing through this Council.' Meanwhile, among the more eccentric additions to the DUP team was the Rev Eric Smyth – later to gain immortality for his unintelligible welcome to Bill Clinton during his first Belfast visit. He got off to a dream start: 'If I'm a bigot, I'm proud to be a bigot', he announced in the *Belfast Telegraph*. 'I'm a Protestant and I know where I stand.'

A war of words erupted in the new Council when unionists at the June meeting approved the expenditure of £48,000 on the commemoration of the Battle of the Boyne. They rounded off a good night's business for the Union by hijacking every imaginable position available to the Council on outside bodies. The vacancies included 47 posts on the education and health boards in the city, as well as top jobs on the museum and university boards. However, fearful of being accused of monopolising all the available positions, they did allocate the SDLP one position: a seat on the Council's Road Safety Committee, the importance of which can be guessed at from the fact that it was known in City Hall parlance as the Tufty Club. Sinn Féin was barred from the four sub-committees of the Finance and General Purposes Committee – the most powerful on the Council – while the SDLP emerged with just a single seat out of 38 on the same bodies. The gerrymandering binge reached farcical levels when the unionists appointed their own members to the boards of community centres in nationalist areas for fear that Sinn Féin representatives would squeeze in by default. Rhonda Paisley took a seat on the management committee of the Markets' Community Centre while Nelson McCausland, then an independent unionist candidate who advocated UDI for Northern Ireland, was appointed to a similar position in the New Lodge community centre. With a touch of irony, Elizabeth Seawright, became a member of the board of the Whiterock Community Centre, scene of the Tricolour removing incident by her infamous hubbie George.

There was more of the same on the standing committees; Alliance, Sinn Féin and the SLDP were blocked from membership of the reconvened Leisure Services Sub-Committee – the very existence of which was later to be declared illegal. Unionists also made a clean sweep of every chair and deputy chair position on the Council. Not surprisingly, there was nary a disapproving word from the great and the good – later to preach pompously about the need to embrace both traditions equally – over this Council carve-up. The nationalist grass-roots had no such reservations. Fr Des Wilson lashed those in positions of authority who turned a blind eye to the unionist gerrymandering.

> They (the unionists) can't accept that nationalists have the right to select their own representatives. As far as morality is concerned, we haven't heard a thing from the moral leaders of the community. We have heard about the immorality of fighting against the government, about the immorality of working when you are receiving state benefits, and about the immorality of divorce, but nothing about this issue.

The *Sunday Tribune* concluded that Belfast unionists had rejected the example of some of their rural colleagues who had embarked on a shared-power exercise with the SDLP. 'Unionists monopolised officer positions in Belfast, Craigavon and Cookstown – all sectarian beargardens', it said.

Positions on outside bodies became even more prized after the '89 elections because the Official Unionists had decided to back down on their boycott of the bodies – introduced in protest at the Hillsborough Treaty – and take their seats. But the UUP received a rap over the knuckles from the Northern Ireland Office when its slate of nominees for the boards was not accepted. While approving the majority of appointments, the

NIO used its powers of authorisation to oust four unionist nominees from the health and education boards and appoint in their place Alliance and SDLP representatives. The new spirit of NIO egalitarianism didn't extend to Sinn Féin – even though its share of the popular vote in Belfast now exceeded that of the SDLP and Alliance.

To appease DUP hardliners outraged at the UUP climbdown on its boards' boycott, the Official Unionists gave their blessing to the reappointment of the Council's Special Committee against the Anglo-Irish Agreement. Fortunately for the city's hard-pressed ratepayers, wrangling over the legal authority of the Special Committee to spend money prevented it from ever meeting.

Sinn Féin responded to the unionist offensive by issuing a 'have you stopped beating your wife?' challenge to the majority parties. In a statement extending a laurel branch to the unionists, Sinn Féin stressed it wished to see a harmonious Council. 'Stop insulting our religion and identity, stop abusing the little power you have; stop the denigration of our language as "a leprechaun language". Our pledge then is to take part with you in sensible debate to benefit all the people of this city.' 'No answer' was the stern reply as the unionists failed to rise to the bait!

Perhaps they were too busy laying into nationalist groups. When the Antrim team reached the All-Ireland hurling final in 1989, the Council banned leisure centres from advertising in the official team brochure, 'Antrim Advances'. When the Antrim heroes returned – beaten but unbowed – from Croke Park in September, the Lord Mayor broke with the tradition of honouring the city's sporting greats by refusing to invite the team to a City Hall reception. Congratulating the Lord Mayor on his stance, Sammy Wilson branded the GAA 'the sporting wing of the IRA'.

In a series of articles, the *Andersonstown News*, the voice of nationalist Belfast, lambasted the churlishness of the unionists towards the Antrim GAA – and took some incoming flak itself for its impudence. In September, the Council passed a proposal banning all leisure centre ads in the weekly nationalist paper. That motion was the culmination of a long-running Council vendetta against the fiercely independent organ. Six years earlier, Council advertisements had been banned from the paper on the proposal of George Seawright, who described the popular tabloid as 'a republican rag'. Interestingly, the original suggestion that the ads be banned from the *Andersonstown News* came from Nelson McCausland, then the head of the Lord's Day Observance Society – an organisation for people who like to lock up swings on a Sunday. On behalf of the paper, I took a seat on the reporters' benches for the ban debate in March 1983 and earned the steely stare of George Seawright over the next hour and a half for my pains. It was my first visit to City Hall and definitely not a case of love at first sight. The ads were, as expected, stopped, for a total of 18 months, after which, the ban simply petered out.

In August '89 when the issue came before the Leisure Services Committee again, Robin Newton, a notorious hardliner from the ranks of the DUP and most definitely not a regular reader of the *Andersonstown News*, proposed leisure service ads be axed from any paper 'which isn't distributed in more than 75 per cent of the city and which didn't have its sales figures audited'. A complex formula which would have made only one real change to the existing departmental advertising strategy – an end to ads in the *Andersonstown News*. Socialist stalwart, Seamus Lynch, a representative of the virulently anti-republican Workers' Party in North Belfast, found much merit in the DUP proposal; he voted for the new advertising criteria which, as the Ombudsman would later attest, were no more than a ruse to get round allegations of political or religious bias against the *Andersonstown News*.

Ads from the five leisure centres in West Belfast contributed £5,000 annually to the coffers of the *Andersonstown News* – a considerable sum for a then small community news sheet. Although there was some confusion over the reference to '75 per cent of the city' and despite boasting an ABC audited figure, the *Andersonstown News* was deprived of further leisure service ads once the decision was taken. My links with the *Andersonstown News* and the fact that I was on the committee discussing the bar probably added fuel to the unionist fire.

Nationalists reacted angrily to the ban – earning themselves prominent coverage in the *Andersonstown News* in the process. 'The Council should have a policy of putting ads in the local papers, not only because it is effective, but also because it helps to keep the local press in existence', said an SDLP spokesperson. 'I've no doubt that this move is directed at the *Andersonstown News*', added Fra McCann of Sinn Féin. 'The Council is now refusing to advertise in a paper which is widely read in West Belfast, the main area in which there is a demand for the leisure service facilities. This is plain stupid bigotry.' Nationalist anger was compounded by the appearance of a half-page advertisement from the Shankill Leisure Centre in the first edition of a new paper published in June 1990, the *Shankill Bulletin*.

Enjoying a surge in readership as a result of the ban, the *Andersonstown News* gave the unionists the two fingers, stating that it wouldn't be changing its editorial policy to suit the City Hall censors but, in fact, 'would continue to advance legitimate nationalist views'. The newspaper lodged a complaint with the Ombudsman over its treatment at the hands of the Council, while Sinn Féin complained to the Local Government Auditor that the Council was guilty of maladministration by spending its advertising budget on newspapers which weren't as widely read as the *Andersonstown News* but had higher advertising rates. Affronted unionists protested that they were simply engaged in easing the burden on the ratepayer – a worthy assertion which was however undermined somewhat by their decision at the same time to splash out £300,000 on a new football pitch at a leisure centre in a unionist area.

While the *Andersonstown News* was an easily identifiable target for the unionist Hezbollah, many other nationalist bodies were caught in the Council's grapeshot approach to community development. On the proposal of the DUP, efforts were made by officious Council clerks to stop grant-aid to the Falls

Women's Centre. The women of the Falls had committed the unpardonable crime of having a delegation from the Troops Out Movement in for tea and Paris buns during their visit to West Belfast for the annual anti-internment demo. The McCarthyist crusade was pulled up short, however, when the Town Solicitor – one of the most prominent Catholics in City Hall – warned such a move would be illegal. Diverted but not deterred, unionists then decided the real reason they wanted to axe funding for the Falls group's ten workers was because they were replicating services already available from other Council-funded groups. When the proposal came before full Council on 2 January 1990, the votes were evenly cast with as many councillors insisting the grants be maintained as were insisting they be cut. Lord Mayor Reg Empey was called upon to bring his Solomon-style wisdom to bear on this dilemma and immediately saw the solution; he used his casting vote to stop the funding. On the slight chance that a Martian in the visitor's gallery might presume this action was motivated by anything other than old-fashioned Belshaft bigotry, unionists at the same meeting okayed a grant of £2,000 for the Shankill Women's Centre. Oonagh Marron of the Falls Women's Centre admitted the logic of the City Fathers was too torturous for the females of the Falls to understand. 'The Falls Women's Centre does the same type of work as the Shankill Women's Group but one gets money while the other one is refused funding', she said. Ms Marron called in her lawyers and when the case reached the steps of the courthouse in May, grovelling Council officials performed a sharp U-turn promising that funding would be restored immediately – and backdated.

The New Year was marked in Belfast with political fireworks. On 3 January, the genial GP and SDLP councillor Joe Hendron sent an urgent message to the new Stormont Secretary of State Peter Brooke calling for Belfast City Council to be suspended and replaced with a commission to carry out its duties. The impassioned SOS was the product of six months of insults and abuse from unionists as they brought the good fight to the 'political AIDS carriers' of Sinn Féin and the Anglo-Irish

Agreement. Dr Hendron – later to snatch the West Belfast seat from Sinn Féin – made his desperate *cri de coeur* after the unionists unveiled their masterplan for the running of the Council. Their strategy, arrived at without any consultation with the opposition parties, involved wholesale cutbacks. 'When they refused to go through the normal system of consultation within the Council with their proposals, they effectively gave the fingers to all those councillors who aren't unionists', he told *The Irish News*.

Though often disgusted at their treatment at the hands of the unionists, the SDLP, partly for fear of playing second-string to Sinn Féin, only rarely voiced its displeasure. There was always the forlorn hope among the most anti-republican councillors of the middle-class Catholic party that the unionists would one day distinguish between the irredentist republicans and itself. But overtures to the unionists were rebuffed time out of number. There were few brownie points for being 'a good Injun' in the late 1980s and early 1990s.

All of which enraged SDLP councillors, who had more experience of local government, were better educated, frequently better-off and invariably more articulate than their unionist adversaries. In fact the party's North Belfast spokesman Councillor Brian Feeney – now retired from politics but still a prominent anti-unionist commentator – fumed that unionists were using 'whatever little power' they had 'in a bigoted and sectarian fashion'. Colleague Dr Alasdair McDonnell – one of the most vociferous anti-republican spokesmen on the Council – delivered the same verdict: 'They have behaved like bigots and adolescents over the last three years', he declared. 'They can keep their seats as far as I'm concerned because they have wrecked any sense of fair play or justice in City Hall. It is all a charade with a gerrymandering committee. It has been rendered useless and a waste of time.'

But the SDLP insisted on keeping their distance from Sinn Féin. While publicly critical of unionist exclusion tactics, they yearned for an 'understanding' with unionists whereby the plum positions on the Council would be divided between the 'two traditions', SDLP-speak for the UUP and SDLP. When Sinn Féin proposed in 1989 that a nationalist forum be set up in Belfast to provide a representative alternative to the City Hall shenanigans, the SDLP baulked at the suggestion. Dr Joe Hendron dismissed the idea – admittedly born out of Sinn Féin frustration at the obstructive tactics of the unionists – as 'stupid nonsense' but six months later it's clear that he too was at the end of his tether with the City Hall unionists. *The Irish News*, a reliable echo of SDLP concerns, pitched in with an editorial condemning 'the blind bigotry' of the unionist camp. 'The behaviour of the unionists is narrow-minded, blind and bigoted', the Catholic daily declared. 'There would be delight and relief among the public if the shameful obstruction was to be removed through the appointment of a commission.' For some time, the paper had reported, with undisguised anger, the unionists' appalling behaviour at City Hall, reserving its harshest criticism for their contempt of fair employment laws. Certainly, unionists frequently crossed swords with the Fair Employment Agency (now Commission) – a body set up specifically to ensure the type of anti-Catholic discrimination which once epitomised local government in the North of Ireland was ended. A major point of contention was a unionist tradition of giving preference in interviews for security staff positions to former members of the security farces. The fact that these former forces men were all true blue unionists was, of course, sheer coincidence. Likewise, unionists refused to take down their pathetic 'Belfast Says No' banner protesting the Anglo-Irish Agreement despite fair employment legislation banning symbols, flags and emblems which compromised the neutrality of the workplace.

To their credit, officials did try and shunt the banner ever closer to the cubby hole, declining to re-erect it above the Dome after it had been removed for cleaning work. For years afterwards it adorned the back car park of City Hall before eventually being moved once again for stone-cleaning work. When the work was finished, the banner was gone and even the unionists couldn't work up the enthusiasm to ask for a new one to be put up. I've been told a few senior Council officials know the whereabouts of the banner – and what a wonderful memento it would make in the Felons' Club on the Falls – but they're keeping mum. Attempts to encourage the interest of the trade unions in the Hall – hardly filled with Bolshevik fervour when it came to the matter of anti-Catholic discrimination – in the case came to nought. Even though many trade union leaders in the Council came from nationalist backgrounds, the unions have the dubious distinction of being the only grouping in City Hall never to have challenged religious discrimination. Even the DUP outshone that record – though for all the wrong reasons. Avuncular DUP councillor Wallace Browne, who was traditionally moved to speech about once a year at full Council, rounded on Derry City Football Club 'for masquerading as a community club when it had a policy to keep out Protestant players'. The soccer club responded with a brief statement to the effect that several Protestant players fielded for the Candystripes. That shut Wallace up for another twelve months.

The procedural game of cat-and-mouse continued at full meetings of Council as the unionists deployed their Orange sledgehammer to crack the green nut. Each month, Sinn Féin would table a motion for discussion at the full Council meeting – a declaration of support for the hard-pressed ratepayers or a rallying cry against prejudice. Unionists would walk out to ensure the motion couldn't be debated due to the lack of a quorum. That only deferred the problem, however, as any motion not debated at one meeting of full council would become the first motion up for debate at the next. Unionists wishing to condemn the Anglo-Irish Agreement, Papal whoremongering or the threat of a nuclear strike from Dublin would have to allow the Sinn Féin motion to be debated at full Council before they could have their monthly rant. Lose-lose for Sinn Féin became win-win. And while any motion tabled by the party was certain to be voted down, the unionists, for throwing out our touchy-feely proposals, were cast as Humbugs. In an inspired move, unionist backroom boys decided to change the standing orders so that any motion not debated at two full meetings of Council – due to lack of a quorum – would not be tabled at the third meeting (and, indeed, ad infinitum) as had been the practice previously. In Troglodyte land no-one ever considered the possibility that Sinn Féin might just table a different motion every month ensuring that they still dominated the headlines the morning after each Council meeting.

The luxury of opposition afforded Sinn Féin the opportunity to censure the unionists in formal motions to Council over their plans to cut Council expenditure by privatising costly leisure centres. The centres were built in the late seventies and early eighties by a British government which believed that nationalists pumping iron in sports centres wouldn't have the time to brick their local barracks. Once built, they were turned over to the unionists to run. By 1990, the centres were draining the Council's finances. While the unionists had to accept the advice of officials to cut, cut, cut, Sinn Féin – having been excluded from the Council decision making process – was under no such obligation. I formed a vocal front group, Save Our Leisure Service Lobby, to highlight the leisure centre job losses and to point out that while expenditure on leisure centres in West Belfast was decidedly frugal, there were no such reservations about budget constraints in unionist areas. In 1989 alone, at the height of the cutback frenzy, £400,000 was spent on new facilities in unionist areas. But it wasn't lost on ordinary unionist voters that while their representatives greenlighted the axing of 112 jobs across the board in the leisure centres, the only voice raised in opposition came from the Sinn Féin benches. Councillors who made their name by cutting services and bawling obscenities at Sinn Féin, leaving themselves time only for the odd study visit abroad, became a laughing stock in their own communities. Veteran journalist Jim McDowell, hosting a memorable radio show on the Shankill drew loud laughter when he poked fun at the jet-setting public representatives of the area.

Not so funny was the attack on Cardinal Ó Fiaich after his death in May 1990. Leaflets left in the Members' Room – open only to councillors – gloried in his death. Under the ghoulish title, 'Even Lourdes Could Not Heal Cardinal Thomas O'Fee', the flyer boasted:

> Cardinal O'Fee, so-called Prince of the Church, has gone to answer at the bar of Almighty God where his Cardinal's cloak will bring him no favours and where his priestly claims will bring him no homage or respect... Although Saint Patrick was not a Roman Catholic and taught none of the dogmas of popery, Cardinal O'Fee claimed to be his 112th successor. So much for the accuracy of his widely hailed authoritative history knowledge and expertise. Is it not strange that the Roman Catholic authorities, when the Roman Catholic Primate of All-Ireland was taken ill at the very centre of their Healing Mecca, rushed the Cardinal away from Lourdes to a hospital in Toulouse where he died?

It was never determined which unionist councillor was behind the offensive literature, but there was no doubting it was part of a wider campaign to try and mark out the Members' Room as 'whites-only' territory. When I first went into the Hall, members' mail was placed in open pigeon boxes. However, unionists tampered with the Sinn Féin mail, making off with some letters. I responded by dumping Rhonda Paisley's letters in the waste bin. Suddenly, a problem which the Council could ignore became an urgent matter to be resolved. The joiners moved in and left only when they had created wooden pigeon hole letter boxes for all 51 councillors, accessible only by key. Eric Smyth adopted the Wild West approach. Faced with the overbearing Sinn Féin presence in the Members' Room, he sauntered past the Sinn Féin councillors in the Members' Room with his personal issue firearm on show. Underwhelmed, Sinn Féin stalwart Joe Austin advised him to put the gun away. 'We give those .22 weapons to the Fianna Boys', he told a deflated Eric. 'Now be a good boy and put it away.'

6.

Going Paddy

The June 1990 election of Official Unionist Fred Cobain as Lord Mayor came, perversely, as a fillip to the nationalist camp. For Shankill representative Fred, not renowned for his intellectual prowess, soon made a name for himself as one of the most ardent members of the Council's Holiday Club. Nicknamed the 18-25 Club (a reference to the IQ of its members, it was suggested, rather than their age), the jet-setting group did as much damage to the unionist cause as the flocks of diarrhoeic pigeons were doing to the granite facade of City Hall. Fred had a colourful past to boot. In 1989, he had been acquitted at the Crown Court on fraud charges when a prosecution witness failed to show. The UUP man had been accused of accepting a £250 bribe to ensure an order for a new minibus for the Limestone Youth Training Project went to a named company. The Crown noted that a former salesman with the company was not willing to give evidence against Cobain, who pleaded his innocence of all charges. Later it would emerge in the *Sunday World* that Cobain sat in on interviews for a post with the Shankill Community Council which was eventually awarded to him after all the other candidates were rejected as unsuitable.

It was swiftly business as usual for Cobain as he oversaw a clean sweep by unionists in June of every chair and deputy chair on Council committees and the barring of the opposition from the plethora of sub-committees. It all proved too much for Councillor Brain Feeney of the SDLP who announced he wouldn't be attending any more committee meetings. 'What's the use?', he said. 'It's a waste of time. Unionists will do whatever they wish to do.'

That was certainly the case when Irish hostage Brian Keenan was released from captivity in August 1990. Brushing aside objections by Frank Millar over plans to give Brian Keenan a civic reception ('Stay with your friend Charles Haughey, we don't want you', was the advice of the ever-hospitable Francis, who added, 'when you go Paddy, you go all the way!'), Cobain rolled out the red carpet for the released hero. However, the Lord Mayor banned Sinn Féin from the reception. 'As things stand, Belfast City Council looks suspiciously like a Protestant Council for a Protestant people', retorted *The Irish News*. The sole consolation for nationalists is that they weren't the only community in the unionist firing line. When Northern Ireland's 400 Muslims requested a plot of land in one of the city's cemeteries to bury their dead, unionists shot down the idea. 'Where would you stop?' asked the Chairman of the Parks Committee Jim 'Junior' Walker of the DUP. 'And anyway Muslims refuse to say prayers over a Christian body.' The same Jim Walker later fell out with the DUP and was chucked out of the party after going off the rails and spending nights sleeping in the party's rooms at City Hall. City Hall scribe Jim McDowell recalls how Jim Walker, when High Sheriff of Belfast, the highest honorary post in the city after the Lord Mayor and Deputy Lord Mayor, would describe himself as 'the low sheriff of Belfast'. During his travails, I spotted him one night wandering through Catholic West Belfast with an overnight bag on his shoulder. I stopped my car and offered him a lift, fearful for the safety of a DUP councillor in Andersonstown. He accepted and I drove him to the city centre, where I declined his offer to join him for a drink. Stripped of the need to spew the bitter rhetoric of the DUP, he was as likeable and as frail and as human as the rest of us.

Which wasn't to say that the unionists in general had the same grasp of political PR as the rest of humanity. In December 1990, Cobain railed against Country and Western music star Hank Wangford because he supported the English 'Time To Go' campaign (calling for the withdrawal of troops). The Lord Mayor urged viewers not to pay their licence fees after the BBC appointed the country crooner presenter of a TV programme. He went on to back a unionist enquiry demand into a guided tour of City Hall which Sinn Féin laid on for NORAID chief Martin Galvin. Sinn Féin also revealed that Cobain was something of an art aficionado. As a member of the Arts Council, Cobain was involved in the drawing up of policy decisions affecting the provision of resources (though he alone couldn't be blamed for the Arts Council's disgraceful antipathy towards the nationalist community). Yet research showed that during the 1992-1993 financial year, when he was chairman of the Council committee which deals with the arts, not one penny was provided to nationalist areas. Sinn Féin angrily called for an inquiry into Fred Cobain's record on the Arts Council and, while the Council predictably steered clear of the issue, the *Sunday World* responded with a shock, horror probe story which I was delighted to later see on the notice board in an Arts Council office!

Not to be outdone by their West Belfast colleagues, DUP councillors in East Belfast demanded a programme of positive discrimination for their own bailiwick, long regarded as Belfast's industrial powerhouse. The director of the Northern Ireland Council for Voluntary Action described the call as 'ironic'. He said it was bizarre that the DUP 'suggest robbing Peter to pay Paul when they robbed Paul when they were in control.'

Perhaps it was because he had so much personal baggage to carry that Cobain set out to accentuate his unionist credentials by pushing out the anti-Sinn Féin boat even further than his predecessors. At the first Council meeting of 1991, called to discuss a proposal to invite newly-elected Irish President Mary Robinson to Belfast, Cobain refused to allow any opposition members to speak. Sammy Wilson activated his electronic alarm when Sinn Féin members rose to protest the gagging order. It was to be the first of a stormy series of meetings which ended only when the courts rapped the unionists over the knuckles. The fact that Cobain's ban extended to everyone on the opposition benches and not just Sinn Féin drew the ire of local papers. *The Irish News* alleged that the Council was 'a gentlemen's club for bigots' run by 'pig-headed unionists'. The *Belfast Telegraph* opined that 'the issue is one of freedom of speech, enshrined in every democratic forum in the world, but apparently unavailable in Belfast City Council'.

Ever-hopeful John Carson, an Ulster Unionist who had forfeited the party whip for refusing to go along with the increasingly barmy protests against the Anglo-Irish Agreement, proposed the Robinson invite motion on the back of the new Uachtarán's predisposition towards the unionist cause. Sammy Wilson was having none of it while the Republic remained 'a Ho Chi Minh trail for terrorists' and successfully blocked the move. But Cobain's refusal to allow any input from the SDLP (or Sinn Féin) led to an official protest by Dr Joe Hendron to Secretary of State Peter Brooke. 'I am starting to wonder if it's worth attending meetings at all because of the way unionists conduct business', complained the exasperated doctor. Dr John Alderdice of the Alliance Party branded Cobain's gag on the opposition as 'the sort of thing one associates with totalitarian states in Eastern Europe'. 'It is clear the unionists have not the slightest idea of what democracy means', he added. Cobain took none too kindly to his slating by the press. 'It is ironic that anyone from the SDLP should complain about a lack of democracy when they have supported the imposition of the most undemocratic form of government anywhere in the world *i.e.* the Anglo-Irish Agreement.'

Things went from bad to worse at a special meeting on 11 January called to condemn an IRA firebomb blitz on businesses across the North. Unionists had hoped to get the SDLP on-side for a motion blasting the IRA for throwing scores of workers on the dole, but DUP enthusiasm for the task at hand torpedoed any possibility of cross-chamber unity. During the debate, Sammy Wilson called for the British Army and RUC to be sent into the 'lairs of the terrorists'. This, he admitted, would mean hardship for ordinary Catholics. 'Of course it will hurt the Catholic areas because that is where they make the bombs', he declared. SDLP councillor Brian Feeney cut the unionists adrift, making clear that his party wouldn't be endorsing the motion which had become a unionist repression wish-list rather than a motion condemning the IRA. 'The people I represent are not animals', he said. 'They do not live in lairs and are not there to be hunted down like animals.' Speaking above the insults and cat-calls from the unionist benches, Sinn Féin councillor Gerard McGuigan called on the British to speak with the IRA – something, as it emerged, that was happening at the time anyway. Outraged, Frank Millar proposed an omnibus gag on all the Sinn Féin members present. Twice the Town Clerk advised Deputy Lord Mayor Eric Smyth, chairing the meeting in the absence of Fred Cobain, that such a proposal was illegal. Undeterred, and as impressionable as he was dense, Eric Smyth decided to take his lead from the Lord Mayor the previous week. He called a vote on the motion which was easily passed by the unionists.

Protestations from Sinn Féin were dismissed by Eric Smyth and colleague Sammy Wilson who objected to efforts by republicans to speak on behalf of the ratepayers who elected them on the basis, as reported in the *Irish Times*, that 'Taigs don't pay rates'. But silencing the pugilistic Alex Maskey was more difficult than the easily-led Eric Smyth had obviously been assured by his mentor. As the roars of outrage from the Sinn Féin benches peaked, the Sinn Féin man approached the Lord Mayor's chair to demand he be allowed to speak. When he snatched the order paper from in front of the Deputy Lord Mayor, Smyth grabbed him by the lapel. As the pair grappled, Alex Maskey waved his finger into Smyth's face. 'Don't ever do that again', he told the non-denominational Protestant minister, before Sinn Féin councillors managed to separate the pair. Unionists immediately pushed through a motion that the Sinn Féin man be ejected from the meeting but, after leaving the chamber for a while, Alex Maskey returned to take part in the final vote. None of the unionists decided to challenge his presence.

After the meeting, the ever-imaginative Eric Smyth decided that Alex Maskey's outstretched digit was in fact an imaginary gun and that he had just been subject to a 'silent death threat'. However, the Sinn Féin man had the last word. Immediately after the meeting, he collared Smyth in the corridor and, according to the preacher, told him, 'I'll knock your ballocks in if you ever do that again'. The affronted Deputy Lord Mayor reported the Andersonstown councillor to the RUC for allegedly threatening to kill him. An exhaustive RUC probe followed, with over 40 councillors and staff being interviewed. Eight months later Alex Maskey – who wasn't among the 40 plus interviewed by the RUC – was arrested from his home in the early morning and hauled off to Castlereagh to be quizzed about his finger-waving exercise. He was released without charge and his lawyers managed to sue the RUC for wrongful arrest – and win him a pound or two in damages.

After the January confrontation, Alex Maskey lodged an application for a judicial review of the Council decision to gag all Sinn Féin members. Two meetings, two rows, one fight, one putative court case. 1991 was turning out to be a hell of a year.

For the full meeting of Council in February, I asked community priest and civil rights activist Fr Des Wilson to come along as an observer. But where to seat him? If I applied for a seat in the public gallery, I would have to submit his name 72 hours before (a stricture introduced by unionists after republicans had responded to the packing of the gallery by loyalist heavies by bringing along their own heavies). Such a move would have alerted the unionists to his presence and exposed the mild-mannered cleric to abuse from the serried ranks of unionists below. I took my dilemma to new Town Clerk Stanley McDowell, another honest official struggling to rein in the excesses of unionist councillors, and asked how one brought guests to the VIP gallery – often mistakenly referred to as the Lord Mayor's box. He informed me that there was no protocol governing the use of the small gallery raised above the chamber though it was recognised as a VIP viewing area. A priest he decided would fit the criteria of VIP. When I suggested that I write to him confirming that Fr Des Wilson would like to take up position in the VIP gallery, he cautioned against it, turning on its head the first lesson I learnt at City Hall: ask the right question. If you didn't ask the right question, officials were under no obligation to release information to you. Once you asked the question, however, they were obliged to divulge everything they knew. The trick, of course, was to know which questions to ask. Conversely, to ask about the VIP gallery, was to invite the unionists to examine the question and invent a protocol which would ban nationalist sympathisers.

Fr Des took up position in the VIP gallery on 3 February and witnessed the shortest Council meeting in five years. Alarmed at reports that Sinn Féin was to take the Council to court, unionists decided to rush all business through before the republicans had time to actually raise a hand to seek permission to speak. With the minutes of the seven standing committees – which usually took two hours to debate – voted through in record time, it was all over in less than four minutes (including the obligatory reading of the Bible). Next up on the agenda was a motion I had tabled calling for the ban on the Irish language to be lifted. Unionists marched out rather than listen to my dulcet tones, all of which left the meeting without a quorum. I was somewhat disturbed at the fact that Fr Des hadn't in fact seen the unionists in finest blustering mode but, of course, the brevity of the meeting and the boorish behaviour of the unionists provided a salutary lesson in all that was wrong with City Hall. He had long argued for court action to bring the unionists to heel. That was a belief now hardened by his experience of the mini-Council session. Cobain boasted that unionists had shanghaied the meeting to prevent Sinn Féin from contributing to Council business. Unionists would in future, he announced, restrict the meetings to only a few minutes before storming out to prevent Sinn Féin from speaking. Special meetings would be called to discuss 'relevant matters at hand'. The mini-meetings were just the latest tactic dreamt up by the rocket scientists in the UU Council grouping. And, in fairness, Cobain seemed to be blissfully unaware of the massive damage his shenanigans were inflicting on the unionists' credibility.

The first special meeting was scheduled for 8 February and the 'relevant matter at hand' was the Gulf War. Sporting a *Sun* 'Support Our Boys' badge, Field Marshal Frank Millar pledged full support for the Allied war effort before turning the meeting into yet another rant against the IRA. Calling for sanctions to be placed on nationalist areas (of Belfast rather than Iraq) the World War II veteran beseeched the British government to treat republican prisoners in uncompromising fashion: 'Maybe we could uphold the old Mexican thing and just stick them against the wall'.

But it wasn't only the poor Iraqis and the Shinners who were in the unionist line of fire. Rhonda Paisley, clutching a copy of *The Power of Positive Thinking*, berated ailing Ulster Unionist Billy Gault for passing the time of day with Sinn Féin councillors in the Members' Room. 'She's going to tell her Da on me', sobbed Billy, whose stock was always low with the DUP because he had quit the DUP for the UUP after representing Paisley's party on the Council between 1981 and 1985. Yet again, a long line of unionists were called to speak before Sinn Féin members who had indicated first. Disgusted, I rushed to the Lord Mayor's chair to accuse him of deliberately refusing to list Sinn Féin councillors to speak. I followed that protest by delivering a broadside against the unionists from the side of the Lord Mayor's chair. At the press benches for the bun-fight, *Andersonstown News* editor Robin Livingstone had high praise for my intervention.

> If his speech was as dramatic and heroic as his posture, then nobody could hear it over the catcalls of Sammy Wilson. 'Sit down, you're pathetic.'

The A'town scribe concluded that democracy in Belfast owed more to the music hall than a modern democracy: 'Sammy Wilson and Rhonda Paisley barracked Sinn Féin's Gerard McGuigan incessantly as he tried to speak', he wrote.

He's standing there talking while his friends are out bombing this town', yelled an aggrieved Ms Paisley. 'Away back to your republican sewer', Sammy Wilson added. The two kept this up, in similar vein, without a break. Unscripted and off-the-cuff, it was an impressive piece of heckling. On a point of information, Councillor Maskey inquired whether anyone in the chamber had a Valium for Ms Paisley... Frank Millar rose to finish the debate... it was now after five, and the news had filtered in that traffic in the city centre had come to a complete standstill because of an IRA car bomb. Councillor Millar referred to the fact that a number of councillors had said that sanctions against Iraq should have been given more time. 'We should get sanctions to operate in a part of Northern Ireland where we would put every friggin' republican and take away their light and water and heat.' It seemed a particularly apt way in which to finish. We joined a queue of homebound traffic that was going nowhere fast, leaving a council chamber that, in truth, seems to be doing the same.

Inspired by Millar's vitriol, the unionists backed his proposal endorsing the war in the Middle-East. But the Mexican Ambassador to the UK was less impressed when I wrote to him to alert the much-maligned people of Mexico about the aspersions being cast on their (admittedly dodgy) human rights record by Millar. Ambassador Bernardo Sepulveda wrote back to me to assure the citizenry of Belfast that Frank Millar's remarks 'stem from B-movies and spaghetti westerns that portray stereotyped Mexican characters'.

At the annual special meeting of the council on 15 February to set the rate for the following year, I presented Sammy Wilson with a copy of my rates demand to show that at least one Fenian did pay rates. He tore it to shreds! Unfortunately for the ratepayers, their bills weren't torn up before they were issued for at the same meeting the unionist majority pushed through a ten per cent hike on the rates. However, a unionist proposal to close six play centres was defeated when some of their number broke ranks and joined the opposition to block the move.

The New Year flurry of unionist obstruction entered a brief hiatus after Lord Justice Campbell ruled on the judicial review taken by solicitor Peter Madden – who had come along to the 3 February meeting for a once-in-a-lifetime experience – on behalf of Alex Maskey. Council officials, whose advice to Eric Smyth had been ignored when he slapped the blanket ban on contributions from Sinn Féin at the 11 January meeting, refused to show to defend the unionists. The Crown Court judge ruled that Alex Maskey had the right to be heard: the gag on Sinn Féin members was invalid and a breach of Standing Orders. 'The debate was part of the democratic process', he added. 'Those who elected a particular councillor were entitled to have their views put forward by him.' Costs were awarded against the Council but the tab was, as always, picked up by the ratepayer. Welcoming the court's decision, Alex Maskey vowed that Sinn Féin wouldn't be shut up in the Council chamber. Fred Cobain feigned delight. 'I'm glad that Sinn Féin now recognise British courts, British justice and therefore the British presence in Northern Ireland.' It was gratifying to see he took some consolation from the court decision against him and his colleagues because he was to get plenty more of the same medicine in the months ahead.

But the Keystone Cop tactics of the unionists weren't winning them any friends at the Northern Ireland Office – a body of opinion the Council could no longer afford to ignore now that it was seeking substantial government backing for its £30m concert hall plan. Bowing to the inevitable, in March 1991 unionists abandoned the absurd ban on Northern Ireland Office Ministers and civil servants from Council property – imposed after the signing of the Anglo-Irish Agreement – so that they could meet with Economy Minister Richard Needham to discuss funding for the putative waterfront concert hall development. Welcoming Richard Needham to City Hall after a six-year ban on NIO representatives, Lord Mayor Fred Cobain, who had joined with the DUP to vote against the lifting of the boycott, said he had no regrets about the six-year freeze-out. The move to lift the ban had been championed by Shankill PUP veteran, Hugh Smyth, who was well-briefed by officials. 'If the government decides to grant-aid us to the extent, say, of £10m on the Concert Hall project, does that mean that if the ban stays Richard Needham would not be able to come into the City Hall to present us with the cheque?' he said. 'The situation as it stands is ludicrous.' It was all the more farcical because unionist councillors had been regularly ferried by minibus to Stormont over the previous five years months to discuss a host of issues with NIO ministers. In his memoirs, Needham revealed that unionist councillors had been drifting back to the NIO as early as 1986:

> As I had so many purse-strings and they had so many pet projects, it was inevitable that the boycott would not hold forever, particularly as SDLP and Alliance councillors could claim credit out of any meeting they had with the minister, which I naturally encouraged.

Some commentators opined that the NIO Ministers obviously weren't being told the full truth about City Hall meetings by their solitary scout who observed all Council meetings from the VIP gallery. If their courageous envoy had given them a warts-and-all report on his visits, surely ministers wouldn't have been so keen to meet with the unruly City Fathers. The split in the unionist camp over Stormont ministers was mirrored in the chamber where diehard DUP duo Sammy and Rhonda had broken with a unionist policy to leave the chamber when Sinn Féin members spoke. Reverting to type, Mutt and Jeff now stayed behind to taunt the Sinn Féin members.

The misanthropic DUP approach to politics inflicted other collateral damage on the Council. In February 1991, unionists closed the door on a Stormont offer of 75 per cent funding towards a community relations programme which had been endorsed by all but three Councils in the North. The entire programme was tarred with the Anglo-Irish Agreement brush by unionists who moaned that the £360,000 community relations grant would be used 'to hype up the Anglo-Irish PR machine'. Alex Attwood of the SDLP branded that position 'a scandal'. 'This is a case of Belfast Council fiddling while community relations in the city continue to burn.' The previous month, unionists had stormed out of a meeting with NIO officials, called to discuss the funding package, because Sinn Féin members were present. 'The bizarre little vignette', commented *The Irish News*, 'is by no means unusual at a council peopled by characters who seem to have walked straight off the pages of one of Charles Dickens' more colourful novels.' But still there were those in City Hall officialdom more concerned with stymying Sinn Féin that bringing the unionists to book. In May 1991, I organised a small press occasion for local reporters to highlight our demands for the democratisation of the Council. But just moments after Alex Maskey, Gerard McGuigan and I presented our press material to the few reporters who had managed to overcome attempts by security officials to bar them from the committee room in which we met, Deputy Town Clerk Robert Wilson was banging at the door and demanding we vacate the room. Speaking to the press was forbidden under Council regulations, it seemed, in Council rooms – although only days previously Sammy Wilson had given a lengthy television interview in the Council chamber. It seemed there were two Council protocols – one for unionists and one for the second class councillors. The occasion was more notable not for the 21-page report, *Belfast City Council – A Bastion of Bigotry*, which we released, but for the fact that in his enthusiasm to prevent *Irish Times* journalist Anne Maguire from entering the room where our mini-press conference was taking place, a council official knocked her glasses off. Always a professional, Ms Maguire, who died shortly afterwards in a car accident, filed her report for the following day's *Times* without mentioning the difficulties she had encountered in getting the story.

At the June 1991 annual general meeting of Council, a high-spirited delegation of women from the Right to March group – a nationalist women's grouping demanding the right to parade to the city centre, previously sacrosanct unionist territory – packed the public gallery to put their case. As the meeting got underway, the defiant group unfurled a banner over the edge of the balcony and into the chamber below. As Lord Mayor Fred Cobain abandoned the meeting before the vote for his successor, angry unionists grabbed the banner and engaged in a tug-of-war with the women above. Only by physically swinging on the banner, bearing the legend '1969-1991: What has changed?', did Lord Mayor-in-waiting Nigel Dodds – aided by gravity – manage to snatch the 'right to march' sign from the female protesters. At the same time, the RUC waded into the demonstrators, removing them forcibly from their vantage point. Aiding the charge was Rhonda Paisley who marched into the public gallery and urged her fellow-councillors, as the *Belfast Telegraph* reported, to 'come up and get them'. There were no takers. Moving to help protesters being jostled out of the hall by the RUC, Alex Maskey allegedly punched an officer on his flak jacket. An hour later, after tempers had cooled and councillors were making their way home, the RUC arrested the Andersonstown man. Four months later he was given a conditional discharge in the courts despite his protests that the RUC had been acting in a heavy-handed manner. Six of the women ousted from the viewing gallery subsequently filed suit against the RUC.

After the chamber hullabaloo, I spotted Nelson McCausland scurrying down to the back door entrance of the hall to seize the official document on which the names and addresses of the visitors to the public gallery were written. As devious as he is devout, Nelson hoped to compromise the demonstrators and the councillors who had signed them in. He arrived at the back door before me and had already relieved a security man of the list when I grabbed him by the throat and demanded it back. After a brief scuffle, he gave it up and ran off to find a bobby on the beat. The Lord Day's Observance Society stalwart subsequently complained to the RUC that I had assaulted him. Aided by the temporary blindness of City Hall staff, I counterclaimed. The RUC eventually wrote to me saying that no action would be taken. Nelson told the press he was 'disappointed to say the least' that the RUC had failed to act on his claim that I had punched him in the face and tried to throttle him. Savouring the moment, I blasted a 'pathetic' McCausland: 'I may have had to restrain him but to allege that I beat him up is going a bit far.' Frank Millar meanwhile, in the wake of the demo, led the charge for increased security precautions at City Hall – including a bullet-proof screen between visitors and the chamber. 'The Council has been good enough at disrupting its own business', he said with a perfectly straight face. 'It doesn't need any help from outside.'

The women tossed out of the Council had the last laugh over Sammy Wilson who predicted they would never be allowed to rally in the city centre when they succeeded – on their fourth attempt – in reaching City Hall. The unwritten law which barred nationalists from holding demonstrations at City Hall was no match for the Beat the Ban protesters who, having been banned originally in March 1991, challenged the block again in April, May, June and, finally with success, in July. Another little footnote was written in Belfast's history as, for the first-time ever, nationalists gathered in protest outside City Hall with their national flag flying. 'It has taken us 70 years to get here', Sinn Féin councillor Sean McKnight told the rally in the front of City Hall.

When the annual general meeting of Council reconvened a week after the chamber fracas, Sammy Wilson nailed his colours firmly to the mast. 'Would this Council be prepared to congratulate all those who have done a good job on two sides of the border?' he asked the Lord Mayor before formal business had begun. It was a none-too subtle reference to the UFF murder of Sinn Féin councillor Eddie Fullerton in Buncrana the previous week. Not surprisingly, there were no attempts by unionist councillors to suggest that Wilson's comments contravened the oath of non-violence given by all councillors when they stand for election. Conversely, when Sinn Féin's Gerard McGuigan had referred to the IRA killing of top Tory Ian Gow, unionists had exploded in paroxysms of outrage and demanded a full-scale

Council enquiry into how the Ardoyne representative could be prosecuted.

In the run-up to the annual meeting, there had been some half-hearted attempts by the UUP to cajole the SDLP into a Council pact but failure to meet the nationalist party's demand for a crack at the Lord Mayor's position and a fair allocation of outside board positions doomed the talks to failure. In fact, rather than bow to SDLP demands that one of their number be given the chair of a committee, unionists joined forces to propose the appointment of the sole Workers' Party representative, Seamus Lynch, to the chair of the Community Services Committee. Unionists could claim that for the first time in six years a non-unionist held a committee chair while in reality they knew the same Seamus Lynch was more than keen to do their bidding, so keen in fact, that the nationalist voters of the New Lodge dumped him at the next election. I once went eyeball-to-eyeball with Seamus at a particularly heated committee meeting but, conscious of the fact that I was giving him about five stone and four inches and that he was an ex-docker, I decided that discretion was, indeed, the better part of valour.

In the event, unionists shafted all the SDLP nominees because, explained Fred Cobain, the nationalist party had made 'derisory' remarks about the UUP. The writing on the wall could never have been clearer for the City Hall unionists but they seemed woefully illiterate. In August 1991, Sinn Féin saw off the opposition to fill the vacancy on the Council caused by the death of Ulster Unionist Billy Gault. Coming in on the back of a massive IRA bomb attack in Markethill, Co Armagh, new boy Joe Austin said he wished to hold out 'the hand of friendship' to unionists. The result had been a resounding vindication for the party's high-profile City Hall campaigns with Joe Austin picking up over 1,000 votes more than the SDLP candidate and shifting the City Hall power balance to 27-24. 'Whatever is the right approach to Sinn Féin, it can be said without a shadow of a doubt that Unionist tactics in Belfast are not working', moaned the *Belfast Telegraph* after the election. Joe, a consummate politician who was as cute as a jailer and as cool as mid-day in Montserrat, was an invaluable asset to the City Hall team.

But it was all proving to much for Rhonda Paisley. The shit hit the Féin at Joe Austin's first full meeting of the Council in September. Sammy Wilson decreed that the vote for the Sinn Féin veteran was irrelevant because all those who had voted or transferred from the SDLP to the North Belfast councillor, 'were sub-human animals'. During my contribution to a debate on the proposed Springvale university development, an emotional Ms Paisley – who a week previously had revealed that she was to quit the Council to teach English in Greece – declared that Sinn Féin was the 'dung of the city' and I was 'a shit'. 'It's all Greek to me', I muttered. The pontificating preacher's daughter had lost her cool. The innovative Springvale campus in West Belfast was 'an insult to the Protestant people in the area', fumed the South Belfast councillor. 'If I was an elected representative in West Belfast, I would tell Richard Needham where to stick his proposals.' Where could the sectarian siren have learnt such risqué language? Moments later she ripped into Nelson McCausland (perhaps I had misjudged him after all) for misrepresenting Lord Mayor Nigel Dodds in the hugely popular magazine of the Lord Day's Observance Society. All that was left were the tears and the recriminations. She wasn't running away from Sinn Féin or former boyfriend Sammy Wilson, she later sobbed to reporters. But clearly broken by her Belfast City Council experience, the former firebrand could only plead with the voters of Laganbank not to elect a Sinn Féin councillor in her place. She found little sympathy on the Sinn Féin benches. As she lashed out at all and sundry at the September meeting, the ever-understanding Alex Maskey had some hometown advice for the teetotalling terror: 'Just you get over to Greece and get the Ouzo down your neck.' I got my own retaliation in by penning a spoof love poem in Irish language paper *Lá* to she who would scorn me. 'If you lose your sense of humour in City Hall you're really in the shit', I told reporters, though Rhonda failed to respond to my rhyming invitation, in the very rough translation which appeared in the *Sunday World*, 'to elope to Bundoran and entwine our dodgems'. The bad news was that Rhonda was no better at keeping her word than her papa who once promised to retire from politics if a loyalist workers' strike failed. It did, he didn't. Though Rhonda jetted back and forth to Greece over the next two years, becoming an absentee councillor, she never gave up her seat.

But there were plenty to fill her shoes. DUP colleague Eric Smyth declared the same month that All-Ireland champions Down wouldn't be given a civic reception to mark their victory because 'the GAA is a Catholic organisation'. As well as sparking a storm of protest, the snub also showed how far Belfast City Council had travelled – backwards – since 1968 when Down had last won the All-Ireland. On that occasion, there was a mammoth City Hall party. The Alliance Party took the reception proposal to full Council in December 1991 only to have it thrown out at a meeting noteworthy for the fact that Gerard McGuigan was again tossed out after protesting the refusal of Lord Mayor Nigel Dodds to allow him to speak. The previous month, the new Lord Mayor had gone out of his way to show it was business as usual following his last stint in 1988. He backed a successful motion to adjourn the full Council meeting in protest at the presence of Sinn Féin. It was a pitiful attempt to turn back the clock but one which characterised Dodds' tenure. The unionist *News Letter*, of all papers, best caught the pathetic nature of the unionist charade in an unusual full-page feature – 'Chamber Potty' – by staffer Geoff Hill after the October meeting of City Hall. It remains one of the most powerfully evocative pieces ever written about the Council.

> Tommy Patton, the former Lord Mayor best remembered for his malapropisms like 'the police are no detergent against the IRA', interrupted the meeting before it began, if such a thing were possible. Tommy was insisting that the word 'approximately' had somehow become lodged in the minutes of the previous meeting. Fine, said Nigel Dodds, the moderately equable Lord Mayor, let's take the word out. A perplexed look passed briefly across Tommy Patton's face at the thought that he would have to sit down and shut up.

Instead he plunged feet first into an eight-minute monologue, becoming increasingly puce about the gills as he apparently insisted that the previous meeting start again... Next in line was Máirtín Ó Muilleoir, the Sinn Féin man who comes to meetings in an open-necked shirt, leather jacket and battered chinos. That's about the only revolutionary statement he's ever likely to make, since as soon as a Sinn Féin member gets up to speak, virtually all the unionists get up and troop out the door. It's rather ironic that the answer to the question, 'What does a unionist councillor do in response to Sinn Féin?' is 'Troops out.' When he had finished, the division bell brought the unionists tramping back, like schoolchildren after the break, to vote on an argument they had not heard. 'You're against this one', said one to a returning colleague.'

Rhonda Paisley – back from Corfu for the Council meeting – did not go unnoticed by the *News Letter* correspondent:

Finally it was the turn of the travelling people to pass before the Council's withering eye, as it debated whether or not to provide more sites for them. Rhonda Paisley's currently nomadic existence between Belfast and Greece failed to nurture a degree of empathy with the concept of rootlessness, and both she and Sammy Wilson disagreed with travelling people as a principle, feeling that they shouldn't exist at all. They were backed wholeheartedly by Independent Unionist Frank Millar whose considered and publicly stated opinion on travelling people is that they should be incinerated. Sadly, the recurring incompatibility of City Hall microphones and the Belfast accent made his impassioned five-minute speech sound as if he was shouting into a tin can tied to a length of string, and the only intelligible words were 'Provisional IRA', 'Sinn Féin', and 'Gippos'. By the time he finished, he too was speaking à la Ó Muilleoir to empty seats, for the next item on the agenda was a proposal by Sinn Féin's Paddy McManus to mark the bicentenary of the formation of the Society of United Irishmen, and most of the councillors were heading down the corridor pulling on their overcoats. And so the curtain came down on another Belfast City Council meeting, and on an attempt by a radical Catholic ignored by the establishment to pay tribute to a society of radical Presbyterians ignored by the establishment.

7.

Dome Dream Team

For the unionists, it never rained but it poured. In 1991, the Ombudsman ruled on the complaint lodged by the *Andersonstown News* on the 1989 ban on leisure service advertising in the weekly paper. The Council was ordered to ditch the ban and pay the newspaper £4,700 in damages. Unfortunately for the ratepayer, the Local Government Auditor didn't surcharge the errant unionists. I have always believed that recidivist unionists might have been cured of their inclination to break the law if the costly court cases had to be paid out of their own pockets, rather than those of the ratepayers.

As the four-year Council term came to a close in May 1993, unionists were left surveying the unholy mess they had created. They had suffered so many defeats that it was hard to believe that they had a 27-24 majority over the opposition. Bless them, they smiled through their troubles, diverting attention from their legal Waterloo by doing what they did best: trumpeting their Britishness. A bronze plaque memorial to the UDR and a stained glass window to the British Army were erected in a City Hall already groaning under the weight of Union Jacks and British Army memorabilia which bedecked its walls. For good measure, they planted 40 trees to mark the 40th year of Queen Elizabeth's reign, threw a dinner to celebrate the 200th anniversary of the Royal Ulster Rifles Association, and gave permission to the shadowy Ulster Society to host an Ulster Day talk in City Hall. There was also a short-lived attempt in 1993 to twin Belfast with Caen in France. The idea was aborted after Brian Feeney said he would 'oppose any attempt to twin Belfast with any town in the universe'. He also revealed that when a similar twinning arrangement with Berlin had been proposed the previous year, he had written to German civic representatives making them aware of the Council's record. The Germans decided not to take up the link offer.

Perhaps they had heard of the traumatic experience of Dublin Lord Mayor Gay Mitchell TD who foolishly accepted an invitation from the cerebrally challenged Belfast Lord Mayor Herbie Ditty to be the first Dublin First Citizen to visit City Hall since the signing of the Anglo-Irish Agreement in 1985. Nationalists and sports-lovers of all creeds were already gunning for Ditty over his refusal the previous year to invite Irish Olympic gold medal winner Michael Carruth to attend a City Hall reception for his neighbour, silver medal winner Wayne McCullough – even though the Belfast boxer had publicly asked for his fellow-Irish team member to be included on the guest list. He was dubbed 'Lord Muppet' by the *Sunday World* City Hall hack Jim McDowell and was ridiculed in the same paper for demanding staff be barred from a councillors' toilet. In response to his complaints that he couldn't pee in private, a lock was put on the door to the toilets and each councillor was issued with a golden key. The Dublin visit had been devised by the Unionists as a public manifestation of the new City Hall glasnost. It swiftly turned into a nightmare when the media – minus Jim McDowell who was stopped at the door by Ditty – were invited into the Lord Mayor's parlour to witness an exchange of gifts.

A scowling and obviously uncomfortable Ditty was backed up by fellow-political dinosaurs, Tommy Patton (then the High Sheriff) and Deputy Lord Mayor Frank Millar – Millar and Ditty were popularly known as unionism's Dome Dream Team. The Lord Mayor failed to reciprocate the warm words of thanks from his Dublin counterpart. Presumably his mind was on the upcoming local election where the number of seats in the

Shankill had been reduced from six to five in line with the area's dwindling population. Playing to the home gallery, diplomat manqué. Ditty, who had refused to wear his chain of office, branded Mitchell – standing just two feet away – 'a foreigner'.

The obsequious Fine Gael TD assured the press corps that he didn't take offence at the term as the Lord Mayor of Belfast was 'entitled to see people as he sees them'. In fact, Mitchell added, he would use the opportunity to invite Herbie to Dublin. All of which proved too much for the 74-year-old Belfast Lord Mayor. 'No way', he retorted. 'I have already told this man that I wouldn't go to Dublin. I wouldn't put my foot over the border because while they have a claim of jurisdiction over Northern Ireland, I don't want any part in it.' He then brought the press conference to an abrupt end by walking out of the Lord Mayor's parlour, leaving the embarrassed Mitchell to find his own way out. When the images were broadcast on BBC, UTV and RTÉ that evening, Ditty found himself lambasted by all sides. The public lashed his bad manners, fellow-unionists bemoaned a public relations disaster and the Alliance Party and SDLP put down a motion of censure. 'Like so many other citizens of Belfast, I just wanted to crawl under the settee and hide', said Independent SDLP councillor Cormac Boomer. There was no need for motions of censure for election day was Herbie's last hurrah. The Lord Mayor who declared, 'I don't support anything that is not British' – but didn't turn down a chance to attend the Irish Day Celebrations in Brussels – found his brand of politics rejected by the unquestionably British citizens on the Shankill.

Even by City Hall standards, the Council's reputation was in the toilet. Mancunian *Irish News* editor Nick Garbutt lambasted the Dream Team:

> Men like Ditty and Millar do not just represent those daft enough to vote for them at Council elections. They represent every single person who lives within the Belfast City Council area. They don't act as if they do…Those people who live in Belfast and are not extreme, bitter and

bigoted loyalists, therefore, do not have a council, an elected body to look after their interests. They are effectively disenfranchised, ignored. They are second class citizens…This is tragic. Belfast people are warm, generous and hospitable. Men like Ditty and Millar are not truly representative of the city. The damage they are doing to the city's image is incalculable.

An *Irish News* survey found that, while eight out of ten people in Belfast knew who Herbie Ditty was, 98 per cent of their number felt he failed to project a positive image of the city. Jim McDowell didn't miss and hit the wall either in his inimitable weekly missive to 'Sir Patrick Mayhem' in the same paper. Furious at being banned by Ditty from the Lord Mayor's parlour for his traditional post-meeting pint with the rest of the councillors (with the exception of Sinn Féin) and press, McDowell let him have it with both barrels:

> Mayor Ditty is short on political savvy. He fails to appreciate that since he took over the mayoralty of the Dome in June, the image of the city of Belfast has plunged to its worst ever. The public relations image of Belfast has been wiped through the mire – or the mayor. His conduct and that of some of his colleagues during the Olympic dispute over gold medal boxing champion Michael Carruth was abysmal. Now it is time for the gloves really to come off and for the decent people who are councillors in Belfast City Hall to realise that the Gerriatria are dragging them into the mud. The only compensation I took from being barred from the Lord Mayor's parlour is that I will no longer have to have a jar with people, and the Lord Mayor in particular, who I consider to be bumbling buffoons. The time for compassion has passed. The City of Belfast, and its ratepayers can no longer afford to tolerate such dinosaurs of the political past-tense in their midst.

Lest anyone think Donegall Pass native Jim McDowell was 'saft' on Sinn Féin or too hard on the unionist City Fathers, it should be noted that during the broadcasting ban, he alone among Belfast hacks voiced his support for the measure.

The proximity of the election also brought a rare sighting of that most delicate of City Hall species, the Alliance Party councillor. South Belfast councillor Mark Long wrote to the press accusing Sinn Féin of failing to make a constructive contribution to City Hall debate. In response, I noted my surprise that Councillor Long claimed to be an elected official but conceded 'that after an extensive search of City Hall record books there is indeed an Alliance councillor of that name…Mr Long says he "has yet to perceive one of the Sinn Féin councillors make a constructive proposal",' I added. 'It gives me no pleasure to point this out to a man with his finger so obviously on the City Hall pulse, but if he checks the Council Minutes book for June 1992 (these, Mr Long, are the large brown books that the staff hand out to you as you enter the chamber) he will find under A312 that not one, not two, but three Alliance councillors voted for an amendment proposed by myself.' (Yes, even I thought I was insufferable.) Long was rarely heard of again and went down in flames at the May elections.

Frustrated, the unionists sought additional items of militaristic memorabilia to adorn the walls of City Hall. Someone with a particularly bizarre sense of humour decided to place a portrait of General Henry Wilson, shot dead by Michael Collins' men in London in 1921, on the wall facing the men's toilets on the first floor. A staunch supporter of the Orange Order who had urged the 'Troubles' be solved in 1919 by shooting the Sinn Féin leaders, he was doomed to spend eternity watching the present-day Shinners spend a penny. But the pendulum was swinging. As part of his new-brush approach to City Hall, Chief Executive Iain MacDonald introduced separate party rooms for each political grouping on the Council. The Council ban on bilingual stationery was also body-swerved by inviting each councillor to apply for their own personalised letter-headed paper and complimentary slips.

The new committee structures were rubber-stamped by the Council in May 1993, just days before the local government elections. Rhonda Paisley, who had decided to quit after a bruising eight years at the hands of the Sinn Féin members whose lives she had vowed to make intolerable, didn't turn up for the Council's last hurrah. However, Sammy Wilson carried the torch for yesterday's men, opposing the new structures because they would increase Sinn Féin representation 'by 35 per cent'. 'We have done a good job in Belfast City Council in closing out these people', he boasted. As tempers flared, Alban Maginness of the SDLP commented that it was fitting for the Council term to end as it had begun, 'in bitter sectarian division'. While the *Belfast Telegraph* noticed the whiff of changes in the air as the term came to a stormy close, Sammy Wilson was having none of it. 'Since October 1991, Sinn Féin have tried 151 times to put motions and 151 times they have been defeated', he told the Council. Alex Maskey rejoindered: 'It doesn't matter how many motions were lost, in 1983 we had one councillor and now we have nine. I'm confident that'll soon be ten.'

As the 1993 elections neared, observers speculated on how long it would be before the unionists lost their majority. 'After more than 100 years of unbroken rule, their overall control of the city council looks shaky', reported the *Irish Times*. Brian Feeney, who didn't stand for re-election to the 'madhouse' cautioned that unionists would maintain their dominance in the largest elected forum in the North for one more term:

> But there can be no doubt that time is running out for unionist domination of Belfast City Council. None of the unionists seemed to notice. John Major went to Derry's Guildhall during his last visit; he didn't come to the City Hall and that is going to be the pattern. The message is that visitors and investors will not come to Belfast because it would suggest there was official approval of the council's appalling behaviour.

'It began with a roar', reported Mary Kelly of the *Belfast Telegraph*, 'but last night, Belfast City Council ended its four year term of office on a strangely subdued note. When the outgoing councillors took their seats in May 1989, the first meeting was marked by angry scenes, two hours of shouting, walk-outs and the beginning of a stormy chapter in the council's history. Unionists deployed a range of tactics to silence Sinn Féin... but four years on, there are some signs of change in the air.'

8.

M'Learned Friends

In a world where apparently everyone with clout – media, church, trade union leaders, political pundits – was agin us, our solicitor Pat Finucane provided a useful counterbalance. Listening to him demolish the arguments presented by our enemies to justify our harassment in City Hall was both revelatory and reassuring. Authoritative, incisive, teasing, he projected an invincibility which was infectious. After a session with Pat, I always returned to the fray refreshed and even more determined to turn the tables on those who would disenfranchise our voters. Pat told us time out of number that our duty was to discharge our responsibilities as elected representatives. Any illegal bar on our ability to represent our electorate was an attack not on us but on the very people we represented. To deny Sinn Féin councillors the right to represent their electorate was to disenfranchise the majority of Belfast's nationalists. His legal partner Peter Madden and colleague Kevin Winters took an equally brusque approach to unionist attempts to play fast and loose with the Standing Orders of City Hall and resolved to defend the few rights Sinn Féin councillors had under the Northern Ireland Constitution Act (1972) which forbids discrimination on grounds of religion or politics. The threat of legal action had previously halted the unionist freeze-out of Sinn Féin in the wake of the Enniskillen

Belfast City Hall 1990: The 'Belfast Says No' banner protesting against the Anglo-Irish Agreement takes pride of place. The courts eventually ruled that the sign was being displayed without planning permission. As a result it was moved to a position inside the dome before being removed for stone-cleaning work in 1992. When work was complete, the banner wasn't replaced. (Photo, courtesy of Belfast Exposed.)

(All photos courtesy of *Andersonstown News*, unless otherwise stated.)

Putting the boot in: An RUC man attacks a protester with a boot after nationalists tried to stage a rally at Belfast City Hall in April 1981.

H-Block protest: People's Democracy councillor Fergus O'Hare, elected to City Hall in May 1981 on a platform supporting political status for republican prisoners, addresses a rally at Casement Park, Belfast, in June 1981 while the hunger strike protest was at its height.

Community stalwart: Ardoyne independent councillor Larry Kennedy who was murdered by loyalists in 1981.

First meeting: Newly-elected Sinn Féin councillor Alex Maskey (bearded, front) is accompanied by supporters as he leaves City Hall after his first Council meeting on 4 July 1983. To his front and right is Bairbre de Brún, now Assembly member for West Belfast.

Team success: Sinn Féin candidates for the May 1985 elections pictured at the City Hall count are (back, l-r) Mick Conlon (who was unsuccessful but is now a councillor), Sean McKnight, Fra McCann (partially hidden), and Bobby Lavery, (middle, l-r) Gerard McGuigan, Alex Maskey, and Máirtín Ó Muilleoir, (front, l-r) Sean Keenan, Lily Fitzsimmons and Tish Holland.

Salute: Máirtín Ó Muilleoir (left) and Fra McCann are raised on to the shoulders of their supporters after their October 1987 by-election victory.

Topsy-turvy: Máirtín Ó Muilleoir pickets City Hall in 1991 with an obvious message for the City Fathers. The cartoon by 'Doll' shows a unionist standing on his head and misreading '1991' as '1661'. The 'Belfast Says No' banner dominated the City Hall car park at that time.

Bigot's bigot: Frank 'Putsy' Millar revelled in the nickname of 'SuperProd'. (Picture courtesy of Sunday World)

Show of strength: Lord Mayor Sammy Wilson (centre) beside DUP party leader Ian Paisley at the inaugural rally of loyalist paramilitary group Ulster Resistance in the Ulster Hall in 1986.

Vote catcher: The late Paddy Devlin of the SDLP who obtained four quotas in his West Belfast constituency in the 1977 elections to City Hall. Today, Sinn Féin holds four of the five seats in the same electoral area.

Upper Falls representative: The late Alliance councillor Pip Glendenning. She and husband Will resigned their council seats in 1987. The by-elections were won by Máirtín Ó Muilleoir and Fra McCann of Sinn Féin.

Fiery: DUP and, later, independent councillor, George Seawright at a Shankill Road protest. (Picture by Sean McKernan, Belfast Exposed.)

Targeted: Sean Keenan, who served for Sinn Féin on Belfast City Council from 1985 to 1989, was shot twice by loyalists.

Palestinian policeman: Lord Mayor in 1987-1988, Dixie Gilmore.

Belfast ambassador: Lord Mayor Herbie Ditty (1992-1993) at the opening of a children's play park.

Shankill representative: Unionist councillor Joe Coggle who travelled the world for Belfast before losing his seat in the 1997 elections.

Taking on Sinn Féin: Dr Joe Hendron of the SDLP who captured the West Belfast Westminster seat from Gerry Adams of Sinn Féin in 1992.

SDLP voice: West Belfast SDLP councillor Alex Attwood.

Council battler: West Belfast Sinn Féin councillor Lily Fitzsimmons who retired from the Council at the 1993 elections.

Triumph: Councillor Sean McKnight and Josie Quigley on the site of the Whiterock play park which was denied equipment by City Hall unionists. Ms Quigley led a successful court battle to have the Council discrimination overturned.

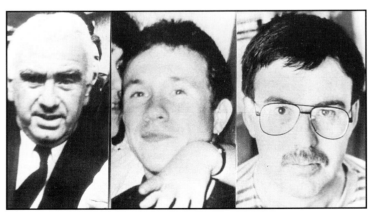

Murdered: Shot dead in the Sinn Féin advice centre on the Falls Road in February 1992 by an RUC man were (l-r) Paddy Loughran (61), Michael O'Dwyer (24) and Pat McBride (40).

Extremists: How Irish News cartoonist Blotski (Ian Knox) saw the unionist troika of Wilson, Dodds and Millar in 1991. (Courtesy of Ian Knox)

Election hopefuls: Sinn Féin candidates in the 1993 election. (Back, l-r) Bobby Lavery, Gerard McGuigan, Máirtín Ó Muilleoir, Paddy McManus (RIP), Tom Hartley, (middle, l-r) Joe Austin, Una Gillespie, Marie Moore, Joe O'Donnell, (front, l-r) Pat McGeown (RIP), Alex Maskey, Fra McCann, Sean Hayes.

Cool customer: Joe Austin (left), who served for Sinn Féin on the Council between 1991 and 1997, canvassing support in his North Belfast constituency.

It's all Greek to me: Rhonda Paisley who moved to Greece while holding on to her council seat until 1993.

Animated? Shankill UUP councillor Chris McGimpsey who came on to the Council in 1993.

DUP stalwart: Nigel Dodds.

The eyes have it: Councillor Liz Seawright pictured outside the council chamber beside Sinn Féin councillor Sean McKnight

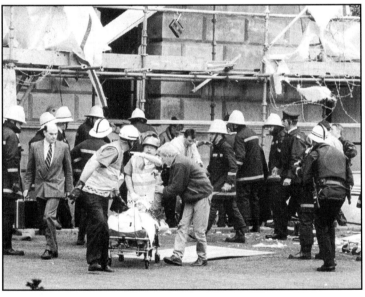

City Hall attack: An injured workman is rushed to hospital by paramedics after a loyalist bomb attack on Sinn Féin's City Hall offices in 1994. (Picture courtesy of Sean McKernan, Belfast Exposed.)

CITY OF BELFAST

THE ASSOCIATION OF PAEDIATRIC ANAESTHETISTS
OF GREAT BRITAIN AND IRELAND — ANNUAL MEETING

*The Rt. Hon. the Lord Mayor
and the City Council*
request the pleasure of the company of

Councillor and Mrs. M. O'Muilleoir

*at a Civic Reception in the City Hall, Belfast
on Thursday, 11th March, 1993 at 6.30 p.m.*

R.S.V.P. to the Lord Mayor's Secretary,
City Hall,
Belfast BT1 5GS.
(Tel. 320202 Ext. 2212)

Finger Buffet

PLEASE PRESENT THIS INVITATION AT THE CITY HALL

Just what the doctor ordered: After Sinn Féin successfully overturned the ban on its members from attending civic functions organised by Belfast City Hall, the first invitation extended to the party in 1993 was to a Civic Reception to mark the annual meeting of the Association of Paediatric Anaesthetists of Great Britain and Ireland.

Play Plea: Backing a campaign by the parents of North Belfast to keep a play park open in the New Lodge area are Workers Party/Democratic Left councillor Séamus Lynch, Councillor Brian Feeney (SDLP) and the late Paddy McManus of (Sinn Féin).

The ego has landed: Stormont Minister Richard Needham who approved policies to ostracise Sinn Féin.

Cash for questions: Stormont Economy Minister Tim Smith.

Céad Míle Fáilte: Former Lord Mayor and DUP Shankill representative Eric Smyth who welcomed US President Bill Clinton to Belfast in 1995.

Flying the flag: DUP councillor Robert Cleland lunges at RUC lines with a flagpole during a Lurgan protest in 1995

bombing and, of course, memories were still fresh of the successful Alliance Party court challenge to the deferment policy which followed the signing of the Anglo-Irish Agreement. But what had gone before was hardly enough to prepare the unionists for the legal thrashing they were to take in the late '80s and early '90s.

Solicitor Pauline O'Hare scored the first major court victory for the nationalist electorate when she successfully overturned by judicial review, on behalf of local mother-of-three Josie Quigley, the 1988 Council decision not to place equipment in a West Belfast playground. In April 1991 Lord Justice Nicholson found that the Council had discriminated against the people of the Whiterock by refusing to put swings in the Whiterock park. The judge ruled that the unionist tactic of meeting in caucus before committee meetings to discuss the agenda and agree an approach which could be pushed through without Sinn Féin input was to turn the very purpose of local government on its head. He rejected farcical claims by Frank Millar, Parks Committee Chairman, that the decision not to place play equipment in the park had been taken because Whiterock Leisure Centre was underused. He was distinctly underwhelmed by Frank's suggestion that Sinn Féin wanted to take the play equipment earmarked for Whiterock and redirect it to 'another dump on the Falls Road', known to most people, never mind the Chairman of the Council Parks Committee, as Willowbank Park. Sporting the surgical collar which he wore for formal occasions, Frank Millar failed to cut the mustard in the witness box, drawing audible moans of distress from the judge with his sectarian reminiscences. 'I have been a member of Belfast City Council for 20 years and I have never seen any discrimination practised there', Frank told an incredulous courtroom. The only unionist to accompany Frank to the courtroom showdown was that legal heavyweight (well, heavyweight at any rate) Dixie Gilmore. Our QC Michael Lavery later compared the performance of Sean McKnight in the witness box to Frank Millar's debut as 'racing Arkle against a donkey'. Confidential documents revealed by the Council under the process of legal discovery subsequently showed that secret meetings had taken place immediately after the Parks Committee decision between the unionist whips and City Hall officials to 'ascertain the reason for the (Whiterock) decision'. Minutes of the meeting reported counsel for City Hall arguing strongly against any attempt to defend the decision. That advice was studiously ignored by unionists who instructed Council lawyers to fight the challenge all the way to the High Court.

'I am satisfied that the unionists' hostility to Provisional Sinn Féin spilt over and led to the decision not to spend money on the playground at the leisure centre', said Lord Justice Nicholson, adding:

> Unionist councillors on the Parks Committee decided to delete Whiterock from the list because parents of children at Whiterock who would make use of the facilities there were seen by the unionist councillors as supporters of Provisional Sinn Féin in view of the fact that they had voted in four Provisional Sinn Féin councillors out of five.

As he announced his decision, Nicholson allowed himself a smile at Josie Quigley who was in court for the verdict and had led the David against Goliath encounter. 'The people of the Whiterock will be pleased even if it comes late in the day', he said to Mrs Quigley across the courtroom. Attempts had been made during the case by counsel for the Council to portray Josie Quigley as a republican puppet by suggesting that Gerry Adams had once lived in the house she now occupied and by insinuating that she was too lazy to use a playground just half a mile from her home. In fact, Gerry Adams never lived there (and what if he had?) and the playground in question was indeed only half a mile away but on the loyalist side of the peaceline. It wasn't until November 1992 that the freshly kitted out Whiterock play park was finally opened, complete with brand new play equipment. The same week, Council lawyers revealed that the court defence of the unionist action had set ratepayers back £25,000. Frank Millar, by then Deputy Lord Mayor, declined my suggestion that he resign. 'I would be a sad person if I responded to calls from Sinn Féin', he said.

Sadly, the officials charged with upholding fair play for all the ratepayers of Belfast, were sometimes keen to defend unscrupulous practices targeted for legal action by Sinn Féin. In fact, a few officials were quite content to operate systems which were clearly illegal – and swiftly acknowledged to be so by the courts – rather than speak up for the civil liberties of those they really served: the citizens of Belfast. We always felt shortchanged when faced with officials rather than politicians during our court cases; a case of fighting the monkey rather than the organ grinder! But it was often only when put to the pin of their collars that officials stood up to the unionists.

That was certainly the case in regard to the CHAMPS (Change Management Planning and Strategy) Sub-Committee of the General Purposes and Finance Committee which was set up to prepare the council for the privatisation of services. Sinn Féin was the only opposition party barred from the GP&F Committee and thus its representatives were the only ones excluded from the CHAMPS Sub-Committee. That wasn't necessarily a bad thing since the Sub-Committee, which met in semi-secret session with £600-a-day consultants Price Waterhouse, was charged with chopping up to 600 jobs from the 2,700 workforce and cutting back services. Under the chairmanship of Eric Smyth, the CHAMPS sub-committee refused to allow Sinn Féin sight of the recommendations of its expensive consultants, who tied themselves up in knots when challenged on why they failed to speak with Sinn Féin councillors while drawing up their report. At a face-to-face meeting, the consultants told Sinn Féin councillors that they had been authorised by senior officials to interview only members of the GP&F Committee and the chairs of other standing committees – which conveniently meant no Sinn Féin councillors would be consulted. Town Clerk Stanley McDowell dismissed the accusation in unequivocal terms but it was a sign of the worrying times in City Hall that any hired consultant would consider a crucial report on the future of the Council complete without any attempt having been made to speak to representatives of the second biggest party. However, Sinn

Féin's sniping at the sub-committee was small beer when set against the unerring ability of the unionists to shoot themselves in the foot. In November the grouping repaired to a four-star hotel in Portrush for a two day brainstorming session on its cutback strategy – a move which went down like a fart in a spacesuit for ratepayers bracing themselves for the decimation of Council services under Compulsory Competitive Tendering – a sophisticated cover name for privatisation.

Alex Maskey was appointed by the Sinn Féin grouping to 'shadow' the CHAMPS group and duly went along to its meetings. Even though he was denied access to the documentation under discussion and was forced to sit back from the table, the unionists found the Sinn Féin man's presence unsettling at a time when they were preparing to shaft hundreds of workers. As a result, they resorted to pre-meeting meetings of the key players: members of the CHAMPS committee, the consultants and senior staff. Decisions agreed by this kitchen cabinet, the CHAMPS committee then met for the briefest of meetings to rubberstamp the resolutions formally put before it. But even that didn't go far enough for CHAMPS chairman Eric Smyth who resorted to holding meetings of the group in the most inaccessible part of City Hall – on the third floor – and in September 1992 locking the door to bar Alex Maskey from entering the room. Councillor Maskey went to the press to slam the CHAMPS closed-shop. 'This report has massive implications for our constituents, especially those employed by the Council', he said, 'yet we are denied any input into how it is considered.' Raising the Damocles sword of court action, Councillor Maskey warned that vital Council decisions 'were taking place behind closed doors'. Frank Millar was unmoved. 'I'm past the stage of worrying about Sinn Féin using the courts', he said. 'They know they have a honeymoon period in the courts but eventually it'll run out – then they'll claim there's no justice. I haven't heard that one in a while.' But the SDLP had no wish to be on the wrong side of a Sinn Féin court action. Alarmed at the public perception of the sub-committee, the SDLP announced they wouldn't take part in any further

CHAMPS meetings if they could not be shown to be open and 'of benefit to the Council'. Fred Cobain retorted that Sinn Féin had to been 'excluded for a very good reason which everyone knows about'. But with the Council's reputation in tatters, that was never going to be enough to satisfy the SDLP. Weary Council officials, wary of another Custer's last stand, cut the potential court action off at the pass by ensuring the door to the CHAMPS Sub-Committee meeting remained unlocked during all further meetings.

In the summer of 1991, Sinn Féin sought by means of judicial review to abolish the patently bogus sub-committee system in the City Hall. I drafted lengthy affidavits on behalf of my colleagues, backed by an affidavit from the SDLP's Brian Feeney, alleging that the Leisure Service sub-committee, our test case, was being used to exclude Sinn Féin. These sub-committees had effectively replaced the kitchen cabinets which unionists had convened before committee meetings in 1987 and 1988 in order to discuss agendas and agree on decisions which could be pushed through without allowing Sinn Féin to speak. I argued that the Sinn Féin members were more active on leisure centre issues than the very unionists denying them representation from the sub-committee. Fra McCann and I were the only councillors to draft an official written response to the proposed privatisation of the centres and alone among the Council group to regularly visit the complexes to meet staff and users. That was not to mention our prominent (arguably sole) membership of the Save Our Leisure Services Committee! Our trump card was the fact that the Leisure Services' Sub-Committee membership had been proposed by DUP councillor Robin Newton, best known for his belief that West Belfast is 'a parasites' paradise' and that, as he told the *Belfast Telegraph*, 'the law-abiding people in North, South and East Belfast are sick, sore and tired of the West Belfast moaners and spongers'. Newton had tabled a similar proposal at subsequent meetings of the annual meeting of the Leisure Services Committee while efforts by Brian Feeney to scrap the sub-committee were voted down. Newton's keen interest in the make-up of the sub-committee belied its real purpose: to ostracise Sinn Féin. In his submission, Brian Feeney said that at one committee meeting when he sought to have the sub-committee system abolished, a former Lord Mayor defended the sub-committees because they had been set up 'to keep gunmen off them'.

However, the defence of the Rubik's Cube of discrimination which was the sub-committee system of City Hall didn't come from its unionist architects. The unionist bush telegraph had quickly relayed news of Frankie Millar's High Court drubbing, making his comrades understandably reticent about facing the same humiliation at the hands of our counsel. The unionists took a rain check on the entire defence of the case but, astonishingly, Assistant Town Clerk, Robert Wilson rushed to their defence. Amazingly, as he was to tell the court, Robert Wilson did not regard the sub-committees as part of a unionist ploy to exclude Sinn Féin from Council business. Yet every breathing moment of sub-committees was dedicated to frustrating Sinn Féin. I couldn't even find out when it was to meet. As I wasn't a member of the sub-committee (though I did serve on the principal committee), I had no right, Town Clerk Cecil Ward had originally ruled, to be informed of the times and dates of its meetings by post several days beforehand – as was the case for members of the sub-committee. He did agree, however, to inform me if the sub-committee was meeting if I was to call and request that information on the morning of any such meeting. This led to the farcical situation where I would call City Hall at start of business each morning to find out which bogus sub-committee was meeting that day.

Robert Wilson argued, somewhat disingenuously, that the sub-committees had been set up to enable members 'to get more involved in the detailed workings of the Council' and 'to review existing services'. In his affidavit, the Assistant Town Clerk stated that the sub-committee system did not prevent Sinn Féin members 'from carrying out their normal business'. His pitiful defence of the convoluted unionist exercise in apartheid even involved a belated justification of the unionist ruling that councillors not on the sub-committees had to sit at the back of the committee room. Though he kindly did cut us some slack: 'It is indicated by Councillor Ó Muilleoir that it is difficult to follow the meeting of a sub-committee from chairs behind the main table. I would accept that acoustics generally in the main committee rooms are poor.' The solution, however, wasn't to bring all members round the one table, as he explained. 'The Council has recently taken a decision to provide a sound enhancement system which should considerably improve acoustics.' Fortunately, Sinn Féin had consistently refused to accept the ruling that we sit, like blacks in '50s Alabama, at the back of the room. On one occasion, Fra McCann shuffled his seat forward to the table, shot the Chairman his meanest Divis Flats stare and tossed his size 14s up on the oak table. Panicked, the unionists abandoned the meeting. On another occasion, I protested that it was impossible to hear the meanderings of septuagenarian Tommy Patton from the back of the room and insisted on sitting beside the unionists. They brought in an official to ask me to move back but, when I refused, resumed business.

Sadly, Robert Wilson made a trenchant defence of the Council policy of refusing Sinn Féin members excluded from the sub-committees copies of the documentation provided for discussion, including agendas, and even went so far as to stand over the ludicrous Council refusal to provide us with the times of the sub-committee meetings. Thus a sub-committee from which Sinn Féin was excluded could meet and decide to meet again the next week without our councillors being any the wiser.

It was a black day for the officials of City Hall – the ultimate defenders of the civic weal – when Robert Wilson took the stand to defend the abuse of civil rights by the unionists. To this day I can't understand why he, rather than the then Town Clerk, Stanley McDowell, or the Town Solicitor went in to bat for the unionists. Though the Town Clerk drafted a short, explanatory affidavit, he steered well clear of the witness box. City Hall sources would later hint that Robert Wilson was given 'bad advice' by certain officials. Some opined that he was the loyal foot-soldier used as a sacrificial lamb by others – elected and non-elected – who knew he was on a Kamikaze mission (and didn't mind mixing their metaphors). Whatever, he won little sympathy from our counsel. Reduced to an apologist for nihilistic unionists by ruthless cross-examination, Wilson came across as a myopic civil servant unable to see the reality of what was going on around him. He painted a picture of a Council where all matters were carried out with a meticulous attention to Standing Orders and a devotion to fair play for all, only to be reminded by our barrister when the case finally came to court in December 1991 that the night before he gave evidence, Sinn Féin members had been shouted down by unionists – at a committee meeting he had attended. Asked the straightest of questions, 'Is there anything that you have observed – either seeing or hearing – to indicate that the sub-committees were set up by the Council to frustrate the participation by Sinn Féin councillors in the work of the Committees?', Wilson answered 'No'. However, under pressure from our counsel, he did admit that unionists 'will seek to frustrate Sinn Féin within the Council', and that on some occasions they 'go too far' and had to be advised by officials. Whether Wilson classified the habitual screaming at Sinn Féin members by Newton, Wilson and Paisley whenever they tried to speak at committee and sub-committee meetings, as 'too far' wasn't entirely clear.

Lord Justice Murray's 30-page judgment in the sub-committee case was finally handed down in November 1992, a full 11 months after he had heard the arguments. It was a resounding vindication of the Sinn Féin position. The sub-committees were declared 'invalid and unlawful' and claims by counsel for City Hall that the Sinn Féin allegations of a unionist conspiracy were 'paranoia' dismissed. I had rushed from work to try and catch his formal ruling in the High Court but was only in time to meet my Sinn Féin colleagues leave the courthouse. We were divided by a security gate which kept apart visitors to the court from those leaving. I shouted across to them to find out how we had done. 'Hands down', said Alex Maskey. 'All of it?' I asked. 'Lock, stock and barrel', he replied, sporting a grin as wide as Royal Avenue.

Noting that the bashful unionists had not taken advantage of the court case to defend their practices in person, Lord Justice Murray pointed out that the Council officials were in no position to explain the motivation behind the unionist decision to set up the sub-committees. Unionist cowardice in ducking the court clash rebounded on them. The judge found that the allegations against the unionists 'must carry weight' because they had refused to make any statement rebutting them. He ruled that the Sinn Féin side had proved that the 'dominant purpose' of the sub-committees was to exclude. Sinn Féin members and, as such, was 'an invalid exercise' of the Council's powers. There was a pointed dismissal of Robert Wilson's defence. As Lord Justice Murray stated in his written judgment:

> Mr Wilson in his affidavit explains that one of the reasons for the subcommittee is to allow individual councillors to get to grips with the work of the Council and to do this on a body which is not under the same pressure of time as the Council itself. If this is so, then what is one to say of a decision which not only denies Sinn Féin councillors any representation on the Leisure Services Sub-Committee, a body which deals extensively with services in that part of the city which Sinn Féin councillors represent, but also will not allow those councillors to speak at a meeting of that Sub-Committee and which they are entitled to attend and at which they may be the only persons in the Committee room with first-hand knowledge of the subject in hand? It seems to me that such a decision cannot be defended on any reasonable or lawful grounds.

Wilson's suggestion that Sinn Féin members barred from sub-committees could raise matters discussed at the main committee meetings was also rubbished by the judge who accepted that minutes were pushed through without allowing any input from Sinn Féin. While sympathising with unionist hostility to Sinn Féin because of its association with the IRA, Lord Justice Murray warned the unionists:

> A duly-elected Sinn Féin councillor is entitled to take his seat on the Council and to enjoy the same rights and protection under the law as any other duly-elected local government member. Unionist councillors may find this statement of the law very hard to accept but accept it they must if they are not to fall foul of the law.

The Council moved immediately to disband sub-committees which had been set up to exclude Sinn Féin by the Community, Leisure, Parks and Technical Services Committees. The aftershocks reverberated around City Hall with Alex Maskey, in no-nonsense mode, informing a chastened Robert Wilson that Sinn Féin would be demanding his resignation – an unprecedented move in a Council where Sinn Féin endeavoured to criticise the elected representatives of unionism (who were ultimately responsible for policy) rather than the officials who implemented it. But, in our view, Wilson had crossed his Rubicon by agreeing to go in to court to defend the illegal sub-committees, a decision which effectively let the unionists off the hook. Yet it was difficult not to feel some sympathy for him. He was forced to be the fall guy for a failed system of gerrymandering at the very time when the shifting sands of demography were about to transform the Council. Sinn Féin never fully forgot his role in the defence of the sub-committee obscenity, but relations did improve considerably in the following years as Wilson proved himself more than able to adapt to the changing face of City Hall.

The sub-committee's decision was a landmark victory for Sinn Féin. Not only did unionists abandon the sub-committee subterfuge post haste (the Council decision was handed down on a Friday afternoon, on Monday notification was circulated among councillors and officials that the sub-committees were toast) but they also caved in to pressure from the Council officials – most notably new English-born Chief Executive Iain MacDonald who had taken over the Town Clerk's position – to replace the gerrymandered committee system introduced back in 1987. From the start of the new Council term in June 1993, all committee places would be handed out according to the principles of proportionality; the more Council seats a party had, the more committee and sub-committee seats it was entitled to. DUP zealots protested the new departure but, battered by a series of court cases and mauled by the media, the UUs agreed to the move in the hope that it would improve the Council's tarnished image.

Unionists branded the promised new era as 'power-sharing' though it fell short of that as, even though Sinn Féin members were to be allowed committee positions according to their party strength, they were still to be denied committee chairs or the position of Lord Mayor. Pressing unionists to dismantle the 'discriminatory machinery at City Hall', Alex Maskey warned the beleaguered majority at City Hall that 'democracy wasn't theirs to hand out'. But the unionist approach to the discussion did signal an increasing awareness that the tactic of isolating Sinn Féin had simply worsened their PR position. They were also aware of threats by the Local Government Auditor to surcharge councillors if they continued to waste the rates on futile court defences of their illegal practices. 'Yes, it is a sea change', unionist whip Fred Cobain said of the committee shake-up in the *Irish Times*. 'We need to make Belfast work'. A unionist deep-throat, presumably the same Fred Cobain, conceded in the same article that Sinn Féin was trouncing them in the publicity stakes. 'I think that we have such a bad image that even when we are right, we are wrong', he bleated. 'We need to do a major repair job.'

For the first time, the Ulster Unionists consulted the Alliance and SDLP about the changes and showed a flexible face to the media, moves which held the real possibility of wrongfooting Sinn Féin and indicated that they had taken seriously an *Irish News* survey in December 1992 which showed just six per cent of the city's ratepayers felt the council provided a good standard of service. Asked if Belfast City Council projected a positive image at home and abroad, not one respondent said yes. It was only a green shoot but there was nevertheless a feeling that the principles of partnership being pushed by the new Chief Executive – and increasingly becoming a core value of all the state agencies – were putting down roots in City Hall. Unfortunately for the unionists, the SDLP didn't take kindly to the stipulation that the new power-sharing arrangements wouldn't cover the rotation of the Lord Mayor and Deputy Mayor position. 'The unionists have put this forward as a power sharing deal but nothing could be further from the truth', insisted Brian Feeney. Feeney may have been a tad too hard on the unionist proposal for it did have one beneficial spin-off, Deputy Lord Mayor Frank Millar branded it 'a sell-out' and revealed that in protest he wouldn't be standing for the council again in May. Belfast, still reeling from his latest outrageous statement in the *Sunday World* – that Travellers 'should be incinerated' – breathed a sigh of relief.

The new equitable committee system was a red rag to DUP bull Eric Smyth – who had taken to wearing short-sleeved shirts to meetings and giving clenched fist salutes while shouting 'No Surrender'. The man of God was tossed out of the January 1993 meeting of Council on a 35-8 vote after refusing to shut up when Alex Maskey tried to speak. Brandishing a placard with the words 'The face of the earth is against them that do evil', Minister Smyth warned that God would bring judgments on the Sinn Féiners and their ilk, collectively known in Biblical times, apparently, as 'Commanches'. Lord Mayor Herbie Ditty tolerated 15 minutes of the tirade – it was, after all, an election year – before asking his Shankill colleague to sit down. When he refused to do so, the meeting was first adjourned, and then, when Smyth resumed his tub-thumping, a vote was taken to toss him out on his ear. New chief executive Iain MacDonald, attending his first full Council meeting, could certainly say that he had received a baptism of fire. But Smyth's eruption was the death throes of the campaign to shout down Sinn Féin councillors. The UUs tried instead to propose a system where all councillors walked out in protest when Sinn Féin members spoke but Sammy Wilson, always spoiling for a fight, again refused to leave the chamber and gradually the all-walk-out-all-walk-in-again tactic petered out.

Parallel with the sub-committee case came a Sinn Féin challenge to the ban on Sinn Féin members from all civic functions. Under a Council motion rushed through, virtually unnoticed, by the all-unionist General Purposes and Finance Hospitality Sub-Committee, shortly after the arrival of Sinn Féin onto the Council in numbers in 1985, civic hospitality was not to be extended to republican councillors. Ulster Unionist Chairman John Carson endorsed the one-sentence motion – 'that invitations be not extended to members of Sinn Féin to attend any functions organised by the Council' – at a meeting which was mostly taken up with more weighty matters of civic governance such as the menu for the Imperial Orange Council luncheon (egg mayonnaise followed by braised rump steak and, appropriately, raspberry pavlova). Not only did this condemn visiting dignitaries to the crushingly boring small-talk of unionists during civic banquets but also meant that Sinn Féin councillors were denied access to events in which they or their constituents were involved. The first action of newly-elected councillor Joe Austin in October 1991 was to challenge his exclusion from the official opening of the Council's new Cecil Ward building (named in honour of the retiring Town Clerk), just yards from the City Hall itself. However, the courts decided not to rule on his challenge because the sub-committee case was being considered. The ribbon-cutting ceremony went ahead in the absence of Joe and his colleagues, enabling the Council to erect an official plaque stating that the building had been opened in the presence of named councillors – none of whom were members of Sinn Féin. Throughout the city, similar plaques with their awkward wording can be seen, replacing the previous signs which used to list the names of all the committee members responsible for the facility.

In March 1992, councillors Tish Holland and Lily Fitzsimmons were barred from attending a Council seminar and dinner held in conjunction with the Equal Opportunities Commission to mark International Women's Day. Among the day's events were a workshop on 'Women and Politics'; neither of the Sinn Féin women was invited. Tish Holland went to the High Court to seek legal redress only to be stymied again by a Council plea to the courts that the issue not be considered until a ruling had been made on the challenge to the sub-committees which was trundling its way through the courts. To their credit, a number of women refused to meekly accept the Council ban, staging a protest outside City Hall and disrupting the lavish dinner in protest at the absence of Councillors Holland and Fitzsimmons. Joe Austin returned to the fray in September 1992, arguing that the imminent visit to City Hall by the President of the European Commission for a civic function made it imperative for the courts to hear his challenge to the functions' ban. 'An important point of democratic principle is at stake here', he argued. 'All votes are equal and therefore no member returned by the votes of the electors of Belfast should be discriminated against by his or her fellow-members.' He pointed out that while Sinn Féin had attended recent Council ceremonies conferring the freedom of the city on the emergency services (Sinn Féin members refused to stand for the excruciatingly embarrassing singing of the Queen during the ceremony, much to the chagrin of the upstanding SDLP members), they had then been denied access to the civic function immediately afterwards to mark the event. As it turned out the Euro dignitary never went ahead with the City Hall visit but unionists, perturbed at the leaking of the proposal, compounded their unlawful activities by introducing a new ruling that all parties but Sinn Féin were to be informed about the visits of senior politicians to City Hall. In an affidavit filed in court by Nigel Dodds in defence of the functions' ban, he argued that RUC or British Army members wouldn't attend City Hall events if Sinn Féin members were present. 'The majority of councillors in Belfast City Council consider it to be wholly inappropriate that at functions, events and meetings organised and hosted by the Council that guests should be compelled to meet or to be confronted by or to be engaged in conversation by Sinn Féin councillors', he said.

In January 1993, Lower Falls councillor Fra McCann demanded the right to be invited to a gala hosted by City Hall to celebrate the centenary of the Irish Amateur Swimming Association. As a representative on the Leisure Services Committee and a councillor for the area taking in the Falls Baths – home to two of the city's oldest water polo clubs – he argued that he had as much right to be there as any other councillor. The previous year, Sinn Féin members had been the only councillors who bothered to attend an international racquetball tournament held in a West Belfast leisure centre and hosted by the Council. They were also the only councillors barred from the Council function to mark the end of the tournament. Again the officious Council side managed to stall the new challenge, citing the impending decision on the sub-committee question. However, a chink in the armour emerged at a meeting with Town Solicitor John Fox OBE, the most senior Catholic in City Hall, when he revealed that the Council's Hospitality Sub-Committee was reviewing its criteria for guest-lists ahead of the court challenge to the ban, now listed for 25 February. The Council was preparing to fold rather than take another court drubbing. But John Fox also urged patience, assuring Sinn Féin that if it held fire on a court challenge, the ban wouldn't be renewed in the new Council due to come together after the May elections. He also indicated that some concessions could be made before then. Access to the documentation of committee meetings from which Sinn Féin was barred would be provided within weeks, he pledged. For months, Sinn Féin had protested the effective 'in camera' nature of the CHAMPS Sub-Committee which was overseeing the introduction into the Council of Compulsory Competitive Tendering. Further court cases would sour the new atmosphere of reconciliation in the Council, Fox warned. Unionist noses shouldn't be rubbed in the dirt now that Sinn Féin was set to score a string of court victories. Neither should the call for Robert Wilson's resignation be made public. He was understandably sensitive on how the Council had decided to fight the sub-committees' court case. The Town Solicitor was effectively seeking a six-month honeymoon period for the 'reformed unionists'.

There was also a bid by some senior officials to split the Sinn Féin ranks by portraying me as a hot-headed extremist unwilling to compromise with unionism. At one meeting between senior staff and a Sinn Féin group (including myself), one official told a long yarn about how officials had successfully manoeuvred the unionist bloc away from Frankie Millar by convincing his colleagues that he was a liability. The message was clear: I was Sinn Féin's Frankie Millar. The attempt to undermine my standing within the Sinn Féin grouping caused me some concern, not because I thought my belt-and-braces approach to unionist discrimination was wrong but because I feared some of my colleagues might fall for the politicking of the officials. After a discussion at our regular monthly meeting, however, the Sinn Féin team agreed to send Alex Maskey along to the officials to reiterate Sinn Féin's unity of purpose, and the party's unqualified support for my approach.

Sinn Féin did show a willingness to compromise by writing to Fred Cobain with an offer to scrap all pending court cases if the unionists lifted the functions' ban and agreed to provide all councillors with access to crucial documentation on the privatisation process. Fred never wrote back but at the February 1993 meeting of full council, the unionists buckled in the face of the pressure from Sinn Féin and demands from central government that they clean up their act. Patience with the unionists was running thin at Stormont where new Secretary of State Sir Patrick Mayhew was determined not only to force the unionists to abandon their silly protests against the Anglo-Irish Agreement but also to embrace powersharing – if they really wanted to benefit from Central Exchequer largesse. He didn't put a tooth in it: 'I think it may become apparent that there is the question of allocating scarce resources for capital projects of one sort or another and that there is no disadvantage in sharing power in a council', he said. Surcharging could have added to the pressure on the unionists but unfortunately, the

Local Government Auditor failed to surcharge the unionists for the costs of their court crashes. Though I lodged objections against the expenditure of the rates on covering the council's court bill, the Auditor responded that he could not be satisfied that the abuses constituted 'wilful misconduct'. Many City Hall observers believed that the unionists would have cleaned up their act a lot sooner if they thought that every abuse of power which led to a court case would have hit them in their pockets.

The ban on Sinn Féin from functions (and the ruling that we be not told about the visits of leading politicos to City Hall) was abolished at the February 1993 meeting of Council. As part of the horse-trading with officials and in a bid to build bridges with thinking unionists, we agreed not to crow about the climbdown. Ironically, the first civic function after the ban was lifted was a reception for the British Army Bomb Squad. Fortunately, the abolition of the bar on attendance came too late to ensure an invitation to that particular knees-up but I did frame the first official invitation I received to a civic function, a finger buffet to mark the annual meeting of the Association of Paediatric Anaesthetists of Great Britain and Ireland. Later, Pat McGeown, a Sinn Féin councillor for Lower Falls, was to pose for the papers with his gilt-edged invitation to a civic dinner to mark the 75th anniversary of the RAF. Squadron leader McGeown considered scrambling his crew but then reported to the media that his pilots were all grounded for the event. That was probably a wise decision since the invitation specified dress as 'formal or uniform'. There might have been a few eyebrows raised if Pat had have come along in his old IRA uniform.

Sinn Féin attendance at civic functions did move another City Hall 'tradition' into the spotlight: the toast to the British Queen at every event which involved hospitality. Sinn Féin councillors remained glued to their seats while others – including shamefaced SDLP councillors – rose to their feet to toast the health of the grande dame on every occasion at which bread was broken in City Hall. Suggestions that the Loyal Toast be replaced with a toast to the people of Belfast received short shrift from unionists. Likewise, efforts to get the Council to follow the lead of Queen's University which scrapped the playing of the British National Anthem at graduation ceremonies were unsuccessful. Unionists preferred to take their lead from local (and loyal) BBC chiefs who insist on playing 'the Queen' at the close of programming on TV and radio – even though the same ditty isn't played by the BBC in Wales and only occasionally by BBC Scotland.

Some traditional republicans had harboured deep reservations about using the British courts to bring the unionists to boot but I had no such qualms. As for the judges, they appeared quite nonchalant about the prospect of ruling on matters brought before them by republican politicians who wished to make them redundant. In fact, if anything, they frequently exhibited more sympathy to the Sinn Féin side than to the boorish and loutish unionists who they saw as letting down the pro-British cause, as much by their disgraceful flouting of the democratic process as their bigoted behaviour. One wonders just how comfortable Lord Justice Nicholson, Lord Justice Campbell and Lord Justice Murray might feel at finding themselves listed in the Pantheon of republican heroes – beside many of those they sentenced to lengthy prison sentences.

9.
Carry on camping

The person who coined the phrase 'travel broadens the mind' had never visited Belfast City Hall, for in Belfast City Council the ruling unionist junta returned from ever more exotic destinations on 'urgent civic business' with minds as narrow as the Panama Canal (one of the few locations not on their junketeering itinerary).

Council perks, junkets, free transport, lavish beanos and even the odd courtesy pint of Bass were the skeletons in the unionist cupboard – a fact I didn't realise until I was fully orientated to the City Hall scene. But, once uncovered, Council junkets became a rich seam for the diligent debunker of the grandeur and mystique which unionists threw up around City Hall. Despite the broadcasting ban and the ability of the unionists to counter Sinn Féin charges that they were wasting ratepayers' money by pointing an accusatory finger at the republican bombing campaign, junkets became the Achilles heel of unionism. Revelations about their high-flying lifestyle exposed them to the ridicule of their own electorate at a time when they sought to portray themselves as the principled vanguard opposing Sinn Féin. From the off, unionists banned Sinn Féin from the frequent forays to foreign climes. Only rarely were SDLP members allowed aboard the free trips bandwagon. Being blocked from the all-expenses-paid junkets was supposed to be a punishment for Sinn Féin but, of course, it just helped to confirm our squeaky-clean image. While civic indignation rose as swiftly as the 747s which carried a contingent of unionists from Belfast International Airport on a weekly basis, only Sinn Féin's hands were unsullied by the grime of graft and self-aggrandisement. Now if only the unionists had been cute enough to offer us a fact-finding mission to Bermuda!

On my arrival in City Hall in 1987, unionists assured their electorate that they were involved in a do-or-die battle with the Anglo-Irish Agreement and the dreaded Shinners. In reality, they were quite happy to leave the petty affairs of Belfast behind when business beckoned. Thus did Frank Millar take three weeks off in April 1988 to visit the Land of Oz for the Eighth World Rose Convention, stopping off on the way in Los Angeles and Singapore. Admittedly, garden parties were popular among the councillors and staff; throughout July 1988, the Council dispatched 25 representatives, made up of councillors and officials, to the Glasgow International Garden Festival on numerous occasions – at a cost of £7,784. Even while unionists were refusing to conduct meetings properly, they still ensured that they voted through regular trips to conferences in every far-flung destination imaginable. The illegal Leisure Services Sub-Committee, from which Sinn Féin was barred, took time off from slashing jobs in leisure centres in March 1989 to take all its 11 members on a 'fact-finding mission' to Britain. In fact, in the 1988-1989 financial year, when only the bare minimum of Council business was carried out, unionists managed to splash out £53,600 on 41 separate trips in the service of the people of Belfast.

While the plum postings on 'study trips' were usually reserved for the (invariably unionist) committee chair and deputy chair, there were occasions when the trips became free-for-alls. Though Belfast City Council's powers were strictly limited, unionists developed an insatiable appetite for information about housing, health, policing and myriad other issues which were outside of their political remit. No destination was too far away when it came to searching for tips on how to conduct the business of local government. Expenditure on unionist flights of fancy rocketed from £39,000 in the 1989-90 financial year to £98,000 in 1990-91. In that year, Frank Millar had travelled to 11 conferences, two fewer than in 1989-1990. Jim Walker of the DUP also went on 11 trips, Herbie Ditty of the UUP went on 10, Fred Proctor of the UUP eight, and Dixie Gilmore of the UUP seven, including a journey to Toronto.

In November 1989, when I first asked for the details of the trips enjoyed by councillors over a 12-month period, and the costs involved, officials were less than helpful. Their reluctance was as much to do with resisting change – such questions had never been asked before – as with a desire to defend the already damaged reputation of the unionist ruling clique. Nevertheless the figures for the trips undertaken in the 1988-1989 financial year were eventually released to me in July 1990.

There was continued resistance to the release of the junketing register with all its juicy details; information about the number of trips and their cost in the 1990-1991 financial year, which I had first requested in July 1991, wasn't released until March 1992 and only after I had to fulfil the silly precondition of stating why I wanted the information requested. Further, officials insisted my right to know was limited to committees I served on, obliging me to redraft letters requesting information I had already asked for in the names of my fellow-councillors.

But regardless of the foot dragging, the flood gates had been opened. A few delightful themes emerged immediately and were to remain constant from 1989 to the virtual cessation of junkets in 1996; the unionists with the biggest mouths were also those with the largest store of air miles and the most egregious ambassadors imaginable for Belfast were those most often representing the city abroad.

Among the destinations visited by councillors in 1990-1991 were Amsterdam, Milan, Gothenburg, London, Rotterdam,

Toronto, Antwerp, Swansea, Paris, Stockholm and Padua. One
bizarre 20-day car trip by Lord Mayor Fred Cobain and
sidekick Councillor Fred Proctor took the pair to Holland,
Belgium and Berlin. While unable to list the benefits of this
European odyssey, Fred Cobain insisted 'much hard work was
done'. Love-hearts Rhonda Paisley and Sammy Wilson, rare
participants in the junket free-for-all, attended a three-day
conference in Brighton. (Sammy Wilson was so disdainful of
the Council junketeering that he once jibed Frank Millar for
wanting to attend a conference in Birmingham during the
Belfast Somme commemorations. Millar gubbed him.) No
fewer than seven councillors had also taken part in a week-
long Rotterdam conference. During the year, Frank Millar had
enjoyed 11 trips, to add to his total of 13 and 14 in the
previous two years, while seasoned travellers Councillor
Walker and Alderman Herbie Ditty had taken part in ten
apiece. As well as having hotel and travel costs covered,
councillors also enjoyed a handsome subsistence allowance
for each day on Council business.

Of the 88 places on trips outside Northern Ireland in the
1991-1992 financial year – at a slightly reduced cost of
£86,100, only five were allocated to non-unionist members.
'It was a dirty job but somebody had to do it' was the Council
motto as nine councillors (including the SDLP's Cormac
Boomer) were ferried to the Somme commemorations in Lille
and Caen for nine days of mourning in June 1991. Trips to the
sombre Somme commemorations were especially popular
among unionists as the four-day excursion usually included
'an evening at leisure' in Paris and 'a sumptuous banquet' in
the Versailles palace. There was also onerous Council work to
be carried out during the year in Philadelphia, Brussels,
Rotterdam, Barcelona and Sundsvall in Sweden (where I
wrote to the local Mayor advising him to alert the citizenry to
the impending visit of Frank Millar).

The fact that leisure centres and community facilities were
being closed across Belfast at a time when junkets were
peaking wasn't lost on the electorate. As unionists sampled

the delights of Copenhagen, Rotterdam, Toronto, Gothenburg, Antwerp, Philadelphia, Sydney, Blackpool (Blackpool?), Caen and Berlin, council workers were being given the heave-ho and their jobs privatised. The cost of free trips soared to almost £100,000 in 1990-1991. Of the 111 places on trips during that year, 108 were taken by unionists, just two by the SDLP and one by Alliance. Sinn Féin didn't get a look-in. The salt in the wounds for ratepayers was unionist claims that a 17-strong delegation, representing the entire membership of the General Purposes and Finance Committee, sent to Britain in February 1992 would examine ways of saving money. Independent SDLP councillor Cormac Boomer withdrew from the trip to councils which had already implemented Compulsory Competitive Tendering, branding it:

> [...] a waste of ratepayers' money. They (the committee) have had the consultants' report explained to them in detail at a weekend seminar, again paid for by the ratepayers. Now, if they haven't got clear in their own minds what they are going to do about Belfast, then there is nothing they are going to get over there which will make them any the wiser.

But the junketeers' downfall was the proverbial slow boat to China: a decision by Parks Committee Chairwoman Margaret Crooks to attend a nine-day conference in Hong Kong in late 1992. When pressed on the need for the city of Belfast to splash out £10,000 on the Hong Kong excursion, Mrs Crooks rejoindered in *The Irish News*, 'I work hard as a Chairman of a Committee, so there is nothing wrong with playing hard.' Among the deeply relevant topics up for discussion at the conference were Urban Forestry, Oriental Landscapes, Restoration of the Malaysian Rain Forest and Converting Former Military Sites to Parks (sadly not in demand in Belfast), and Feng Shui – the belief that places exert power over people. If the pressure got too much for the South Belfast UUP councillor she could always relax on 'a luxurious air-conditioned vessel for a cruise through the harbour while the night falls over the South China Sea', according to the conference brochure which helpfully added: 'Unlimited free drinks and relaxing live music are available on board.' After that, it was a PR penalty kick. Crooks' decision to back a Council block on a £100 grant to the Ulster Deaf Sports Council as the controversy over the Hong Kong extravaganza mounted showed just how out of touch with public feeling she really was. The cat was out of the bag for unionists who professed that conferences abroad were all work and no play. Controversy over the Hong Kong trip was to dominate coverage of the Council throughout 1992 and was the hook on which criticism of other trips could be hung. In fact so many unionists were set to be out of the country during the autumn of 1992 that Sinn Féin could, tongue in cheek, call on Secretary of State Patrick Mayhew to appoint a commissioner to run the Council's affairs.

One of the many foreign destinations patronised by the unionists in the run-up to the Hong Kong beano was Brussels. In October, the City Hall dispatched 11 of its councillors, swiftly dubbed a football team on tour, plus six officials to Brussels for a week of 'fact-finding' at a cost of £14,000. Bristling at its hostile treatment from the media, spin-doctors in the PR office at City Hall, reduced to a ghost town due to the absence of almost the entire unionist contingent, refused to release the itinerary of the trip or even the names of the participants. Not surprisingly, the press howled in outrage and savaged the entire affair. Unmoved, a further five councillors packed their bags and headed for Madrid and Barcelona in the company of officials. Frank Millar, who had been on 38 trips outside Ireland in the previous three years, got into the act in the summer by jetting off to Copenhagen. But he didn't miss out on the autumnal trips bonanza either; in October he returned to Belfast from Brussels for only the briefest of breaks before setting out to Barcelona to represent Belfast at the 'Neighbourhoods in Crisis' conference. His shameless jetsetting did provide food for thought for local newspaper editors. 'Of all the councils in Northern Ireland, Belfast's has become the laughing stock', fumed *The Irish News*. 'Its monthly meetings are a source of constant embarrassment. The antics of some of its members would disgrace the monkey enclosure in the city zoo.' Immune to criticism, unionists refused to scale down their junketing even as they bemoaned the fact that they couldn't find £10,000 in the Council budget to fit out a new community centre in loyalist North Belfast. Likewise, they knocked back suggestions that senior citizens be admitted free of charge into the Council's leisure centres, pleading a loss of revenue.

The *Irish News* launched a campaign against the junketeering, publishing regular lists of the most-travelled councillors, complete with details of previous 'placings'. In true Pavlovian style, unionists dismissed criticism of their junketing excesses as Sinn Féin propaganda. The concept of 'when you're in a hole, stop digging' was to them a foreign country. Even as consultants Price Waterhouse issued a report recommending the shedding of 600 Council jobs to ease privatisation, Frank Millar and Ian Adamson were jetting off to Copenhagen for a clean air conference. (Ten years later and the quality of air in Belfast remains the worst in these islands.) Given the inbuilt City Hall unionist majority, there was little opposition councillors could do about the junkets except embarrass the hell out of our high-flying colleagues. When I tabled a motion for full Council in March 1992, calling for a nine-month freeze on junkets, unionists pushed through business in eight minutes to ensure that by the time I reached City Hall the majority of the councillors were on their way home. I fell back on that favoured republican scapegoat, the British Army checkpoint, as an excuse for my bad timekeeping and rolled the motion on to the following month's meeting. Unionists blocked it there too but the motion, including a statement censuring Margaret Crooks for her 'work hard, play hard' statement, finally got an airing at the May meeting of Council, before being voted down.

Fortunately, the Local Government Auditor, the ultimate watchdog on Council spending, took as dim a view of the junketing as the average ratepayer. On the eve of the Hong

Kong outing, I wrote to Auditor Jack Bailie and objected to the trip. Already he had warned the Council in his annual report issued in May 1992 that 'trips outside Ireland or Britain should be kept to a minimum and numbers restricted'. The unionists responded by commissioning a five-page report by Council officers the same month into the enormous benefit of their free trips regime to the hard-pressed populace of Belfast. It was a toe-curlingly embarrassing attempt by unionists to pull the wool over the eyes of the citizenry and a belated response to the jibe by SDLP councillor Brian Feeney that the unionists didn't bring written reports to committees on the bountiful benefits of their free trips because they couldn't read or write. The unionists' risible efforts to justify their jet-setting rebounded on them with devastating effect when the BBC current affairs programme 'Spotlight' devoted an entire programme to an exposé on the junkets.

Programme makers surreptitiously followed five of the most prominent junketeers to Spain for a two-venue conference in late October 1992, at, in fact, the very time when Margaret Crooks was enjoying a junk trip in Hong Kong. I had written to Fred Cobain as Chair of the Development Sub-Committee asking for the Spanish trip to be abandoned in solidarity with Council employees losing their jobs as part of the Compulsory Competitive Tendering process. He declined to reply. The BBC programme was an eye-opener. In Madrid, tub-thumping fundamentalist Eric Smyth went AWOL from the conference to go shopping, while an Alliance councillor along for the ride had to admit to the cameras that he missed the keynote speech of the event because he had gone to his room for a nap. The session of the Madrid housing conference which was, according to Belfast City Council, the most relevant of the entire event, passed without even one of the local representatives attending. The shenanigans of Fred Cobain and co-pilot Fred Proctor (due to Cobain's infamous fear of flying, the pair had driven across the Continent to the paella-fest) were even more memorable. The pair failed to show at the Barcelona leg of the conference where they were supposed to be picking up vital tips about staging the Olympic games. When 'Spotlight' eventually caught up with them in Belfast, former Lord Mayor Cobain admitted that he was 'sightseeing at the ratepayers' expense' before storming out of the interview. Red-faced and stuttering a feeble defence throughout the 'Spotlight' grilling, Cobain, declared the *Sunday Life*, was 'neatly and thoroughly filleted'. The programme also threw up a few other titbits, including the fact that like-sized Bristol council spent just £2,000 per year on trips and study visits. What was supposed to be a crucial conference in Spain was, in fact, ignored by most councils in the Republic of Ireland and Britain, where unlike Belfast, councillors had responsibility for housing issues. The freeloading Belfast delegation found itself making up 25 per cent of the entire UK representation at the event.

The only surprise in the Spanish debacle was that fiery independent councillor Frank Millar, unionism's Alan Whicker, wasn't among the freeloaders. For his propensity to travel was in inverse proportion to his ability to behave in a civilised manner. Some argued that his famed xenophobia and rabid right-wing views made him the perfect ambassador for Belfast unionists and certainly, wearing his Council cap, he saw more of the world than Marco Polo. Surprisingly smitten by the Celtic wanderlust, Frank Millar was oblivious to criticism from the 'rubbish that represents Sinn Féin' because, he proclaimed, he could get the message across to the people he met that Northern Ireland is a great place to visit. It's not known if the Tourist Board ever kept figures of how many sociopaths succumbed to the globe-trotting unionist's charms and visited the North. Frank didn't take kindly to criticism from the Alliance Party either. When North Belfast councillor Tom Campbell branded the unionist's three-week trip to Australia 'scandalous', Millar hit back in *The Irish News*, charging that his Alliance colleague had 'nothing to offer other than snide, sleekit, slimy comments. He is not big enough to get his head ducked. He is a know-all who knows fuck-all.'

Millar declined an offer to publish full details of the Australian tour, insisting simply that it had been essential to win support for the proposal that the World Rose Convention come to Belfast in 1991. It subsequently emerged that the decision to bring the event to Belfast had been taken in 1985, a fact not exposed to examination at the December 1987 Parks Committee meeting which sanctioned the trip because unionists forced through business without debate. In a series of more reasoned letters, perhaps written for him by the Council's Public Relations officers, Millar wrote to the press to defend the junket culture in City Hall. On their travels, he wrote, unionists 'always correct or challenge misleading or ill-informed comment relating to the position of Northern Ireland in the United Kingdom'. Trips were more a labour of love than a perk, he explained, adding, 'the present daily rate of £52.95 has to cover full hotel and food, booking into the cheaper type hotel and generally looking for the cheaper places to eat'. Rather conveniently, Frank had forgotten that the cost of conference attendance invariably covered hotel accommodation and meals.

In a two-page apologia for his junketing excesses in *The Irish News*, the independent unionist dismissed my criticisms of him made in a fax to the Copenhagen organisers of a conference he attended, as 'the ravings of a megalomaniac'. I was in good company. Journalist Jim McDowell, whose weekly missive from the Dome of Delight was keeping *Irish News* readers spellbound, was 'if not exactly a public relations officer for Sinn Féin, alternatively… a most willing message boy for such body'. He went on to give a point-by-point 'rebuttal' of the 13 charges I had made against him, ranging from sectarianism to loud-mouthed hooliganism. It was one of the most astonishing pieces of writing ever penned by an elected representative. His diatribe included an admission that he had been fined £100 for disorderly behaviour when he challenged 'republican rabble' supporting Cliftonville football club, had indeed called for 'so-called travelling people' to be incinerated and did view gays as deviants. He added: 'Sinn Féin's concern for homosexuals and/or lesbians is their own business. However strange or weird as it might appear, one can only say, freedom of choice; mind your handbag.' Just as archaeologists could speculate on the lives of our Neanderthal ancestors based on their cave wall etchings, Millar's ravings gave political anthropologists a unique insight into the wondrous workings of the unionist mind.

Councillor Jim 'Junior' Walker was more concerned about justifying his jaunting when he topped the hit parade of most-travelled councillors in 1990-91 with eleven separate trips, especially as UUP councillor John Carson had added his voice to the chorus of disapproval over 'wasteful trips'. When pressed by the *Independent* to detail one benefit from his travels, Councillor Walker recalled that he had once seen a poop-scoop at a Rotterdam conference which he decided would literally clean up Belfast's dog-fouling problem. On his return, officials told him the idea wouldn't work. 'And when it was explained to me (that it wouldn't work) I went, "Right, okay, that's fair enough".' Almost £500,000 had been spent on trips overseas yet, with his back against the wall, that was Walker's best shot at justifying the expense. 'If these trips are of any benefit, it's been kept a very big secret', opined Brian Feeney of the SDLP. 'Nice work if you can get it.'

But while unionists in public played hardball on the need for junkets, declining the sensible advice of Alliance Party councillor Tom Campbell to lash the 'hypocrisy' of Sinn Féin for participating in trips organised by other councils, including Derry, but opposing them in Belfast, the penny was dropping. A sign of the times was the letter in the *Belfast Telegraph* from 'UNIONIST' which berated Sammy Wilson for defending the expenditure of £98,000 on Council trips. 'I for one object strongly to ratepayers' money being frittered away needlessly and I would remind Alderman Wilson that £98,000 is an absolute fortune to most Belfast people', wrote the letter-writer. 'Top marks to Sinn Féin for highlighting this scandal, maybe there is hope for them yet!'

Increasingly, officials, when tabling invitations to conferences before committee meetings, would recommend non-attendance. Even when visits did go ahead, the number of participants was pared back and trips outside Britain or Ireland became a rarity. By the time, Margaret Crooks flew off to Hong Kong in the autumn of 1992, unionists were becoming afraid to touch free trips. Their fear of flying was reflected in the expenditure on junkets from April 1992 to March 1993 when costs dipped to £60,000. Amsterdam, Brussels, Barcelona and Madrid all got to enjoy the scintillating company of Belfast's civic leaders but a combination of our propaganda blitz and the Spotlight coup de grace had combined to make homebirds of Belfast's once travel-crazy councillors. Indeed, trips virtually stopped between Margaret Crooks' jaunt to Hong Kong and the May 1993 elections. For years, unionists had insisted that 'study trips' were an essential part of civic governance but suddenly it appeared that the city could function admirably from home. Appropriately, as the junket bandwagon imploded, among the very last of the free trips was an excursion to Sellafield. Chastened by the response of the electorate to the junket furore during the election, incoming councillors steered clear of free trips. The Holiday Club's spreading infamy was illustrated all too painfully for unionist councillors when the audience at an election forum in the heart of the Shankill, being broadcast live on Radio Ulster, erupted in laughter when the presenter mentioned the globe-trotting antics of local representatives.

Just £32,000 was spent on trips in the 1993-1994 financial year. The vast majority of visits involved just one councillor and one official, gone forever were the days of the 25-seat charabancs to the Glasgow Garden Festival. But I did manage to notch up my own first trip when I represented the Council at a University of Ulster conference in Belfast Castle in February 1994. Ultra-sensitive, I covered the £100 cost of the conference from my own pocket, which created an unusual situation for the Town Treasurer's office which had never before been faced with a councillor wanting to pay for a Council freebie.

While the cost of attendance at conferences did rise again in the mid-nineties, not least as a consequence of the Council's involvement in economic missions to the US, unionists were careful to involve councillors from other parties. And they found willing soul-mates in some of the new SDLP members; two of the party's councillors joined a five-strong Council delegation to a planning school in Harrogate immediately after their 1993 election. In previous years, just one councillor had represented the city at the event. But even the SDLP couldn't stomach all of the excuses pedalled out to justify junketeering; in July 1993 the party voted against a decision to send Lord Mayor Reg Empey to the unveiling of an Orange Order memorial in Thiepval, France. There was a justifiable suspicion that incorrigible jet-setters among the unionist ranks misunderstood the Council's new-found responsibility for tourism as obliging them to travel abroad even more frequently. In the space of two weeks in April 1994, Jim 'Junior' Walker flew off to Canada and Rotterdam for tourism conferences...though he didn't manage to make it as far as Belfast Castle for the aforementioned economic conference that he was slated to attend.

But public fury at the antics of Belfast City Council wasn't confined to the ceaseless junketing. There was also the matter of extravagant expenditure on banquets and beanos for the chosen few. Ratepayers, already shaken by multi-thousand pound bills for trips abroad, were rocked by the revelation that expenditure on civic hospitality soared by 400 per cent in just four years. In the 1991-1992 financial year, £118,000 was spent on banquets, dinners and luncheons for councillors and their guests. That was more than double the figure for the previous year, three times the figure for 1989-1990 and four times the amount spent in 1988-1989. The real obscenity wasn't the gratuitous waste of Council rates on the hooleys but that many of the unionists stuffing themselves at the ratepayers' expense were professional people well able to pay their own way rather than get fat on the pennies of pensioners. In July 1991 alone, councillors lined up ten dinners at City Hall. Averaged out among the 51 councillors during that year, expenditure on slap-up meals worked out at £2,000 a head, but of course Sinn Féin councillors were barred from all functions – an ideal position to be in for a party which staked its reputation on its opposition to freebies.

Contained within the hospitality expense figure was the cost of free drinks before meals, the cost of the food itself, and the cost of controversial aprés-dinner free bars. Conservative estimates put the cost of free drink for councillors and their cronies at £20,000. Hard-pressed Council staff unsuccessfully appealed for an end to the post-bash free bar which sometimes kept them at work until the early hours of the morning. But their plea, like my suggestion that councillors pay for their own drinks' bill, fell on deaf ears. Shankill councillor Joe Coggle refused to countenance the prospect of unionists putting their hands into their own pockets in order to finance their high-living. In response, I argued that he must be hard-up and called on ratepayers to send him their spare 50p coins. Joe later told me he had given my donation to the Orange Cross fund for loyalist prisoners' dependents, which was no more than he was entitled to since he had a son serving an 18-year sentence for attempting to shoot up a Falls Road taxi depot. Unionists exhibited none of the fundamentalist abstemiousness the public might have expected from such a Christian crew. In fact, even when the pubs and clubs of Belfast closed on Good Friday, unionists still managed to splash out on drinks' parties. On Good Friday 1991, Parks Chairwoman Margaret Crooks hosted a drinks' reception in the bar of Belfast Castle to mark the opening of a new facility. Margaret declined to be drawn on my suggestion that she organise a whip-round to cover the cost of the knees-up and challenged me to raise the money myself. In response, I promised to eat the minutes of the recent parks department meeting which approved the closure of six Council play centres if she would refund the cost of her free trips abroad.

Thankfully for my digestive system, she didn't take up the challenge.

But even when their drink was free, unionists were reluctant to share their sup with Sinn Féin. Bass Breweries in West Belfast were somewhat embarrassed when Sinn Féin discovered in 1991 that they were providing their famous brews gratis to the Lord Mayor's parlour so that councillors could enjoy a relaxing pint after council meetings. Their generosity was tainted by the unionist policy of forbidding entry to the Lord Mayor's den to Sinn Féin councillors. But while blushing Bass executives stressed that the free ale was intended as a gift to the entire Council body, unionist Fred Proctor was more concerned about the refusal of Lord Mayor Nigel Dodds to roll out the barrel. Teetotaller Dodds discontinued the practice of serving up pints after the Council meetings during his 1991 tenure. 'That means that when the breweries come to replace the three barrels, much of it is simply being poured down the drain because no one is drinking it', moaned Proctor.

During Fred Cobain's 1990 tenure as Lord Mayor, undrunk beer was never a problem. The heart of the roll, Fred merrily set up drinks for councillors and constituents. An anonymous caller to my Saturday morning clinic in the Sinn Féin offices in Andersonstown tipped me off to the fact that in October 1990, Fred had hosted a wedding reception for a constituent in the Lord Mayor's Parlour, at public expense. True to form, Fred wasn't even in the country at the time, though my source was able to tell me that he rang through his best wishes from the International New Towns conference in Rotterdam! The Local Government Auditor defended the function on the basis that how Cobain spent his £15,000 hospitality allowance as Lord Mayor was his own business. However, backed by officials, Cobain declined my request to examine the fine detail of how his hospitality allowance had been spent. 'My conscience is clear', he insisted.

Embattled unionists soon found the brakes being put on another City Hall 'perk': the free use of Council vehicles. At a meeting of the General Purposes and Finance Committee in February 1991, which I attended as an observer as Sinn Féin was barred from the Committee, I witnessed Frank Millar fly into high dudgeon because he had been refused a lift home in a Council vehicle. The Council driver, complained Millar, had pretended he had messages to do when in fact, he was 'sitting on his arse'. My antennae rose. Until that date, I hadn't been aware that unionists – who could be spotted daily being chauffeured around by Council drivers – had no right to this service. Another can of worms was opening. I wrote to the Local Government Auditor asking for clarification on the use of Council vehicles for private business and was delighted when the normally ponderous Mr Bailie agreed to immediately examine the log-books for the City Hall vehicles. 'As far as I am concerned neither Council cars nor any other Council property should be used to carry out private business', he wrote to me as he set out on his probe. 'Council assets should only be used for the benefit of the Council.' While Town Clerk Stanley McDowell stressed that he was 'not aware of the use of any (Council) vehicles by councillors for private business', the Local Government Auditor found Council vehicles had been used repeatedly to ferry Alderman Millar from the City Hall to his home 'on welfare grounds'. That practice, branded an 'abuse of privilege' by the Alliance Party's Tom Campbell, was halted once the Auditor's investigation began. My efforts to be allowed access to the Council log books were blocked by officials but media exposure of the abuse led to new conditions on the use of vehicles being introduced.

It was a depressed and deeply unhappy unionist group which faced its electorate in the May 1993 poll. Some of unionism's elder 'statesmen' bowed out of city politics to make way for younger faces who were under orders to clean up their City Hall act. For nationalists the real victory wasn't in seeing the sun set on the political career of holiday club veterans such as Frank Millar and Herbie Ditty. The real triumph was in seeing unionism's Lord of the Manor existence in City Hall, the lavish banquets, the free trips, the private taxi service and the nod-and-a-wink arrangement with officials, crumble before the very eyes of unionists, elected and non-elected, who had created a culture of perks and pork-barrel politics. The unionist junk had sprung a leak and, boy, did they know it.

10.
Minding Your Language

E nter stage left the Irish language and the already sorely-pressed City Hall unionists lost the plot. It was bad enough to have the sanctity of City Hall defiled by Sinn Féin while the IRA campaign was in full throttle, but for their councillors to speak in tongues was the stuff of which nervous breakdowns were made. Having been elected on a platform of promoting the Irish language within the City Hall, I had no hesitation in putting the issue on the political map, but even the most diligent student of the antediluvian behaviour unionists call politics couldn't help but be impressed by their reaction to An Ghaeilge. The game plan was to modestly demand the same rights for Irish as are available to Welsh speakers in Wales. The blue touch paper having been lit, I had only to withdraw and let the unionists get on with the job of putting the Irish language rights campaign where I wanted it: on the front page.

You had to take your hat off to Sammy Wilson. Every time I tabled a motion on the Irish language, he responded with a reactionary and racist counter-proposal. To every DUP action there was a nationalist reaction. As the unionists railed against Irish, interest in the lingo soared in nationalist areas. Building on his 'leprechaun language' snub, Wilson reacted to a motion I put forward in December 1989 calling for more support for Gaelscoileanna by proposing an amendment which decreed that Irish was a 'a dead language promoted by terrorists and Sinn

120

Féin'. His stance won the support of the UUP councillors, including Ian Adamson, an Ulster-Scots aficionado who, to his credit, spoke a few words of Irish. Those credentials were enough to earn him an appointment to the board of the Ultach Trust, an organisation which brought the Northern Ireland Office's favourite Irish speakers around the one board table. A quixotic character, Adamson is the author of several weighty tomes of dubious academic standing which argue that the Ulster Presbyterians are in fact the descendants of the Picts driven out of Ireland by the Gael before making a comeback with the Plantation. To Adamson's great embarrassment, for he is, in truth, a decent chap with a witty after-dinner speech routine, the National Front, as the *Sunday Life* revealed, put his *Identity of Ulster* on their recommended reading list. At my last Council meeting in May 1997, I had to ask the permission of Ian Adamson, then Lord Mayor, for my eight-year-old daughter to view the proceedings from his viewing gallery. He kindly agreed, showing that he wasn't as anti-nationalist as his voting pattern might suggest. Shortly afterwards, the ageing paediatrician married a twenty-something clerk, so perhaps he wasn't that whacky after all.

Not to be outdone by Sammy Wilson, UUP members were at pains to demonstrate their own deep knowledge of the Irish language. Shankill representative Joe Coggle, who sat on the Belfast Education and Library Board, told councillors, 'I want to have nothing to do with your Irish language'. That view was endorsed by his unionist colleagues in a series of votes with Sammy Wilson popping up as an unlikely ideologue for the anti-Irish vanguard with his observation that 'leprechaun language' was a suitable description for An Ghaeilge because 'it would be easier to find a leprechaun in modern-day Ireland than an Irish speaker'. Warming to his subject, he later responded to a university student's letter regarding the Irish language with the following salvo: 'As we do not either understand the language or give any support to it, we have no intention of answering your letter which is written in a foreign tongue, what is more a dead foreign tongue.' Inspired, Rhonda

Paisley, an underachieving part-time artist, (critics dubbed her work 'naive art' which basically means it was the sort of stuff you were slapped for when you handed it up at school), opined that discrimination against Irish ó was permissible because, she informed the *Irish Times*, 'English is the national language of Ulster'. The DUP woman whose art gallery was in Ballyhackamore (which translates in Irish as the Town of the Big Turd) was also something of a linguist. When the commissioners responsible for public hearings into the Belfast Urban Area Plan agreed in 1989 to provide me with a translator so I could address them in Irish, Rhonda insisted that her Huguenot background entitled her to simultaneous translation in French. The Commissioners duly obliged, but when it came Rhonda's turn to address the august body, she had to admit that she could only speak faltering 'school' French. Conradh na Gaeilge and the European Bureau for Lesser-Used Languages (the latter in embarrassingly cringing terms) did write to the Council, at my urging, to call for a linguistic change of heart, but without success.

Consequently, like Oscar Wilde, I could have it both ways: portraying the unionists as Neanderthal supremacists with *bata scoir* in one hand and sash in the other while garnering buckets of publicity for the cultural renaissance then taking hold across nationalist areas.

The introduction of Irish was certainly a case of culture shock for the unionists who decided the solution to the growing clamour for Irish language recognition was to outlaw the practice. Intellectual giant (or should that be gnat?) Frankie Millar (with the support of UUP councillor John Carson) responded to a letter I penned to the Town Clerk Cecil Ward asking for bilingual stationery, standard stuff in Welsh councils, by rushing through a motion which effectively banned Irish from Council business. From February 1988, English was the only language in which Council business could be conducted. It had taken me all of four months to get the unionists to place a symbolic burning cross on the lawn of every Irish speaker in Belfast, courtesy of Proinsias Ó Muilleoir.

It was hats off too to Nigel Dodds who did his bit to vindicate the Sinn Féin position that the unionists were incapable of reform or affording nationalists basic rights. He ruled that no councillor would be allowed to speak 'a foreign language' in the chamber, earning Belfast City Council the dubious distinction of being the only local government forum in Ireland or Britain where the indigenous language was banned.

The Sinn Féin response was to work with the emerging Irish language organisations in the city to set up skittles for the unionists to knock down. A blizzard of applications for funding engulfed the Council, only to be rejected by unionists.

Even the season of goodwill did little to temper unionist fury at any expression of Irishness. In the run-up to Christmas 1988, unionists experienced emotional meltdown at the news that the Andersonstown Leisure Centre had teamed up with a local youth training scheme, Glenand, to erect a sign in Irish on its roof with the seditious message 'Guíonn Glenand Beannachtaí na Nollag oraibh' (Glenand Wishes You a Happy Christmas). Opposition to the festive greeting was led by East Belfast representative Robin Newton of the DUP who, bizarrely, had been alerted to the existence of the signage by Colin Abernathy, a senior figure in the shadowy Ulster Clubs movement (later shot dead by the IRA). Unionists moved swiftly to ban the festive billboard, only to be ignored by the community of Andersonstown. The sign stayed.

The one Council responsibility which impacted on the Irish language was its power to name streets. In 1949, the then thrusting young politician Brian Faulkner had amended a Stormont Act to ban street nameplates in Irish, a phenomenon which had become all too common in nationalist towns like Newry. Ignoring that legislation, many nationalist areas of Belfast began erecting bilingual street names in the wake of the H-Block hunger strikes. City Hall unionists were unimpressed. When Liam Andrews, a fluent speaker of Irish and Welsh, who lived in West Belfast's Shaws Road Gaeltacht, a community of some 60 souls whose first language is Irish, wrote to the Council asking to change the name of his twenty-yard *cul-de-*

sac to Cois Cluana, he was given short shrift by the Council. Undeterred, Andrews engaged in a two-year correspondence with the Council during which he pointed out that many of the names in his neighbouring Andersonstown were already in Irish. Learned Town Clerk Cecil Ward, who enjoyed a month's holiday each summer on the Great Blasket, responded with typical eruditeness that names such as Ballaghbeg Way, Greenan and Rosnareen were not in Irish. 'They are Anglicised etymologies thereof as indeed is the word Belfast itself!'

Not that the unionists banned every vestige of Irish from City Hall; the First Citizen's chain bears two mottoes in Irish, 'Eirinn go Brá' and 'Lámh Dhearg Abú'. The Lord Mayor's chain in Dublin contains nary a word of Erse! The bug was even picked up by unionism's elder statesman, Tommy Patton, who once memorably called for two gondolas to be bought for Belfast zoo, rather than the one recommended by officials, so that they could be bred. During a heated debate in City Hall, he invited the Sinn Féin members to 'póg mo thóin'. It's not known what Cormac Boomer, an independent-minded SDLP councillor who eventually became an unsuccessful independent candidate in West Belfast after he and the party parted company over his support for internment, made of all this. He declared the vibrant Irish language community on the Shaws Road in West Belfast, a beacon of hope for language activists nationwide, a 'ghetto' and blasted Sinn Féin for 'contaminating every aspect of our noble heritage'. Cormac limped home on the SDLP ticket in a series of elections before bowing out in 1994 as an independent with just 400 votes. But he did leave behind a lasting contribution to civic life: a lengthy campaign against dog doo-doo resulted in a Council bye-law banning pooch pooh in Andersonstown. Red signs forbidding dogs from shitting on the pavements peer down from every lamppost in Andersonstown. Sadly, much like Cormac's overall contribution to the body politic, they are studiously ignored by the local populace and their pets.

I wasn't lost for campaigning issues beneath the Dome. With their unionist-only mentality, the great and the good in City

Hall had created a mammoth cross between a Gospel Hall and an Orange Hall, a Gosorange Hall, where Catholics were only meant to be admitted as hired help. Armed with the knowledge of what made good copy for the press, especially the Irish language press, the City Hall was my free-fire zone.

No monthly meeting was complete without a motion from Sinn Féin denouncing the denial of Irish language rights. All of which in itself wouldn't have been terribly newsworthy if it hadn't been for the sophisticated response of independent unionist Frank Millar. In his racist response to even the most docile, cap-in-hand demand for recognition for Irish, Millar made Alf Garnet look like Lionel Blair.

Ulster Unionist sage Ian Adamson frequently entered the fray with his weird musings on the Irish language. 'It was unrealistic at present to see a wider use of the Irish language in Belfast', he decreed as the number of Irish schools in Belfast soared. For every motion I would propose on relieving the plight of the long-suffering Gaeilgeoir, he would have an amendment calling for more support for Ulster-Scots, a mishmash of Scots Gaelic, native Irish, Lallans and olde worlde English rather unfairly dubbed 'a DIY language for Orangemen'. No unionist ever managed to satisfactorily explain why their politicians failed to promote Ullans within the Council during the 100 years or so they held sway in the City Hall and why it was only the sight of gurning Gaeilgeoirí which sparked their love of the lingo.

Every motion put in front of committees, sub-committees and full council demanding fair play for Irish was ambushed. But I did have one famous victory when in April 1991, due to a botched unionist attempt to force the scrapping of the meeting by leaving it without a quorum, a motion calling on the Register of Births, Marriages and Deaths at City Hall to provide bilingual forms was passed. Unionists were outside the chamber on one of their interminable protests when I rose to propose the motion. Before they could return, the motion was put to the vote. The SDLP, showing the political courage which has made them an endangered species in West Belfast, abstained, and the motion passed on the six Sinn Féin votes with no votes against. On my homemade, bilingual Council stationery, I banged out a press statement predicting that the decision would give the campaign to have the Council ban on Irish overturned a timely fillip.

In fact, the unionists swiftly overturned the decision. 'It would not be in the interests of democracy to let this decision stand', declared Ulster Unionist Margaret Clarke at the next Council meeting, but it was a sweet moment nonetheless, especially since it was recorded by the *Belfast Telegraph* with the memorable billboard poster (which now adorns my study wall) 'Sinn Féin Scores Irish Victory'. And this was no trivial issue; there was no greater humiliation that could be heaped on the bereaved family of an Irish speaker than to outlaw the language in the official record of death. There was no great surprise though when the Stormont Minister responsible for the registration of births, marriages and deaths refused to take any action to introduce bilingual forms on the back of our Council breakthrough. Adopting a more sober approach than that evident in its fly-posters, the *Belfast Telegraph*, though miffed, assured readers that the government-sponsored Ultach Trust would 'guard against' efforts to win measures such as bilingual government forms by 'helping with grants towards non-political bodies run by lovers of the language rather than republican activists'. (At the time of writing, Irish is still banned from use in civic marriages at City Hall.) True to form, the Ultach Trust was never sufficiently moved by the Council's rabidly anti-Irish policies to ever bring itself to issue as much as a mild rebuke of the unionists. But then again two of the Council's chief censors, Ian Adamson and Chris McGimpsey, sat on the Ultach Trust Board.

The Council attitude to Irish was merely a reflection of official government policy which failed to acknowledge the existence of Irish. There were no official forms in Irish, no television service in the language, a churlish attitude to Gaelscoileanna and a marked hostility to any attempts to celebrate Irish as a living community language. In 1991, the government announced plans for an additional 200 hours of TV programming in Scots Gaelic, bringing the total allocation to 300 hours. In the same year, there wasn't a full hour of programming on the local stations. Things haven't improved dramatically either. In the whole of 1999 the BBC didn't produce even one Irish language programme. If the government didn't view Irish as a 'leprechaun language', it certainly saw it as part of the white man's burden. The figures bore that out. While 142,000 people declared themselves as having a knowledge of Irish in the 1991 census in the North, only £2m was spent on the promotion of Irish by the British in the year 1994-95 (including expenditure on Irish schools). In the same year, £11.3m was spent on Gaelic in Scotland, a language spoken by fewer than 70,000 people. According to the bean counters, that translated into £14.24 per Irish speaker in the Six Counties, and £159.09 per Gaelic speaker in Scotland. Aprés-ceasefire, I was one of ten prominent Irish speakers in the North who had a testy exchange with Secretary of State Sir Patrick Mayhew on his treatment of the Irish language. The correspondence was sparked by his refusal to provide an Irish language translation of the Frameworks for the Future document, one of a long list of documents thrown up by the diplomatic dancing between the participants in the peace process deliberations. Sir Patrick wrote to me to suggest that Irish speakers should go to Dublin to have the document translated, a recommendation which led us to ask if he believed we should also look to Dublin to have the North's Irish schools funded. We demanded parity of esteem. Mayhew retreated behind the defensive mantra that his treatment of Irish, including the fact that the language wasn't officially recognised, represented 'a parity of esteem'. But, as the post-ceasefire 'decontamination' of Sinn Féin wasn't complete, Mayhew refused to sign the letter himself or agree to meet with Sinn Féin to discuss our language demands.

For my part, I maintained my one-man rights roadshow for as long as I held a Council seat. Sinn Féin's boast was that the ban would go; that the Council would, eventually, be forced to acknowledge the existence of Irish and provide funding to Irish language development activities. As with so many other issues, the unionists found themselves stranded by the shifting sands of time. Not only did they witness increasing, if still dilatory, British government support for Irish as the prohibition on Irish street names was lifted and Irish schools were funded, but even below the Dome, the sound of conversation in Irish was to be heard. The famed Donegal scribe Seosamh Mac Grianna once referred to Irish as a warm language within cold prison walls: 'Nach te an teanga an Ghaeilge istigh anseo idir ballaí fuara, an teanga a d'fhaibhir is a d'fhás agus a tháinig i méadaíocht i dtír nach raibh príosúin ar bith inti!' (Which roughly translates as, Isn't Irish a warm language in here between cold walls, a language which developed and grew and came of age in a country where there were no prisons.) Many nationalists viewed Irish as an equally inspirational language within the marble halls of City Hall; it was the ultimate language of subversion and of change in an institute built to preserve the British-unionist way of life (whatever that was!).

Emboldened by the changing City Hall demographics and a series of small victories, I took to speaking at length in Irish during Council debates, thus cocking a snoop at the 'ban' on Irish but failing to dent the unionist stranglehold on policy. My regular proposals before full Council, calling for the setting up of an all-party committee to promote the language and for the scrapping of the ban on Irish certainly exercised the unionist camp. One motion in November 1993 fell when Ian Adamson won support for an amendment which read like a chapter from Lord of the Rings. After blasting Sinn Féin's efforts to promote Irish, Adamson's amendment committed the Council to 'replacing eventually Latin in future official mottoes by early British, the most ancient discernible language used in Ireland and the native tongue of the Great Magonus'. So devoted was Adamson to the Great One that he refused to withdraw his amendment to allow an Alliance proposal calling for some restricted recognition of Irish to go through. I later asked Chief Executive Iain MacDonald, whose father was a Gaelic speaker from the Scottish islands, what progress he had made in implementing Adamson's proposal. That was a question he knew better than to answer.

Encouraged by the new open atmosphere which accompanied MacDonald's arrival, though he later left the Council in controversial circumstances, with rumours abounding that he had been pushed out by unionists who didn't like his partnership approach to local government, I also began to lodge applications for the use of the City Hall for Irish cultural events. The new Chief Executive was keen to blow away the sectarian cobwebs which enshrouded much of City Hall politics and urged Sinn Féin to organise activities which would demonstrate that the Council belonged to all its people. He did his own part too; he circumvented the Council ban on bilingual stationery by introducing a new policy whereby every councillor was entitled to personalised Council stationery in whatever language they chose. Obtaining City Hall for an Irish language event required a similar dose of lateral thinking. The illustrious hall, traditionally, was only available for special events, such as the annual shindig of the Royal Irish Regiment and centenary celebrations. Unable to find enough Irish speaking squaddies, I commandeered for the nation the centenary of the Gaelic League and wrote off to the Chief Executive in the name of a one-member West Belfast branch of the League asking for the use of the City Hall in December 1993 for a commemorative event.

Unionists, furious at seeing the hall host events celebrating the Irish tradition of Belfast, could huff and puff, but denying the use of Council premises in the face of a legitimate request wasn't feasible. Thus on 3 and 4 December 1993 did the TV crews record the invasion of City Hall by scores of Irish-speaking youngsters to mark the opening of a mini-féile within the once sacrosanct City Hall. For the first time since the opening of City Hall in 1906 did the city's premier building serve as the venue for a mammoth celebration of Irishness. Over 50 artists from across the country donated pieces of art for a two-day exhibition under the auspices of the annual Gaeilge fest An tOireachtas. Town Solicitor and acting Chief Executive

John Fox proffered an olive branch by opening the Council cheque book to buy two works of art from the exhibition while a string of unionist councillors were among those who viewed the paintings and sculptures. Then on the evening of 4 December, 250 Gaeilgeoirí packed into the Banqueting Hall for a night of revelry and craic. A local theatre group staged a series of irreverent skits as *Gaeilge* while I organised impromptu tours of the chamber for Irish speakers from my constituency who had, like the vast majority of their fellow-citizens, never been in City Hall. Their disbelief at being at an Irish night in City Hall was palpable and brought home to me the seismic nature of the changes which were taking place in an institution which had been created to keep nationalists at the gates. Unamused, the stony-faced portraits of former First Citizens peered down on the raucous proceedings as Pádraig Pearse's 'Óró Sé do Bheatha Abhaile' got its first City Hall rendition. It was a night laced with irony and vindication for the city's Irish speakers as they danced and drank the night away. As the mood soared, I made my way up a little-known back stairway behind the stage and out onto a balcony of one of the mini-domes which flank the green dome of City Hall. Braced against the December cold by the success of the celebrations below, I looked out over Belfast and allowed myself a little holiday in my heart at the lengths we had come on the journey to have our people respected by a Council which built its strength on the rates and rents of nationalists but treated their identity and traditions with contempt. A proud people who refused to wear the mantle of second-class citizenship were now at play in the Brahmins' very citadel of bigotry. Armed with nothing more dangerous than their language and their culture, the nationalists of Belfast were serving notice on the dolts and the diehards, the hustlers and the hatemongers who had ruled City Hall for a century that their days were numbered.

City Hall not only opened its doors to Irish events but paid for the privilege. In April 1993, the first-ever grant to an Irish language project went to the Pléaráca festival in West Belfast. When my thoughts turned to celebrating St Patrick's Day beneath the Dome, I also tapped into Council coffers. Disgracefully, St Patrick's Day was ignored by Belfast City Council. Staff took a day off, though not a public holiday in the North, the Patron Saint's Day is a bank holiday, but there was no official celebration of the day that was in it. All that changed in 1995 when, taking the 100th anniversary of the setting up of the first Belfast branch of Conradh na Gaeilge as my passport to fulfilling City Hall criteria, I threw a St Pat's Day céilí in City Hall. On the morning of the event, we brought back the Oileán exhibition to City Hall and organised a presentation of shamrock in a City Hall where ne'er a sprig of shamrock was traditionally to be seen on St Patrick's Day. It was a red letter (or should that be green letter?) day for Belfast.The céilí itself was a sight for sore eyes as the famous McPeake family from West Belfast led a 50-strong troupe of youngsters in a selection of traditional tunes before the céilí-hoppers took to the floor. During the day, we had invited along children from the city's all-Irish schools for a party. Unionists looked on aghast. They couldn't come to terms with the audacity of elected representatives who would use the hallowed rooms of City Hall for a children's hooley. For our part, we couldn't understand why their own voters didn't rail against the snobbery and elitism associated with a building which may have been a bastion of Britishness but which was never a haven for the working class people of the Shankill or Sandy Row.

In 1996, the 150th anniversary of the Great Famine was the St Patrick's Day cue for a lecture in Irish in the City Hall before a barnstorming sets' céilí. On every occasion that we pushed for support for the Irish language, Sammy Wilson and his DUP colleagues countered with proposals to postpone a decision until more information could be obtained about the organisation requesting grant-aid or hosting an event. But, all the relevant criteria having been fulfilled and with officials increasingly nervous about drawing down the ire of the courts, the best the unionists could do was stall, rather than block, funding or permission for the Irish language initiatives.

In the wake of the first IRA ceasefire, I had joined forces with a number of likeminded Gaeilgeoirí who recognised the urgency of creating jobs for young speakers and using Irish as an economic driver in West Belfast. We formed Forbairt Feirste (literally, Belfast Development) and swiftly secured funding from the government agency, Making Belfast Work, and the International Fund for Ireland. The advent of Forbairt Feirste brought added weight to our Council initiatives. In September 1994, the Council's Economic Development Sub-committee adopted a proposal to forge links with the new Irish language TV station, TnaG, with a view to creating jobs in Belfast. Nary an objection was raised from the unionist ranks. Attacking job creation was like attacking Santa. Thus did the previously Hibernophobic Council approve a £5,000 grant for a West Belfast conference in 1994 to examine the links between employment and the Irish language and councillors were later sent to a local government conference in Donegal on the promotion of Irish. There was a suspicion in the latter case that the unionists' love of junkets may have outweighed their antipathy towards Irish as they insisted on monopolising the few places for the weekend Irish language beano! Change was in the air; in 1996 when Conradh na Gaeilge held their ard-fheis in Belfast, the Lord Mayor, fundamentalist minister Eric Smyth, threw them a party; the invitation card to that fleá quickly became a collector's item.

But while the ban on Irish street names was lifted, the red tape surrounding the new legislation meant that the first official street names in Irish (and, indeed, Ulster-Scots) were a long time in coming. In April 1997, Shaws Road Gaeilgeoir Liam Andrews' marathon effort to have his own street named in Irish was defeated when unionists voted to block the move, even though a majority of residents supported Andrews' proposal to change the street name from Rosgoill Park to Ros Goill. Fifteen years previously, the Council had hidden behind the petticoats of the legislation banning Irish street names to block Andrews' bid to have his *cul-de-sac* off the Shaws Road named Cois Cluana. Ignoring the city edict, Andrews erected the name plate

Cois Cluana outside his house where it can still be seen, even though the tiny terrace house is now subsumed into the newer Rosgoill development. But in 1997, unionists argued, with the law clearly on their side, that while the new legislation did permit bilingual signs, Irish-only signs were still outlawed. Thus, Ros Goill was sunk. 'The saddest aspect of the whole affair is that 11 years after the signing of the Anglo-Irish Agreement, it is still illegal to erect a simple street name in Irish, even where, as is the case in Rosgoill Park, that is the wish of 95 per cent of the residents', said Liam Andrews. Alex Attwood branded the unionist block on Ros Goill as 'more of the same, resistance to equality'. 'This is a core abuse of power by the unionist majority', he said. 'It amounts to the rejection of the overwhelming wish of local people and the rejection of equality for the Gaelic language and culture. The unionists may use legal niceties to explain away a decision based on inequality and intolerance but that won't make the issue go away.'

I bade my own slán to the Council's notorious anti-Irish language policy by cocking a snoop at unionism's abominable men in a novella as Gaeilge, *Ceap Cuddles*. As with three previous books I had written in Irish (one about the council, Comhad Comhairleora), my publisher asked permission for the new satirical romp to be launched in City Hall, in the Lord Mayor's parlour to be precise. Ian Adamson, then occupying the First Citizen's seat, pleaded a busy schedule and 'regretted' being unable to make his rooms available for the December 1996 launch. Perhaps the subject matter had given him the jitters. *Ceap Cuddles* was a juvenile – some might say surreal – tale about a sex-obsessed Sinn Féin councillor, Cuddles Cooper, who aspires to be the first Catholic Lord Mayor in Belfast. Backing his bid are his colleagues, Jim 'Car Park' Keenan and Linda 'Schmeisser' Simpson (to balance things out the unionists had the Reverend Thompson Gunn) and the whole thing ends in a King Kong style denouement on the Dome of City Hall. It wasn't meant to be taken seriously but you just can't tell some people: Sammy Wilson responded to news that my publisher was seeking to launch the book in City Hall by gifting it some free publicity. 'I would never want to read anything Councillor Ó Muilleoir would write, especially in that leprechaun language he likes to spout – and there will never be a Sinn Féin Mayor of Belfast', he barked. Innured to literary criticism, I went on to organise a book launch in the spacious Sinn Féin offices of City Hall and issued invites to all and sundry. Among those popping by to pick up their signed copies and sip a glass of wine, as a uileann piper bounced a hornpipe off the walls of City Hall, were several senior officials. It was either a sign that they too realised the times they were a-changin' in City Hall or that they had heard that Pamela Anderson makes a cameo appearance in *Ceap Cuddles* and were hoping she'd turn up for the launch!

On the outside, changes in the Council's policy towards the Irish language came dripping slow. The first street names in Irish didn't go up until 1999. By then a Cultural Diversity Sub-Committee had been in operation for two years, for one 12-month period under the chairmanship of Sinn Féin Councillor Seán Hayes. While the Cultural Diversity Committee didn't make the rapid headway Irish speakers might have wished for, its very existence signalled the start of a new era for the Irish language in Belfast.

11.

Tell Us Something
About Yourself Then...

One of my all-time favourite cartoons shows an aspiring candidate for a civil service vacancy present himself at interview sporting an Orange sash. 'And tell us something about yourself then' the head of the interview panel is asking him. Funny? Yes. Outlandish? Not in Belfast City Council. Allegations of anti-Catholic employment bias have dogged Belfast City Council, and its predecessor the Belfast City Corporation, for as long as both bodies have existed. I was still a new boy when the first major case of discrimination by the Council was proven. In October 1988, the Council was found by the courts to have discriminated against Catholic cleansing worker Alex Johnston who was subsequently awarded damages of £3,600. Two Protestants who worked with the West Belfast man were promoted in the Technical Services Department in charge of street cleaning – even though they were less well qualified than their Catholic colleague. But a council which wasn't used to having its employment practices challenged didn't take the finding lying down. It later emerged that the Council continued to victimise Alex Johnston after the 1988 judgment because he had dared to take a complaint over his treatment. In 1992, the Fair Employment Commissioned ordered the payment of an additional £7,500 to Johnston to compensate him for the victimisation he had endured. A spokesman for the FEC said the case was 'a particularly odious form of discrimination'. 'To have the initial hurt and offence compounded by being further penalised is intolerable.' The original Alex Johnston finding came hard on the heels of an allegation by Councillor Alex Attwood of the SDLP that the Parks Department in the Council was a veritable Orange empire. He charged that the Department was employing relatives of existing workers, the vast majority Protestant, on short-term summer contracts. The Town Clerk angrily refuted the allegations.

Rumours that senior staff were Masons, Orangemen or both were traditionally difficult to prove in the Council. However, there was little doubt that a culture of discrimination had taken hold in many areas of the Council. That culture was bolstered by the display of British paraphernalia throughout City Hall, the display of the 'Belfast Says No' banners, the flying of the Union Jack at the Council's Duncrue Street offices and the hanging of the Queen's portrait in Council offices.

The first major Fair Employment Commission report into the Council's employment practices, leaked by Sinn Féin in March 1992, showed that Catholics held just 28 out of 162 senior management posts. Sinn Féin councillors had met with senior officials to press for sight of the draft report which had been in the Council's possession since early 1991 but had been distributed only to the General Purposes Committee (which had no Sinn Féin members). Sinn Féin threatened court action if the report wasn't made available to republican councillors on the same basis as it had been circulated to unionists, a threat only withdrawn when the report was mysteriously dropped in my lap. I was later told that one of the officials we were pressing for the release of the document was a senior Mason. Whatever, I found as a rule that an officer's membership of the Orange Order, unionist party or Masonic Lodge never prevented him or her from dealing fairly with Sinn Féin when the heat was on. During the Gulf War, I complained to one of the senior officials responsible for fair employment matters about security men at the main gate to City Hall sporting newspaper stickers with a

Union Jack and a headshot of a British soldier marking 'Sun Flag Day, A Defence of the Patriotic Spirit'. A poster backing 'Our Boys In The Gulf' was also erected in the security lodge at the back gate entrance to the Council car park. Over a cup of tea in the Robing Room where councillors gathered before Council meetings, I asked this officer what his reaction would be if I was to lodge an objection to the wearing of the badges (which were in blatant contravention of FEC guidelines). He replied that he would say I was stirring up trouble. Wrong answer. I went to the Town Clerk over the attitude of this official to an offensive breach of FEC policy. Shortly afterwards, security staff were told to remove the stickers or be suspended. The signs disappeared, despite the protests of unionist councillors and DUP threats to carpet officials involved in instructing staff to take down Union Jack posters and remove badges.

Even given the resistance to change in some Council quarters, it beggared belief that the FEC, faced with foot dragging and obstructionist tactics from the Council, had been a full four years in drawing up its draft employment report. It emerged that questionnaires were issued to staff, as per the instructions of the FEC, in September 1988. At a time when unionist hostility to FEC 'interfering' was at its height, one third of the payroll never returned the forms. An analysis of those employees who failed to return the forms wasn't completed by City Hall until May of the following year. It then took six months for the Fair Employment Agency (it became the FEC in 1990) to carry out a validation exercise on the figures, but tables provided by the Council did not provide all the required information. Collection and analysis of the information on the workforce's composition wasn't completed until September 1990.

Overall figures for September 1988 showed 2,187 or 68.2 per cent of the Council's permanent employees were Protestant and 909 or 28.4 per cent were Catholic. A breakdown of the figures revealed that the Gas Department employed 177 Protestants and only 36 Catholics. The Council's Technical Services

Department employed 792 Protestants and 289 Catholics, a respective 71.4 to 26.1 per cent ratio. In the Parks Department, 367 workers were Protestant and 94 were Catholic, a 75.4 to 19.3 differential. At the time, the religious breakdown in Belfast was estimated to be 55 per cent Protestant and 45 per cent Catholic. 'Although Belfast City Council signed the Fair Employment Agency's Declaration of Principle and Intent in 1978, there is no evidence that any serious commitment has ever existed to promoting economic equality for all sections of the community in the Council's workforce', said Oliver Kearney of fair employment group, Equality. When the final report was issued in July 1992, FEC head Bob Cooper called on the Council to take more action to promote equality of opportunity. Insisting an equal opportunities programme be put in place, Cooper said:

> The Commission would have expected the Council, as a major employer in Belfast, with approximately one third of all local government employees in Northern Ireland, to have taken a more active and visible role in this regard.

Brian Feeney laughed off both the results of an alternative report into fair employment, commissioned by the unionists at a cost of £2,000 and issued to the FEC as a response to the official draft report, and predictable unionist calls for the resignation of Bob Cooper. The figures, he said, confirmed Belfast City Council's standing as 'the worst council in Ireland'. Sammy Wilson went on the counterattack by successfully proposing a motion at full Council in July for an investigation into the religious make-up of a County Down building firm which had been awarded a substantial Council contract, while Hugh Smyth declared the FEC report proved 'the Council has a fair employment record second-to-none in the country'. That said a lot about the 'country'!

However, the FEC report side-stepped some of the controversial issues Sinn Féin had been highlighting. There was no comment on the flaunting of British flags and emblems on Council premises while the display of two 'Belfast Says No' banners, while 'questionable', would merit action, only if an employee was to complain to the Commission. But in correspondence with the FEC, I did win a commitment that the Council policy of giving preference to a candidate who had been a member of 'the Security Forces or Armed Forces' when two candidates were equal in all respects amounted to 'indirect discrimination'. I had less luck in a one-man attempt to have the 'Belfast Says No' banners removed. After lodging a complaint as an employer – in theory the councillors employed the Council staff – I was invited along to the FEC offices where among those who interviewed me was barrister Tim McGarry of 'Hole in the Wall Gang' fame. Though he may have gathered some material for a comedy sketch, McGarry didn't come up with a strategy to have the banners pulled down and the Council subsequently had my objection struck out on the basis that I had no standing in the matter. Ironically, the Council's own Equal Opportunity Policy Statement, adopted in 1990, stated: 'The Council is committed to the provision of a working environment free from flags, emblems, posters, graffiti or other materials likely to be provocative, offensive, intimidate or in any way likely to cause discomfiture or unease for employees.' Council officials and officers were well aware that it was more than a staff member's job was worth to object to the banners which clearly marked out the City Hall as unionist territory and served as a modern-day 'No Catholics Need Apply' sign. However, the Assistant Town Clerk wrote to me in February 1991 to say that he did not believe that there was any conflict between the Council's Equal Opportunity Statement and the banners. But shortly after my complaint was dismissed, the banner on the dome came down to facilitate cleaning, and never went up again. The same fate befell the banner in the main Council car park. I once asked a Chief Executive where the banners were stored and was rewarded only with an enigmatic smile.

While the introduction of Sinn Féin councillors to the body politic seemed to make little immediate impression on the ruling Council clique, there was a growing feeling that many

Catholic employees, emboldened by the changing council, were unwilling to put up with the traditional prejudices of their superiors. In 1992, a Fair Employment Tribunal was told by five Catholic community workers that a recruitment process to find a senior officer for Belfast City Council was 'a sham'. A pre-interview briefing, carried out by the three Protestant interviewers, was unique to the appointment and contributed to the panel's recruitment of a Protestant, who had poorer qualifications and experience than the applicants, all of whom had honours degrees. Under cross-examination, one of the interviewers admitted that even she felt something was 'not quite right' about the recruitment procedure and admitted that she had never previously encountered the pre-interview briefing procedure. Two of the Catholic candidates had three times more experience than the successful candidate, who boasted a single O Level and an unexamined diploma in youth and community work, while one other had twice as much experience. One of the rejected candidates had eight O Levels, a Teacher's Certificate from Manchester University, a Diploma in Youth and Community Work, a BA degree in Social Science, a Diploma in Adult and Community Education (post-graduate) and an MA in Adult and Community Education. Unsuccessful candidate Alanagh Rea had 13 years experience in the department, held a certificate of qualification in social work and a BA degree while colleague Dan Doran, the community officer in charge of West Belfast, held a BA in Social Science and a Diploma in Adult Education. The Tribunal heard Protestant interviewer and Community Service Department official John Doherty had given Alanagh Rea 22 points less than the successful candidate.

The Catholic applicants charged that the Catholic head of the Community Services Department, Brendan Henry, had come under pressure from unionist councillors to ensure a Protestant was appointed to the vacancy. A tall man who seemed to shoulder the pressure of working for Belfast City Council with more difficulty than Protestant chief officers, Brendan Henry had earlier survived a loyalist murder attempt at his North

Belfast home. Community Services Assistant Director Doherty denied allegations by counsel for the five Catholics that he had engineered the recruitment process to appoint the Protestant applicant. But former Community Services Department officer Roisin McDonough, a no-nonsense community leader who in 1998 became Chief Executive of the West Belfast Partnership Board – told the Tribunal that unionist councillors nicknamed the Council's community services team 'the Fenian Department'. In 1988, Roisin McDonough had her own run-in with her councillor bosses when she wrote an article in the *Irish Times* expressing the 'bewilderment' felt by the people of West Belfast by their pilloring after the killings of two British Army corporals. After the article appeared, Brendan Henry told her he 'had no option' but to suspend her because unionist councillors were 'extremely angry' about the newspaper piece. She was reinstated four weeks later and a fair employment hearing in 1990 upheld her complaints of religious bias and interference by councillors in disciplinary procedures. The vacancy in the Community Services Department had been caused by her departure for another job. She told the tribunal that she had been shocked when she heard who was her replacement, but said the appointment would have given the Department a better image in the eyes of unionist councillors. Finding in favour of the five Catholics, the Fair Employment Tribunal noted that two of the three interviewers had no experience of community services. One was the Registrar of Deaths, Births and Marriages and the other a building control officer employed by the Council. In a unanimous 35-page decision, the three Tribunal members said they had no doubt that the successful candidate for the post was the least qualified and had the least training. The Council was instructed to pay damages of £52,000 between the five snubbed Catholics while the ratepayers were left with a £10,000 bill for the hearing. Sinn Féin calls for those involved in the recruitment process to be disciplined and to be barred from future interview panels fell on deaf ears.

Leading a unionist counter-charge in his inimitable bumbling style, Fred Cobain attacked the messenger. He obtained figures of the religious breakdown of *The Irish News*, chief critic of the Council jobs bias, and distributed them to the General Purposes and Finance Committee. For good measure, the budding Machiavelli attacked the Fair Employment Commission's own employment record.

But nowhere were Council double standards more clear than in the case of Catholic road sweeper James Whittson, who was told by fellow worker and loyalist John Dawson that he would be killed if he gave evidence against a UVF gang which had tried to kidnap him. The New Lodge man suffered a breakdown after the attempted abduction which took place as he was leaving a shop on the Shankill Road in April 1991. Three UVF men involved in trying to kidnap the Catholic man were apprehended at the scene by the RUC. Workmate Dawson tried to lean on Whittson to drop the charges but, though terrified, the New Lodge man refused and went to the RUC who set up a sting operation which caught on videotape Dawson and a colleague threatening to kill their Catholic workmate if the court case went ahead. Dawson was charged with trying to pervert the course of justice and was remanded in jail for a year before the courts imposed a two-year suspended sentence when he pleaded guilty. As Whittson battled with bad nerves and eked out an existence on his sickness benefit, Cleansing Inspector Dawson returned to his job. Charged with Dawson was Council employee Rab Robinson whose UVF son was shot dead by the British Army after murdering a Catholic shop owner. At the time, no disciplinary action was taken against either of the men and no investigation ordered, quite a contrast with the case of Roisin McDonough. In a moving letter to Chief Executive Brian Hanna in March 1994, Whittson asked to be told why those who attacked him were back in Council employ while his life was ' in ruins'. However, it emerged that Whittson's *cri de coeur*, addressed to the Town Clerk, wasn't even brought to the attention of the top official in City Hall until 15 months later, in June 1995. When it did reach the desk of Chief Executive Brian Hanna, he ordered an inquiry. The report of the inquiry team was delivered to the Chief Executive in November 1996, by which time John Dawson not only remained in Council employment but had been promoted to a more senior position of Area Contract Inspector.

While FEC restrictions on discriminatory practices started to bite throughout the 1990s, the unionists took advantage of ambivalent rulings by the fair employment body on the flying of the Union flag and the display of portraits of the Queen to insist that these symbols of British rule remained on show in Council workplaces. When a row blew up in August 1996 about a portrait of the Queen at a cleansing depot in Dunbar Link in central Belfast, where the workforce was split 60-40 in favour of Protestants, unionists rushed to the defence of Her Majesty. Nationalist workers took a photo of the portrait which, they complained, they were 'jokingly' ordered to bow in front of, and supplied it to the *Andersonstown News*, which duly plastered it all over the front page. The portrait also had an interesting pedigree: it belonged to John Dawson. Complaining that they felt threatened by the article, unionist workers downed brushes and walked out. Enraged, DUP councillors warned of a situation where the Union flag would be taken down from Council offices while the Tricolour remained on show in the Sinn Féin members' rooms at City Hall. And they really saw red when a Council audit of the number of portraits and flags in Council buildings was published in December 1996, with the instruction that they be removed because they contravened FEC legislation. Legal counsel left the Council in no doubt but that the display of the Queen's portrait and the flying of the Union flag in workplaces where they obviously caused offence was illegal. Unimpressed, the DUP pushed a motion through Council in May 1997 declaring that officials were not permitted to remove the flags or portraits, regardless of the legal position. In a document leaked to the *Belfast Telegraph*, senior counsel responded that this stipulation could result in the Council facing 'an avalanche of religious discrimination claims from Catholic employees'.

And there was considerable bias too in the allocation of resources. SDLP and Sinn Féin representatives in the north of the city were at one in their denunciation of City Hall leisure services strategy which left the burgeoning nationalist areas of North Belfast without a leisure facility while neighbouring Protestant areas, Ballysillan, Loughside and Shore Road, had one apiece. In October 1988, a Department of Education pen pusher, presumably unaware of the reasoning behind this bizarre policy, wrote to the Council explaining that grant aid of £1m would be available if the Council was willing to build a leisure centre in one of the massively disadvantaged nationalist wards in North Belfast. Councillors on the Leisure Services Committee voted to tell the Department where it could put its £1m grant after Robin Newton of the DUP, a brooding character at the best of times who was given to sectarian utterances, told fellow committee members that 'we need a new leisure centre like we need a nuclear explosion'. Things hadn't improved much by 1997 when an internal Parks Department document revealed that eight times more money was spent on the upkeep of parks in unionist areas than was spent in nationalist areas. Over £4m was spent on the parks in unionist areas while less than half a million pounds went to the parks in nationalist districts. A further £1m was allocated to parks in 'neutral' areas of the city. 'It is stark evidence of the inequalities which nationalists at an individual level and at community level continue to endure', said Gerry Adams, while Joe Hendron found the report 'a major cause of concern'. 'Rates come from all city residents and therefore all must be given equality in leisure provision', he added.

12.

And Then There Were Ten

Despite having lost the West Belfast Westminster seat to the SDLP in 1992, the Sinn Féin vote peaked at a new high in the May 1993 elections to City Hall. That turnaround in the party's fortunes came at a time when spirits were in freefall. Indeed, that night and morning in Belfast City Hall the previous April when the marathon count for the West Belfast seat was carried out was the most miserable experience of my political life. As dawn broke, it became clear that Shankill loyalists had succeeded in giving Joe Hendron of the SDLP enough votes to take the Westminster seat from Sinn Féin, but it was almost 8am, 23 hours after the count started, before the Returning Officer made his official announcement. It was as if a trapdoor had opened in my stomach and all my political hopes had gone spilling out.

In May 1993, however, Sinn Féin garnered over 23 per cent of the vote in Belfast, on the back of the Hume-Adams' talks and the improved political atmosphere. The party returned ten councillors, three in Upper Falls where I stood, four in Lower Falls, and three in the Oldpark area of North Belfast. New faces in the Sinn Féin team included former hunger-striker Pat McGeown, who (even if it is a cliché) could truthfully be regarded as a legend in his own lifetime, and former party chairperson Tom Hartley. Pat was the only Sinn Féin councillor who won total respect from his unionist counterparts. When he

145

spoke in City Hall with his measured, determined tone, the banter halted and the unionists sat rapt at his comments. A former leader of the IRA in Belfast, Pat took the place of Lily Fitzsimmons who stepped down after eight years on the front line. The Turf Lodge grandmother had an eloquent parting shot for the unionists:

> For years, the Council had treated the nationalists of West Belfast as nobodies. I suppose the one thing they have learnt over the past eight years is that we are somebody.

The election left the unionists holding on to their century-long stranglehold of City Hall by the barest of margins. While the actual breakdown in City Hall wasn't changed by the election, remaining at 27-24, the writing was on the wall for unionists who had failed to take back the seat won by Joe Austin in the October 1991 North Belfast by-election. The SDLP returned with nine seats, though losing out one seat to Sinn Féin in the Lower Falls, the party gained an additional two seats in outer North and South Belfast where the number of Catholics was on the up, to the Alliance's five. In 1985, the SDLP and Sinn Féin, between them, held 13 seats. In 1989, Sinn Féin and the SDLP had 16 seats; now in 1993 they boasted 19 seats. The unionists scraped 27 seats after they managed to gain an extra position in South Belfast which had been created by the decision of the Boundaries Commission to transfer a seat from the depopulated Shankill ward to Botanic. But the sands were shifting fast in South Belfast in particular. There the SDLP's Dorita Field topped the poll in Botanic where the quota was, ironically, 1690 votes, and gave hope of a second nationalist seat there in the next election. In percentage terms, the party breakdown after the May election was Sinn Féin 23.2 per cent, UUP 21.5 per cent, DUP 16.8 per cent, SDLP 15.6 per cent, and Alliance 10.9 per cent (independent unionists made up the rest). Prescient *Independent* correspondent David McKitterick predicted that the Council would fall into nationalist hands at the next local government elections. 'For more than a century, the proportion of Catholics in Belfast never exceeded 30 per cent, but today it stands at about 45 per cent', he said.

I was the tenth and last Sinn Féin councillor elected at the two-day count and emerged from the count room with a predictable 'Tiocfaidh ár lá' to the cheers of scores of delighted election workers who had all but taken over City Hall. Councillors and workers crowded onto the regal staircase to have their picture taken as Gerry Adams popped a champagne cork before we marched triumphantly from City Hall to the Sinn Féin offices in Sevastopol Street on the Falls Road. Along the way, supporters waved Tricolours from the high-rise Divis Tower or lined the route to cheer us on. There are few things to compare in life with Sinn Féin election celebrations, possibly because the good times are always tinged with memories of absent friends and the after-shocks of blacker days. After the May election, even those involved in the most ecstatic celebrations would have spared a thought for the family of party worker Alan Lundy who had been shot dead by loyalists just weeks earlier while carrying out work on a security porch at the home of Alex Maskey.

The '93 election was certainly a sweet victory on a personal basis as it marked the first time that my wife, Helen, had attended the count. On St Patrick's Day, our son Pádraig had been born dead in the Royal Victoria Hospital. The support of the wider republican family during that time had been unstinting and in stark contrast to the situation at City Hall where our loss didn't merit a mention in the time set aside at the beginning of Council meetings for notices of commiseration or congratulation. The following month, the engagement of an Alliance councillor was deemed worthy of mention. Helen had been out little since the death of Pádraig but was persuaded by Gerry Adams to accept a lift to the count in his armour-plated black taxi. It was a much-appreciated gesture.

The DUP zealots suffered their worst election result in the city in a decade. From a peak of 14 seats in 1985, they found themselves in the new Council with just eight seats. But while the DUP clearly learnt no lessons from their trouncing, the fresh

UUP team, with its mean age reduced from 65 to around 40, certainly saw the error of its ways. From now on, the Ulster Unionists would adopt a semi-detached approach to the DUP's campaign against Sinn Féin. With an eye to the public relations disaster which had been the 1989-1993 term, the larger unionist party took a more aloof attitude to the perennial protests against the Shinners and set out to exploit the opportunities for positive PR thrown up by the new powers over economic development which had been given to councils. A semblance of power-sharing with the SDLP was initiated, with the nationalist party's Alex Attwood being appointed chairman of the Client Services Committee with the support of the Ulster Unionists. Born out of meetings between the SDLP and UUP before the election, the new partnership agreement was designed, said Alex Attwood, 'to purge the past, plan for the future and rotate officer posts, including that of mayor'. Stealing my anti-junketeering clothes, the West Belfast councillor also declared he wouldn't be accepting his £1,300 annual stipend as a committee chairman.

The new 'partnership' programme of unionism also extended to the Alliance Party, but not to Sinn Féin, with the SDLP insisting that they alone could represent the nationalist side of the powersharing equation. But the bar on the SDLP holding the top positions in the city, those of Lord Mayor and Deputy Lord Mayor, wasn't lifted by the unionists, sparking an SDLP boycott of the inaugural dinner of incoming Lord Mayor, and guru of 'thinking unionists', Reg Empey. The new detente between the SDLP and UUP soured swiftly. As Alban Maginness said,

> We have negotiated with the UUP and they made a lot of interesting noises. We thought sanity and civilisation would break out in Belfast City Council but it has effectively got worse. Nothing seems to have changed. They've elected a unionist mayor, a unionist deputy and they have a majority on the most influential committees.

Alex Attwood was also smarting as he detailed the changes that had come about since Reg Empey last served as Lord Mayor in 1988:

Journey man: Blotski in the Irish News casts a cynical eye on Frank Millar's jaunt Down Under. (Courtesy of Ian Knox)

Merry dance: In March 1995, Andersonstown News cartoonist Oisín steps out for the first céilí at City Hall with James Molyneaux and Ken Maginnis

Writing on the wall: Irish street names put up illegally in Belfast. Local councils are now obliged to put up a translation of English street names where there is a demand. However, it remains illegal to name a street or development in Irish only.

Heartbreak: Alan Lundy (39), who was shot dead by loyalists at the home of councillor Alex Maskey in May 1983, with his wife Margaret and their children Alan, Daniel, Clare, Elizabeth and Ciarán

Milestone: The annual internment commemoration march makes it to City Hall for the first time in August 1993. On the evening of the march, loyalists shot dead Sean Lavery, the son of Sinn Féin councillor Bobby Lavery.

Loyalist victim: The funeral of Sean Lavery (21), son of Sinn Féin councillor Bobby Lavery, makes its way through his native New Lodge district in North Belfast.

Bread winner: Blotski in the Irish News portrays a desperate Alasdair McDonnell grasping half-a-loaf after his election as Deputy Lord Mayor in June 1995 while colleague Alex Attwood tries to drag him back. Alex Maskey is not amused. (Courtesy of Ian Knox)

Standard-bearer: 'Eleventh hunger striker' Councillor Pat McGeown who died suddenly in 1996.

Ullans guru: UUP Lord Mayor (1996-1997) Ian Adamson (second from left) at a City Hall book launch.

VIP Visitor: Mayor Thomas Menino of Boston takes time out on a visit to Belfast, during which he addressed a full sitting of the council, to meet with prisoners' campaigner Briege Brownlee (right) in a Falls Road cultural centre while Councillor Marie Moore looks on.

Yes, Minister: Baroness Jean Denton who in 1977 was embroiled in a fair employment scandal within her department which was exposed by the press

Washington D.C. appointment: Community priest Fr Des Wilson, who spearheaded the Conway Mill education and jobs' development, sets out for the Washington D.C. economic conference in May 1995. Community groups in West Belfast banded together to cover the cost of Fr Des' flights and conference fee.

Business first: Ulster Unionist Lord Mayor and businessman Reg Empey who pioneered the council's foray into economic development.

Inspirational: New York State Comptroller Carl McCall who made a plea for fair employment at a City Hall function in 1997.

'Strategist': UUP leader on the Council, Fred Cobain, who once declared that some mandates are more equal than others!

Dinner's served: Councillor Sandy Blair and Belfast's High Sheriff, Councillor Jim Walker line up to be spanked between courses by waitresses at the proposed School Dinners' restaurant. (Picture courtesy of Sunday World.)

Number crunching: Shankill councillor and former Lord Mayor Hugh 'Shughie' Smith.

Green Mardi Gras: St Patrick's Day celebrated in Belfast city centre for the first time in 1998.

Loyalist breakthrough: Billy Hutchinson was elected for the loyalist fringe party, the PUP, at the May 1997 local government elections. He is now a councillor and an Assembly member for North Belfast. (Photo by Thomas McMullan, North Belfast News.)

Outspoken: East Belfast unionist councillor Jim Rodgers who opposed plans to celebrate St Patrick's Day in Belfast city centre.

South Belfast: Carmel Hanna of the SDLP who was elected to City Hall in May 1997 for the South Belfast area after exceeding the quota of 1690 votes.

History maker: Alban Maginness who became Belfast's first Catholic Lord Mayor in 1997. Tidying the Lord Mayor's Parlour for him is City Hall staff member George Hynes.

Never on a Sunday: UUP councillor Nelson McCausland.

New boy: Alliance Lord Mayor David Alderdice launching the 1999 St Patrick's Day parade in Belfast.

Changed: Belfast City Hall today

Making progress: Sinn Féin councillor — and occasional chauffeur for Edna O'Brien — Tom Hartley entering a City Hall meeting room.

The last shall be first: Councillor Marie Moore who became the Sinn Féin councillor to reach the highest-ever position in City Hall when she was elected Deputy Lord Mayor in June 1999.

The Berlin Wall has come down, Mary Robinson has been elected President of Ireland, a Democrat has been elected President of the US, Mandela was released. Power and those in power change all around the world but Belfast remains the same. There was no rotation of senior positions, no acknowledgement of our culture, values or identity, no serious attempt to target areas of disadvantage, protect jobs or save services, in short, the position is now that position that existed prior to 1985. It was manifestly inadequate then and it is manifestly contemptible now.

Meanwhile, stung at the abandoning of their traditional, unionist-only pact with the UUP for a wobbly coalition with the SDLP, the DUP also stayed away from the First Citizen's inauguration bash. Sinn Féin wasn't invited. Unperturbed, Empey added the Lord Mayor of Dublin, Gay Mitchell, to the invitation list; a politician who was once bitten but clearly not shy. 'People like Reg Empey are in the process of making Northern Ireland a mongrel state where you can have a visit by the Queen one week and a visit by the "Queen" of Ireland Mary Robinson the next', bemoaned Sammy Wilson. But Wilson was unequivocal about his party's attitude to the sharing of the key Council posts. 'We will ensure that there is never any non-unionist mayor or deputy in this council', he said. That sentiment was translated into less diplomatic language by Eric Smyth, who alone among unionists refused to vote for Reg Empey as Lord Mayor because he objected to the proffering of even token positions to the SDLP: 'No. No. No Surrender', he shouted across the chamber. 'We will surrender nothing to you, the NIO or those other Commanches.' Virtually without media comment, PUP councillor Hugh Smyth, whose party claimed an insight into the workings of the UVF, was elected Deputy Lord Mayor by the combined unionist bloc.

But the UUP's new-found sense of civic responsibility didn't last very far into the new term. Braving a welter of criticism and the best advice of senior officials, unionists baulked at moves to complement the restructured committee system with access for all parties to outside boards and bodies along the same principles of proportionality. That ban, and the block on Sinn Féin members from holding chairs or deputy chairs of committees and from representing the Council on official cross-party delegations, became the priority targets for Sinn Féin in the four years ahead as the party strove to build on the victories it had scored in the previous decade. The job of forcing change was made all the more easy by the fact that the party was now represented right across the Council. In fact, the new committee system proved a godsend for nationalist councillors determined to get stuck into Council business on behalf of their constituents. Under the old system, Sinn Féin's nine members had been restricted to just 18 committee positions between them. On the other hand, just eight unionist members, Fred Proctor, Herbie Ditty, Dixie Gilmore, Tommy Patton, Nigel Dodds, Frank Millar, Jim Walker and Ian Adamson – held the grand total of 77 positions. The new system also gave the RUC a headache. Immediately after the election, senior officers declared that they wouldn't attend any meetings of the long-standing City Hall Police Liaison Committee if Sinn Féin members were to attend, but even the RUC's famed powers of persuasion couldn't change City Hall standing orders. As a result, the committee, which served no purpose other than to legitimise the RUC and which had never published the minutes of its weighty deliberations, was scrapped. However, unionists continued to hog the positions on outside boards and bodies. Though holding just 53 per cent of Council seats, unionists held on to 93 percent of outside positions. 'The nationalists of Belfast are caught in the classic taxation without representation bind', said Alex Maskey as he led his team in for the new term. Under a proportional handout of committee chairs, Sinn Féin would, he said, be entitled to the chair of one principal committee and three sub-committees. As it turned out, it was a case of the more things change. Sinn Féin got no chair or vice-chair positions, while the unionists snapped up 22 out of 24 chair and deputy chair vacancies.

The DUP had no monopoly on eejits for there were a few colourful characters among the leaner UUP team as well.

Former shipyard worker Sandy Blair spent most of the following four year term downing half-uns in the pubs around City Hall and paying more attention to the head on his pint than to the unionist whip. Styling himself as something of a fist-fighter, working class hero, Sandy once posed with his mitts up for the *Sunday World* to boast of how he had given 'the hand of Prod' to an amorous punter he discovered in a public house disabled loo with a lady friend. Eyewitnesses said he had to be pulled off his victim. 'I hit him a couple of punches on the gub', declared unionism's latest civic ambassador. Sandy's erratic voting pattern and frequent absences during crucial votes was to leave its own mark on the changing City Hall. The UUP man also memorably joined forces with the DUP's Jim Walker to back plans to bring a 'School Dinners' theme restaurant to Belfast. The pair were pictured posing in the *Sunday World* with scantily clad 'teachers' who were extolling the virtues of spanking diners between courses. Sitting alongside Sandy and Jim was East Belfast councillor and children's football scout Jim Rodgers, who once dressed up in full Glentoran strip to canvass votes in East Belfast. Jim's shrill denunciations of 'the terrorists' were matched only by his determination to stop funding for community projects in West Belfast and on the nationalist Lower Ormeau Road.

The new term also brought new faces. Diligent if not exactly animated, the McGimpsey brothers, Chris and Michael, brought fresh blood to the tired Ulster Unionist ranks, while taking her leave of the DUP fold was Rhonda Paisley. Having originally vowed to make life hell for Sinn Féin, Rhonda found life increasingly depressing in the changing Belfast. 'I dread Council meetings and I always leave exhausted', she confessed to the *Sunday Life*, before acknowledging what the rest of us knew from the moment she first blew her own (toy) trumpet in City Hall: 'Politics is not my forté.' What exactly her forté is never became totally clear in the years following her departure, but there was a discernibly less poisonous atmosphere in City Hall in her wake. In fact, before stepping down formally, she had taken on the role of an absentee councillor, going to

Council meetings only often enough to ensure she wasn't booted off for non-attendance and spending full meetings of Council reading trashy novels. So abysmal was the record of the self-styled super-politico, that I presented her with a wooden spoon, courtesy of the *Sunday World*, for having the worst attendance record of any councillor (and that included a terminally ill member of the DUP). In the period January-June 1992, Paisley missed all 11 meetings of the Town Planning Committee and all 11 of the Community Services Committee. In her absence, the DUP's decline continued apace.

Like a punch-drunk old boxer, Sammy Wilson spent the new term walking into Sinn Féin haymakers. With Frank Millar hanging up his councillor's gown, Wilson took up the mantle of Undisputed Champion Bigot of City Hall. Having insulted every other group in the city, schoolteacher Wilson turned his attention to the gay community. Deriding plans for a gay festival, he slated those involved as 'poofs and perverts'. Openly enthusiastic about the ruthless campaign of assassination against Sinn Féin councillors and supporters, he couldn't contain his joy at the assassination of Donegal councillor Eddie Fullerton, though the Lord Mayor ruled out of order a motion congratulating those responsible. 'I defend the right of the Ulster people to prepare to resist', he told the *Sunday Tribune*. 'We have the right to defend ourselves and to uphold our democratic rights. Ulster Resistance has made it clear that it is preparing to defend Northern Ireland against aggression from Britain or the Republic of Ireland.' Gloating over attacks by loyalists on victims alleged to have been involved with Sinn Féin, he boasted: 'When people who promote war become victims of violence then they cannot expect any sympathy from me.' That, for SDLP West Belfast councillor Alex Attwood, was tantamount to 'dancing on the coffins' of those murdered by loyalists.

Sinn Féin started the new term by flagging up other burning issues, most of which centred on the choking British-only ethos of City Hall. Early in the new term Alex Maskey set out the party stall, calling for the removal of stained glass windows dedicated to the British Army and their replacement with a memorial window for all those killed in the Troubles, the opening of City Hall for use by nationalists, the provision of equality of opportunity in employment, the scrapping of the Loyal Toast at civic functions, the removal of the Union Jack from the City Hall dome, the taking down of the 'Belfast Says No' banner in the City Hall car park, and the appointment of nationalist Lord Mayors. 'Belfast is our city too, as is Belfast City Council and Belfast City Hall', he said. 'Unionists should say now what steps they are prepared to take to ensure this Council reflects all the city's traditions. The alternative is to wait until they lose their majority and have parity of treatment imposed upon them.' The Sinn Féin councillor would later call for the commissioning of a stained glass window in City Hall to mark the pogroms of 1969, on the same lines as those already in place which paid tribute to the RUC, UDR and British Army. Unionists responded by claiming that the entire programme of recognition for nationalism within the hallowed portals of City Hall amounted to 'cultural genocide'. And the 'pan-nationalist threat', according to Sammy Wilson, came in the most benign forms. Grant-aid to the Ard Eoin Fleadh, both the fleadh and its counterpart, the West Belfast Féile were to be consistent targets of the unionists, was cut from £4,000 to £2,500 in June 1994 after the DUP man argued money was tight. The same week the Council authorised expenditure of £250,000 on new carpets. The only consolation for nationalists was that the tender for the carpets had to be made on an EC-wide basis and was won by a firm in Tuam, County Galway. Unionists already branded the exquisite Italian marble used in the construction of the elaborate reception areas at City Hall as 'Catholic marble'. The mind boggles at how they described the lush acres of carpet from the dreaded Free State.

Though outwardly cocksure and ebullient, republicans had no guarantee that the changes they struggled for at City Hall could be attained. There was always the fear that the shifting balance of power at City Hall would only nudge the UUP towards a rapprochement with the SDLP and Alliance, an arrangement which would see Sinn Féin forever on the margins. Regardless, the new term saw Sinn Féin parade the corridors of City Hall with growing confidence. While our publicity stressed the unchanging unionist mind-set which pervaded City Hall, the day-to-day reality was that officials treated us like royalty. Visitors, including novelist Edna O'Brien (who had to warn Tom Hartley to keep his eyes on the road as he give her a car drive tour of West Belfast), never failed to be impressed by the courteous and helpful attitude of staff in response to Sinn Féin requests and by the freedom with which our councillors went about their business in the hall. There was a growing feeling among the Sinn Féin group, as we prepared to move into bigger offices set aside for our members, that we had come into our own.

Major breakthroughs, such as the first Irish language celebration in City Hall in December 1993, the first grants to Irish language organisations and the derailing of the junket gravy train, served to give the push for equality added momentum. On the other hand, by their every action unionists betrayed the growing crisis of confidence in their ranks. While there was more than a element of hypocrisy about the unionist protests at having to sit side by side with 'apologists for terrorism', there was no hiding their morale meltdown as they saw republicans of the calibre of Pat McGeown and Tom Hartley enter the Council arena with unrestrained gusto.

That crisis of confidence demonstrated itself at Council debates where unionists – minus Sammy Wilson and the PUP's Hugh Smyth – continued to troop out every time a Sinn Féin councillor spoke. Debates were fiery and laced with invective, slagging and cat-calling. Though never scaling the K2 of bitterness reached in the previous term, full meetings of Council were far from tranquil.

Given to overegging the pudding, I often had my coat tail tugged by colleagues who urged me to cut short apocalyptic speeches. On one occasion, Sammy Wilson voted through a motion that the clerks keep a verbatim account of my musings after I had detailed his connections with Ulster Resistance –

which had been founded in the Council-owned Ulster Hall as Sammy, sporting his mayoral chain of office, looked on. I had also thrown in some titbits about his October 1986 meeting in the Lord Mayor's office with Canadians Harold Wright and Bill Taylor, who were subsequently convicted of running guns to loyalist paramilitaries. The pair testified in court that after Wilson left them in his office, they were joined by loyalist paramilitaries led by John Bingham (later shot dead by the IRA) to discuss their gun-smuggling operation. Only a three-line whip by my colleagues prevented me from making a string of further allegations but at any rate, Wilson's defamation case threat came, unsurprisingly, to nought.

When the committee decisions up for ratification at the monthly council meeting didn't provide the spark for the chamber conflagration, motions tabled by the unionists attacking Sinn Féin and the IRA did. With admirable optimism, unionists came to each monthly meeting with a tendentious motion blasting Sinn Féin for supporting the IRA and calling on the British government to ban the party. In the face of overwhelming indifference from a government engaged in secret dialogue with republicans, unionists raised the anti-Sinn Féin flag at every meeting. Like the anachronistic white trash of the Deep South, the unionists continued to alert the world to their 'negro problem'. Belfast had been a great wee place for years, they would explain, because the Fenians, like the blacks of segregated America, had been content to stay in their own world. That world, of course, didn't include City Hall. But now the uppity Taigs wanted to be part of the 'unionist world'.

Yet anyone looking at the outside bodies on which the Council was allowed representation would have considered Belfast a Sinn Féin-free zone. Traditionally in Belfast, unionists seized all the positions on major public bodies such as the Belfast Education and Library Board, the Ulster Museum, the Fire Service and the health boards, for themselves. By June 1993, and despite the unionist claims of power-sharing, this policy had been liberalised only sufficiently to allow two SDLP members and two Alliance members to serve alongside the ten unionists on the Belfast Education and Library Board. The story was the same on the other outside bodies. Sinn Féin nominations to positions on the Ulster Museum Board of Trustees, the Belfast Harbour Commissioners and the Fire Authority for Northern Ireland were all frustrated.

Hogging positions on outside boards and bodies set up in the wake of the reform of local government in 1972-3 was nothing new for unionism. Up to 1,000 board positions were available in over 60 major quangos across the North and while the majority were appointed by ministers, councils had a considerable say. Belfast City Council alone made 62 appointments. Even before the signing of the Anglo-Irish Agreement in 1985, unionists took all the places going. Lisburn unionists took 100 of 102 up for grabs. A DUP councillor subsequently apologised because one place had accidentally gone to an SDLP member. British ministers made no attempt to intervene in this charade, even when unionists found they were on so many public bodies that they couldn't attend them all because their meetings clashed. 'They didn't care', explained Brian Feeney. 'Better no service to "their own" than let "the other side" have a look in.'

The ban on membership from the BELB was particularly pernicious. The majority of schoolchildren in Belfast were Catholic and Sinn Féin, as the largest nationalist party, represented thousands of parents with children at those schools. Yet, because Belfast City Council refused to appoint Sinn Féin councillors to the Board at the start of each four-year term, no republican voice was ever raised to fight for more resources for the education of local children. Catholic Church collusion in the veto on Sinn Féin was an open secret. I protested to Down and Connor Bishop Dr Patrick Walsh, who responded in November 1994 by requesting Sinn Féin's education policy, but never moved against the status quo. For the Catholic Church, it wasn't a matter of keeping the 'men of violence' off the boards lest they corrupt the minds of innocent children. Rather, for the parish priests, it meant the popular local politicians who represented Sinn Féin couldn't meddle in their educational power base, for every member of the BELB was also entitled to serve on a number of school boards. No Sinn Féiners on the BELB meant no Sinn Féiners on the boards of the Catholic schools in the republican heartlands of West and North Belfast. The Catholic Church had no qualms about joining forces with the most sectarian wing of unionism when it came to keeping the representatives of the meek off the BELB. So much for the Sermon on the Mount. At the time of writing (October 1999), not one Sinn Féin member has served on a board of governors in a Catholic school in Belfast – though unionists have. Sinn Féin councillors were considered good enough to send their children to the local Catholic school but not good enough to bring their considerable expertise – and invaluable contacts – to bear on the problems facing a district with a record of educational underachievement.

Some officials and board members of the BELB itself were less than enthusiastic about tackling the ban. Joe Austin and I met with education board Chief Executive TJ Moag to discuss the ban in January 1992 and left him in no doubt but that we considered BELB officials culpable in the McCarthyism being practised by Belfast City Council because they failed to raise a murmur of protest against it.

While Sinn Féin wore its successful court cases on its sleeve, the unionists were confident that their refusal to play ball with appointments to outside bodies was secure against legal challenge. They made little pretence at justifying the discrimination against Sinn Féin. Unfortunately, our legal advice was that a challenge to the ban on Sinn Féin from outside bodies might very well be found by the courts to be legal. In such a scenario, advised our counsel, the unionists might conceivably expand the policy. Guided by the golden rule that we didn't go into court unless we were sure of success, Sinn Féin drew up affidavits on the ban but didn't file suit, for the moment.

In June 1992, when I had come within a whisker of being appointed to the (toothless) Eastern Health and Social Services Council on behalf of the Council, unionists closed ranks to block the move. The Council had five places on the Council, but two elderly unionists, Joe Coggle and Herbie Ditty, cited overwork and resigned. This was no rare occurrence. Having monopolised all the plum committee, chair and outside body appointments, unionists found they didn't have the time (nor, quite often, the inclination) to attend the boards they were appointed to. All councillors were circulated about the vacancies on the Health Council and asked did they wish to take up one of the positions. Nominated by the Sinn Féin grouping, mine was the only name put forward. Under the advice of Town Clerk Stanley McDowell, the unionists rubber-stamped my appointment at the June 1992 meeting of the General Purposes and Finance Committee only to perform a volte face at the full meeting of Council on 1 July. My nomination was 'taken back' by the unionist chair of the GP Committee Eric Smyth at the request of fellow-unionist John Carson. There was Dumb, Dumber and then Eric Smyth. Oblivious to the fact that he was portraying himself as a dullard, Smyth told the press that he didn't know what was going on when the original committee meeting he chaired approved my name. He was, in fact, made aware of the nomination by officials 24 hours before the meeting and had only made his U-turn after coming under pressure from his hardline colleagues on the DUP benches. By the time the General Purposes and Finance Committee next met in August, Smyth had got his act together. That meeting was told that Smyth himself and unionist Margaret Dunlop had belatedly expressed an interest in serving on the Council. Their nominations were unanimously approved by the Committee. Mine was rejected.

Likewise, Council delegations were a no-go area for Sinn Féin. When Council new boy Michael McGimpsey, still wet behind the ears after his election the previous month, supported a Town Planning motion in June 1993 to send an all-party delegation, including Sinn Féin, to a housing conference in Derry, Sammy Wilson accused him of 'treachery'. McGimpsey was swiftly hauled into line and at the July meeting of full Council amended his own proposal to bump Sinn Féin off the delegation – and set a record by becoming the first ever councillor to propose and oppose the same motion in seven days. The UUP U-turn on the Derry trip signalled an improvement of relations between the two unionist parties in the wake of a fractious electoral battle. In September, both parties voted unanimously to block any visit to Belfast by President Mary Robinson and, for good measure, rapped her over the knuckles, as 'the head of a foreign and oppressive state' for 'giving credibility' to Sinn Féin by shaking hands with Gerry Adams during a visit to Belfast three months earlier.

At the same meeting, unionists unanimously agreed to ignore the advice of the Council's own solicitors and block funding to West Belfast Irish language body, Glór na nGael. They also agreed to differ over the £32m conference-concert hall plan which went though the Council in November with only the DUP voting against. At the make-or-break meeting for the Laganside development, I demonstrated skills normally only seen at Billy Smart's circus, performing a breathtaking feat of acrobatics to reverse Sinn Féin's previously trenchant opposition to the 'white elephant' with qualified support. The Waterfront Hall is in truth a wonderful building which serves as a flagship for the rejuvenated riverfront of the city but the fact that the project was never advertised for open tender and that the professional fees to the architects alone were £1.7m still sticks in my craw. On the plus side, no Union Jack flies from the roof of the building and promotional material has included flyers in Irish. In its early days, the Council's Conference-Concert Hall Sub-Committee had been made up entirely of unionists. In protest at the exclusion of nationalists, I once picketed a meeting of the committee, holding up a cartoon which asked did unionists know it was 1991 and not 1661 (as it would appear if you stood on your head... as unionists do). However, with the introduction of proportionality, Sinn Féin was to hold approximately 20 per cent of the seats on the board set up to run the hall after it opened in 1996. Ironically, Ulster Unionist John Carson, who championed the construction of the hall, and who agreed a truce with me whereby I agreed to stop sniping at the project if he helped an American businessman secure a contract with the Royal Victoria Hospital which would bring jobs to West Belfast, lost his seat in the May 1997 local government elections. The American businessman never got the contract either!

Flirting with the risk of legal action, the unionists continued to block Sinn Féin at every opportunity. However, the proportional presence of our councillors on committees (only the UUP had more seats on each committee than Sinn Féin) sent out its own signal that the culture of City Hall was changing no matter how valiantly the UUP whip Fred Cobain held his thumb in the dike.

In January 1994, an internal UUP document detailing a proposed carve-up of the seats on the Council's community centres found its way into the hands of Sinn Féin. The document listed the council's 15 community centres and the names of the unionist, SDLP and Alliance members who were to be voted on to the board of each centre. The names of Sinn Féin councillors were conspicuous by their absence. Accusing the unionists of returning to 'the failed policies of political apartheid', Sinn Féin released details of the plan to the press and called on the SDLP to oppose the proposal to put unionists on the boards of community centres in nationalist areas. But it wasn't only Sinn Féin which hit the roof over the plan. Council solicitors also blew a gasket at the unionist masterplan which was voted through the Community Services Sub-committee on 31 January, despite Sinn Féin protests, at the proposal of unionism's 'new man' Chris McGimpsey. The same source referred to Lower Ormeau nationalists opposed to Orange marches as 'dogs marking out their territory'.

Unionists elected members to community centres across the city but, while stopping short of putting their own names forward for the boards of nationalist community centres, they refused to appoint Sinn Féin nominees to those same centres – even though no other names were put forward. In a lengthy legal opinion, the Town Solicitor ordered the unionists to 'correct the outcome of having employed a defective procedure' by returning Sinn Féin councillors Pat McGeown, Bobby Lavery, Fra McCann, Paddy McManus and Marie Moore to the boards of community centres in their local areas. Large portions of humble pie were subsequently served up for unionists at the March meeting of the Community Services Sub-Committee as Sinn Féin warned that unreconstructed unionists would be forced to accept power-sharing once they lost their City Hall majority.

The community centres' debacle was a humiliating blow in párticular for Fred Cobain who had vowed that Sinn Féin would never represent the Council on outside bodies. It was a victory a long time in the coming for Alex Maskey; in 1983 he had been appointed to represent the Council on the board of Community Technical Aid by the Community Services Committee only to see the decision overturned by unionists and the vacancy filled by the Alliance Party.

Moves towards a changed Council were given another fillip in February 1994 when the three Sinn Féin councillors on the Economic Development Sub-Committee were appointed (along with all the other interested members of the Economic Development Sub-Committee) to attend a conference on the EC in Belfast Castle. Also attending was unionist MP John Taylor who said the presence of the Sinn Féin trio was 'distasteful'. I countered that his remarks (in 1993) that the loyalist murders of Catholics 'may be helpful' were even more distasteful. Taylor's onslaught was blunted somewhat by the fact that no other member of the Economic Development Sub-Committee bothered to turn up for the conference. Rather than target their anger at absent colleagues, Sammy Wilson and Fred Cobain predictably rounded on Sinn Féin and declared that the party would never again represent the Council on an outside delegation. For the record, the conference itself was addressed by the anaemic Stormont Minister for the Economy, Tim Smith, who later had to resign a different Cabinet position over the 'cash for questions' controversy in the House of Commons. Ironically, the previous year, when the Minister had refused to provide me with a detailed breakdown on Industrial

Development Board expenditure in West Belfast, on the basis
that obtaining the information would be prohibitively
expensive, I had written to him offering to pay for the research
involved. Sadly, he never took up my offer; perhaps my price
wasn't gránd enough.

The IRA's continuing campaign provided the unionists with
ammunition to counter the growing Sinn Féin demands for
equality within City Hall. But with the August 1994 IRA
ceasefire, even that fig-leaf was to be removed. There will
never be a better time to make republican politics, advised Pat
McGeown, as Sinn Féin cranked up the pressure on the City
Hall junta. Others didn't stand on City Hall ceremony when it
came to silencing Sinn Féin. In May 1994, the party's new
offices in the hall were targeted in a UVF bomb attack.
Fortunately, Councillor Marie Moore had left the room
moments before the bomb, placed on scaffolding outside the
office window, exploded. The normally outspoken Council
failed to pass a motion condemning the murder bid which
seriously injured two Catholic workers, one losing an eye.
Committee meetings which took place the day after the attack
made no reference to it – this from unionists who would
adjourn standing orders to condemn the throwing of a rotten
apple at an Orange hall. The same Nelsonian eye was turned a
fortnight later to a death threat written on Council headed
notepaper and delivered to Alex Maskey. 'Next Time Be In The
Room' was the scrawled message slipped into Alex Maskey's
pigeon hole in the Members' Room – where only councillors
are allowed access.

In typical style, unionism reacted to the strengthening of links
between nationalists in the run-up to the IRA ceasefire by
circling the wagons. Turning his back on the embryonic
coalition with the SDLP, Fred Cobain announced in July 1994
that the UUP and DUP were to set up a joint committee to
decide on the best way to spend the Council's £50m budget.
'The good old days of unfettered unionism have returned',
warned Alex Attwood, adding: 'This could have devastating
effects on council services, particularly in sensitive areas like

community services and community relations projects which have not found favour in the past among some unionists.' For Sammy Wilson, however, majoritarianism was everything. 'I can't understand why anyone would be angry or have any concerns about the parties which form the majority on a council seeking to ensure that the council spends its £50m budget in the most efficient way. It's the essence of a democracy that people have to get a working majority. It happens in the rest of the UK and in the Republic of Ireland.' Strangely, the DUP man's staunch support for majority rule was to vanish when his side weren't in the majority. A disillusioned Alex Attwood saw majoritarianism in action when his party lost the chair of Client Services which it had been granted in June 1993 in the following year round of chair handouts. Reverting to type, the unionists abandoned talk of a bright new era and refused to give the SDLP even one of the chair positions on the Council's five standing committees. Rubbing salt in the wounds, Alex Maskey reminded the SDLP – who were refusing to support any Sinn Féin nominations for the chairs and deputy chairs of committees – that there would be little thanks from unionists or nationalists for abandoning nationalist unity in order to curry favour with the UUP. 'There is no doubt that eventually unionists will have to extend proportionality to the chair and deputy chairs of committees', he said. 'However, the SDLP tactic of begging for a unionist change of heart on the issue is no real alternative to standing up for the rights of ratepayers. Slowly but surely, the unionist stranglehold on City Hall is being broken. The question the SDLP must ask themselves is are they going to play a part in breaking that stranglehold?' (Press Release 27 June 1994) As SDLP hopes of a new understanding with the UUP turned to dust, John Hume was moved to remark that the City Hall unionists wouldn't give his party 'fresh air'.

Likewise, unionism had two approaches to paramilitary violence: one for republicans and the other for loyalists. When the UVF's deputy leader in Belfast, Trevor King, was shot dead, Alderman Joe Coggle described him in a *Belfast*

Telegraph death notice as 'the best'. For more years than most unionists cared to remember, popular Shankill Road councillor Hughie Smyth had been a member of the UUP team at City Hall – even though he represented the UVF's political wing, the PUP, and had his offices in the paramilitary grouping's Shankill Road prisoners' centre. Smyth took the UUP whip, attending party meetings in the Hall and, shamelessly leading the charge against Sinn Féin over its 'links' with the IRA. Having completed his year as Deputy Lord Mayor, his unionist colleagues catapulted him into the Lord Mayor's seat a year later. Repairs to the City Hall offices blasted by the UVF – still six months off a ceasefire – had yet to begin when Wee Shughie's elevation to high office took place. When subsequently challenged about his party's City Hall pact with the PUP, David Trimble insisted there was no similarity between his stance and a mooted pact between the SDLP and Sinn Féin. 'Hugh Smyth showed to everyone during his year as Lord Mayor that he is totally committed to peace and the democratic process.'

At least Smyth had a sense of humour. When Ireland faced Holland in the World Cup in July 1994, I pressed him to adjourn the monthly Council conflagration to allow councillors to watch the evening game. The new Lord Mayor struck a compromise by rigging up a TV in a special room outside the chamber. It was a bittersweet concession by unionism as the Orangemen of Holland trounced Jack Charlton's men. But Hugh Smyth wasn't the only one with an electoral success to toast. In the handout of Council positions in June 1994, North Belfast Sinn Féin councillor Bobby Lavery sneaked the position of deputy chairman of the Council's Housing Liaison Committee thanks to a number of absent unionists and the support of the SDLP. Unionists reacted as if he had been elected to the UN Security Council. For Sammy Wilson the vote was 'a tragedy' while the *Belfast Telegraph* deplored the development but noted that Sinn Féin,

> have obtained a mandate to play a full part in Council business. They cannot be excluded...They are generally

effective representatives, doing a good job for their constituents...Councillors in Belfast should realise that the more they try to exclude Sinn Féin by dubious methods, the more support it may obtain.

Slow-learner Michael McGimpsey predicted the election would be overturned by full Council at its July meeting, unaware of the fact that committee appointments were not subject to ratification. With unionist maverick Sandy Blair holding the chair of the committee, Bobby Lavery didn't have to wait long before he was called upon to chair the body's proceedings. When that happened Sammy Wilson was joined in a walkout by Jim Rodgers. The pair hoped to leave the meeting without a quorum, but had to immediately return to the committee room when it transpired that there were enough councillors left to allow business to continue.

Despite falling out briefly over the appointment of Bobby Lavery (the DUP accused the UUP of deliberately staying out of the meeting until the election was over, an allegation the UUP denied), it was business as usual for the unionists when they closed ranks in October to deny All-Ireland football champs Down a civic reception. Alliance councillor Steve McBride, who proposed the motion, accused unionists of scoring an own goal, but unimpressed Official Unionist Nelson McCausland (who had fought the '93 election as an independent before switching to the UUs) successfully proposed an amendment which simply noted the historic victory before calling on the GAA to scrap its Rule 21 ban on the Crown forces.

Council shenanigans proved too much for Chief Executive Iain MacDonald who quit in May 1994, after a mere 14 months in the job, to make way for the urbane and consummate official Brian Hanna who had served the Council as Director of Technical Services. Though a unionist by background, Brian Hanna made no secret of his belief that only partnership government would serve the interests of the ratepayers of Belfast. But Iain MacDonald wasn't the only one to give up on the City Hall unionists. Loose cannon Sandy Blair around the same time announced that he was quitting the UUP for 'ignoring working class issues'. Already in hot water with the party for urging voters to 'show their disgust' with Council junketeering, Sandy's departure wasn't mourned by the UUP, but it did leave their slim majority even more vulnerable.

A determined and doughty figure committed to ushering the Council into a new era of partnership, Chief Executive Brian Hanna urged councillors to embrace the new role of economic promotion, aware of the fact that with such responsibility would come an obligation to ditch the politics of exclusion. He was dismissive of plans to establish a Belfast Forum – a type of Belfast Partnership Board involving the statutory agencies and councillors – when it was clear that it would exclude Sinn Féin and, to a lesser degree, the SDLP. In 1994, pea-brained Stormont Economy Minister Tim Smith joined forces with the DoE to set up the Forum, appointing Lord Mayor Hugh Smyth as his co-chairman and restricting Council representation to the chairs of the five standing committees, none of which were held by nationalists. Fred Cobain had led unionist opposition to an SDLP suggestion that the Council be represented by the leaders of the political groupings. Sinn Féin compared the body to a Johannesburg Forum which contained no blacks. In August 1994 I asked permission to address the Forum, which was meeting in City Hall, only to be knocked back by Smith who seemed unaware of his own claim that the Forum 'is to improve co-operation and understanding between elected representatives and the various public sector bodies'. When I tilted at the Forum windmills by demanding Minister Smith wind up the Forum or face a Sinn Féin picket of its meetings, he remained resolute. Shortly afterwards, however, the 'Protestant Forum for a Protestant People' bit the dust. It was to be replaced with the Belfast Vision Board which accorded Sinn Féin representation according to its strength on the Council and was to go to on to publish its strategy in English and Irish. In conversations with Brian Hanna over the Forum initiative, I got the distinct impression that he had little time for initiatives which were going to exclude one section of the community. He

also insisted staff treat all councillors equally and with respect
– that went not only for Sinn Féin but also for elected
representatives who had earned a reputation for spending most
of the day in a drunken haze.

There was pressure coming on the Council too from a British
government, which was begrudgingly lifting its own
restrictions on Sinn Féin in response to the IRA ceasefire, and
from the business movers and shakers of Belfast. Thus, while
the DUP and co pledged never to do business with Sinn Féin,
Stormont Economy Minister Baroness Jean Denton was quite
willing to come along to City Hall to discuss rising electricity
prices with a cross-party delegation of councillors which
included myself. Business leaders, meanwhile, were scathing in
their comments about the Council's public image and top civil
servants left unionists in no doubt that the cost of increased
grant-aid was an end to the cold war with Sinn Féin. The
political guerrilla campaign against the unionists started to take
its toll. In January 1995, Sinn Féin councillors Joe Austin and
Una Gillespie were included in a City Council delegation
visiting Dublin. Despite complaints by Reg Empey that Sinn
Féin's involvement in the trip designed to lure visitors to
Belfast was 'hypocrisy', the party's inclusion in the visit to the
Mansion House made a nonsense of claims the previous year by
unionists that Sinn Féin would never again represent the
Council. In May, Fra McCann joined Reg Empey as an official
Council representative on the West Belfast job creation agency,
CityWest, thus becoming the first Sinn Féin representative on
an outside board. At the same time, Councillor Paddy
McManus took advantage of in-fighting between the unionist
parties to take a seat on the Eastern Health and Social Services
Council. In September 1995, I became the first Sinn Féin
representative to represent the Council at a planning inquiry –
in Clonard Hall in West Belfast – when I joined a Council
delegation protesting the re-zoning of an industrial site at
Springvale for educational use. Every little victory was creating
a discernible momentum towards a different tomorrow.

13.

Crumbs from the Table

Motivated in part by the sight of their majority going south, the UUP reactivated their discussions with the SDLP in the run-up to the June 1995 election of the Lord Mayor. While unionists tried to trade the top Council positions for an SDLP commitment to ostracise Sinn Féin, the nationalist party held firm, declaring that in the wake of the IRA ceasefire it had 'a better relationship than ever with Sinn Féin'. But not all the SDLP members could resist the UUP baubles. South Belfast councillor Alasdair McDonnell broke ranks with his party at the June meeting to become the first Catholic Deputy Lord Mayor of Belfast. Faced with the grim prospect of seeing a deal being forged between unionists and his party which would see SDLP choice Alban Maginness – rather then himself – occupy the Deputy Lord Mayor's chair, McDonnell went on a solo run. Proposed by Ulster Unionist John Carson and backed by dissidents within his own party as well as by the UUP, he was voted in to serve alongside incoming Lord Mayor, DUP firebrand Eric Smyth (who immediately branded his deputy the 'best of a bad lot'). There were bitter recriminations within the SDLP as the party saw the possibility of negotiating a deal with unionists to rotate the position of Lord Mayor and Deputy Lord Mayor ad infinitum sacrificed on the altar of McDonnell's personal political ambitions. 'It was self-seeking, wrong-headed and not in the best interests of either the council, the party or the city', said Alex Attwood. 'One swallow does not make a summer and Alasdair McDonnell as deputy mayor does not make for full partnership.'

South Belfast GP McDonnell announced his touching faith in the unionists 'to move forward positively' during a victory address which featured a blistering attack on Sinn Féin and confirmation for unionists that he would back policies to exclude the party. For his pains, McDonnell and fellow SDLP 'rebel' Mary Muldoon had the SDLP whip removed from them for six months. 'Dr McDonnell has been handpicked by the unionists as the most acceptable Catholic they could find', said Alex Maskey who blasted unionists and the SDLP for defeating Sinn Féin moves at the same meeting to have the principles of proportionality extended into every facet of City Hall life, including the chairs of committees and the position of Mayor and Deputy Mayor. The Sinn Féin man feared unionists would use the election of Alasdair McDonnell to paint the Council as progressive:

> Nothing could be further from the truth. Indeed, a second deal is being hammered out between the unionists and the SDLP to deny top committee positions to the 25 per cent of the electorate who vote for Sinn Féin. We strongly advised the SDLP, including Dr McDonnell, at a series of meetings before the election for the mayoralty, not to allow the unionists to split nationalists on the council. Though the SDLP ostensibly agreed with this position, some of their group put power at any price before the wider community interest. Dr McDonnell has justified his deal with the unionists by claiming that half a loaf is better than none. The irony of that attitude is that if nationalists were firm in the council they would have a share in the whole bakery.

Shunned by his own party group and ignored by Lord Mayor Eric Smyth, McDonnell struggled to fulfil his civic duties. He confided that Eric Smyth never consulted him about even the most trivial Council engagement, leaving the SDLP man to operate in a limbo, waiting for the 'leftovers', appointments which the Lord Mayor couldn't be bothered fulfilling. But council protocol was fairly low on Eric Smyth's priority list. The man who had called for the TV programme 'The Good Sex Guide' to be banned and wanted to see vigilante groups formed to tackle the rising drug problem on the Shankill was more interested in doing the Lord's work by attacking Sinn Féin.

The finest hour for Eric came when Bill Clinton rolled into town in November 1995 to bolster the republican and loyalist ceasefires – and switch on the lights at City Hall. Growing US interest in the peace process had led to a succession of economic and political emissaries being fêted at City Hall banquets. Briefed to exhibit balance in all their political dealings, the US contingent resisted Sinn Féin pressure to criticise the City Hall regime, but some unionist councillors who made a pitch for American investment realised that they would have to clean up their act. Appealing for investment while council meetings degenerated into name-calling and point-scoring wasn't on. Reg Empey, self-employed businessman and chair of the Economic Development Sub-Committee at City Hall, was one of the first to accept the need to present a united front to potential investors. Under his game plan, unionists could best win back additional powers for councils by behaving in an inclusive and mature manner. In his role as Council economic tsar, he ensured that every councillor had a say on the Economic Development Sub-Committee. For its part, Sinn Féin enjoyed its inclusion in Council events to lure investors and party councillors left everyone they met, in particular US politicians, with the message that investment must be targeted at areas of need, unionist and nationalist, and not used to shore up discrimination.

Sadly the realisation that inclusion was the way forward didn't dawn on Empey before President Clinton's economic regeneration conference in Washington in May 1995 when the large Belfast City Council delegation left Gerry Adams off their invitation list. Not one to harbour ill-feelings, Gerry Adams and fellow Sinn Féin delegates gate-crashed the reception anyway and hogged, to the disgust of unionists, the cocktail sausages and TV coverage of the Council event. The visit of Bill Clinton and

First Lady Hillary was the undoubted high-point of US interest in the peace process. Councillors were lined up on the 'marble', the rotunda entrance to City Hall, to shake hands with the pair – minus several members of the DUP who had boycotted the event. It was a momentous moment by any standards as tens of thousands gathered outside City Hall to give the President a rapturous welcome. Though best remembered for a rambling and largely unintelligible speech by Eric Smyth (which eventually petered out in the face of 'We want Bill' roars from the crowd), the occasion also marked a political watershed for Belfast City Council as, for the first time, the DUP were clearly placed outside the political consensus. Having spent years trying to have Sinn Féin ostracised from Council affairs, the DUP had crossed their own Rubicon into isolation. Their vicious opposition to the peace process had brought them to a stage, albeit temporarily, where every other party on the Council could unite on one side of the fence while the DUP stood on the other. As if that wasn't enough reason for cheer, the night was also memorable for an ebullient rendition by Van Morrison of 'No Religion Here Today'. Singing along with the chorus while childishly jamming my elbow into a surly Nelson McCausland, who found himself seated next to me in the VIP enclosure, was the stuff of which City Hall memories are made.

The collapse of the IRA ceasefire at Canary Wharf in February 1996 provided a brief respite for City Hall unionists as they played 'told you so' with anyone who would listen. However, like the restoration of the ceasefire itself, it appeared to be only a matter of time before the unionist rout was complete. In June 1996, when the unionists again shut out Sinn Féin from representing the Council on outside boards, Tom Hartley wrote to all the organisations involved asking if they condoned the unionist campaign. In the process he rolled out some illuminating statistics about the unionist attendance rate on the outside boards. To the embarrassment of those concerned, it emerged that unionists who coveted positions on the Belfast Education and Library Board actually missed two out of every three meetings. In 1993, when one of their number, Liz

Seawright, was thrown off the Board for non-attendance, unionists responded by reappointing her. During the same term unionist councillor Jim Kirkpatrick was also ejected from the Board for missing meetings for a period exceeding six months. Again, unionists simply reappointed him to the body. It was a case of history repeating itself first as farce then as tragedy when in December 1993, unionists appointed John Carson to fill the vacancy on the BELB created by the death of Tommy Patton. Within nine months, the BELB was forced to write to the council saying that Carson had lost his place because he too didn't attend any meetings for a period of over six months.

It's a sobering fact of City Hall history that not once did unionists, of their own volition, initiate any changes which would enhance equality and fair play within the council. Even the most inconsequential improvement in the lot of nationalists enjoyed their implacable opposition until it came into effect, at which time, with no more than a shrug of the shoulders, unionists got on with it. Similarly, while unionists of all persuasions protested their refusal to do business with Sinn Féin, real business was being carried out at committee meetings which were conducted without rancour or division. Sammy Wilson, while chair of the Town Planning Committee ensured that I, like every other Sinn Féin member, was allowed a full opportunity to contribute to debate, going as far as calling Paddy McManus by his first name when calling him to speak (a privilege I never enjoyed). In truth, he was an excellent chairman and if it really was nauseating for Paisley's party to carry out council business with Sinn Féin, it never showed. With the UUP, the SDLP and Sinn Féin singing from the same hymn book on many of the issues which were coming before council, it was inconceivable that the clock could ever be turned back to the dark days of one-minute committee meetings and kitchen cabinets. Not that the DUP was over enthusiastic about the bright new world opening up. While behind committee doors – and away from the probing eyes of the press – DUP councillors argued the toss with Sinn Féin over those issues which were the bread and butter of Council politics, in public they pledged undying opposition to 'Sinn Féin/IRA'. In reality, that meant trying to block resources from going to Catholic areas.

Despite the ravages of architectural modernisation, Falls Baths remains one of the most imposing buildings on the Falls Road. Renamed Falls Swim Centre in the nineties to reflect the introduction of fitness suites and a five-a-side court, the Baths hold a special place in the hearts of everyone with roots in the Falls – and that's effectively everyone in West Belfast. Its seven old pennies a go hot baths were a Friday night favourite of the mill workers and labourers who made their home in the streets around the Baths at a time when indoor toilets and bathrooms were an unimaginable luxury. No childhood memory of the Falls is complete without recalling the Indian file marches of schoolchildren with towels wrapped around their heads, Arab-style, making their way from their classroom to the Baths for the weekly swim. The Baths had also played a role in one of Belfast's blackest chapters; after the Luftwaffe blitzed the city in 1941, the Baths were drained and used as a temporary morgue. Given the importance of the Baths to the Falls, strenuous efforts were made to have the Department of the Environment list the landmark building. However, DoE officials, who rarely saw anything of merit in West Belfast, rebuffed such suggestions. In fact, the DoE listed just one building in West Belfast – Trench House – and then stood by as it was demolished in 1997!

As it entered its centenary year in 1996, the Baths was showing its age. Council funding was needed urgently to spruce up its dilapidated exterior and to provide the sophisticated fitness suite equipment increasingly demanded by customers. And while the elaborate frontage (still boasted by the equally magnificent Ormeau Baths which is now an arts gallery) had been torn out by the planners in the 1950s, there were still hopes that a revamped building could be the jewel in the crown of a reinvigorated Falls.

City Hall unionists had other ideas. They wanted to celebrate the centenary by closing down the Baths. The charge against the facility was led by Jim Rodgers and Sammy Wilson who showed an extraordinary interest in the affairs of West Belfast

from their East Belfast constituencies. They were unimpressed
by the Council's own figures, which showed that the Falls Baths
served the most deprived district in the city – unemployment
levels in the area topped 80 per cent – and insisted its £37,000
running costs deficit could no longer be found in the Council's
mammoth multi-million pound budget. To underline their
determination to allow the Baths to be run down, unionists
refused to release £70,000 which had been set aside in Council
coffers for the upgrading of the facility. There were no restraints
on expenditure in their own backyard. Not only did unionist
North Belfast boast three leisure centres – Grove, Ballysillan
and Loughside – while nationalist North Belfast had none, but
unionists had carried out continuous improvements at their
favoured centres. The figures in the 1993-1997 term spoke for
themselves:

Nationalist areas:
   Andersonstown Minor Hall converted to fitness suite, £110,000;
   Andersonstown upgrading, £30,000.

Unionist areas:
   Ormeau Recreation Centre Climbing Wall, £50,000;
   Shankill Leisure Centre pool play equipment, £119,000;
   Ballysillan Leisure Centre reception area, £57,000;
   Avoniel Leisure Centre re-roofing, £38,000;
   Olympia Leisure Centre fitness suite, £178,000;
   Shankill fitness suite, £70,000;
   Shankill improved entrance, £60,000;
   New pitch at Avoniel, £400,000;
   New pitch at Ballysillan, £400,000;
   Indoor Tennis Centre at Ormeau Park, £500,000.

Under the guise of an overall review of leisure provision in the
city, unionists moved against three nationalist leisure centres –
Falls, Shaftesbury and Beechmount. There was no attempt by
unionists to take the extent of deprivation or the government
policies of Targeting Social Need into consideration as part of
their review of the £7m annual leisure services' budget, though
legally they were obliged to do so. However, initial proposals to
sell-off unionist Loughside Recreation Centre as part of the
cutbacks were scrubbed by unionists at the June 1996 meeting

of the Client Services Committee. At the full Council meeting on 1 July, unionists voted in favour of a proposal by Sammy Wilson to reduce opening hours at Falls to just one shift a day. The doors would now close at the centre at 4pm each day, sabotaging a popular evening youth club. Neither staff nor users at the centres were consulted. Yet, while Wilson *et al* demonstrated their belated interest in leisure facilities in West Belfast by closing them down, they were reminding their own constituents that their diligence had saved centres in unionist areas from closure. In a lead story in the *East Belfast Herald&Post*, Wilson took the credit for putting 'impassioned arguments' which had saved Ballymacarrett from the axe.

At the September meeting of the Leisure Services Sub-Committee, Deputy-Chair Bobby Lavery made history by becoming the first Sinn Féin councillor to chair a meeting of a Council standing sub-committee. But there was little cause for celebration as Sammy Wilson again forced through a motion to close Shaftesbury Recreation Centre in the nationalist Lower Ormeau – where residents had consistently opposed Orange parades – from 1 January 1997. A second proposal to sell off Beechmount Leisure Centre was defeated on the casting vote of Bobby Lavery. However at the parent Client Services Committee three weeks later, Wilson, backed by Nelson McCausland, won support from fellow-unionists for his proposal to close Beechmount from 4pm each day and to seek expressions of interest from potential buyers. Oblivious to protests by trade unions and users at the centres, unionists forged ahead with their plans. However, worried officials, with very clear memories of recent court cases, pointed out that the same criteria used by unionist councillors to support the closure of Shaftesbury, Falls and Beechmount would now have to be used when they reviewed the future operation of leisure centres in their own constituencies. If it was necessary to close Beechmount because of its annual operational deficit of £400,000, how much more necessary might it be to close Shankill or Grove leisure centres which were losing, respectively, £700,000 and £575,000 per year.

A picket of City Hall and a well-attended meeting in the Falls Swim Centre, organised by our Save Our Leisure Services Campaign – which had finally found a purpose wider than simply manoeuvering Sinn Féin around the broadcasting ban – served to galvanise opposition to the unionist closure campaign. The meeting in the Falls Swim Centre brought out members and supporters of 30 sports clubs which used the centre, including the Cathal Brugha and Setanta water polo teams which have been based at the Baths for over half a century. News that the Council was to spend a sum similar to that needed to save the Falls Baths on a six-councillor trip to Novia Scotia, Toronto and Pittsburgh fuelled the anger of the 6,000 people who came through the doors of the centre each month.

When the decisions to partially close the Beechmount and Falls centres were ratified by full Council on 1 October 1996, local mother-of-three Nuala McKee, a leader with the St Peter's Youth Club which used the centre, signed her name to an affidavit challenging the legality of the move. Mrs McKee argued that the decisions to partially close Falls Baths and Beechmount were unlawful because they were discriminatory and ignored the British government's Targeting Social Need guidelines. She sought an order restraining the Council from implementing their decisions – due to come into effect on 6 October. The court hearing on 3 October was a penalty kick. Mr Justice Kerr instructed the Council to put their shut-down plans on hold until a full judicial review of their decision was heard on 15 October – the day after a special meeting of Council which had been requested by the SDLP and Sinn Féin to discuss the issue.

The opportunity to wax eloquently on the sins of unionism was denied nationalists at the special meeting on the eve of the hearing when unionists started the meeting by announcing that their closure plans were being scrapped. Under enormous pressure from the Council's own legal advisors who were wary of another court battle, unionists accepted the recommendation of officers to initiate a new review of leisure provision. On this occasion, the review would be carried out by professional consultants, would take into consideration the views of staff and users and would look at the potential impact on deprivation any decisions might have. In the meantime, the Centre did have its birthday party. In December, users, old and new, packed into the five-a-side hall for a celebration luncheon and a photo exhibition on the Baths of yesteryear. It was an anniversary which the Council had been set to ignore – until our lobbying began, there were no plans to mark the centenary.

Price Waterhouse began their review of leisure provision in January 1997, meeting with user groups and councillors from all parties. When their weighty report was finally tabled in late March, unionists were hoist by their own petard. They were told by officials that this time round any decisions on cutbacks would have to be carried out across the board – in Catholic and Protestant areas. Faced with that ultimatum, unionists, who had previously been gung-ho about cost savings, now agreed to postpone any further deliberations on the cutbacks until the new Council convened in June. Thus did the last major attack by unionists on council provision for nationalist areas come to an end, not with a bang but with a whimper.

While the DUP, and to a lesser extent, the UUP, liked to portray themselves as staunch defenders of Ulster, manning the Council barricades against the Sinn Féin hordes, the reality was that Sinn Féin had become part of the City Hall furniture. (One DUP councillor took the talk of barricades a little too literally. In a scene right out of 'Zulu', East Belfast representative Robert Cleland was caught by the TV cameras lunging at RUC lines with a six-foot flagpole during a July 1995 loyalist protest to stop nationalists marching through the predominantly Catholic town of Lurgan. His heroics cost him a £100 slap on the wrist from the courts.) But even as the '93-'97 term passed its midway point and the resistance to change seemed futile, Canute-worshipping unionists continued to baulk at the prospect of forging a deal with the SDLP, whatever about Sinn Féin. Even when a major English entertainments company pulled out of a deal to buy over a £800,000 council-built watersports centre, citing the violence at Drumcree in July 1996, unionists forged further into their political *cul-de-sac*. But their once vice-like grip on City Hall was inexorably weakening.

Paddling their own canoe, new independents Jim Walker (ex-DUP) and Sandy Blair – who were both thrown off the board of the BELB for non-attendance – played havoc with unionist policy. The pair joined with Sinn Féin and the SDLP in September 1996 to block plans by the brethren to close the Shaftesbury Recreation Centre in nationalist South Belfast and shorten the hours of opening at West Belfast's Beechmount Leisure Centre. Not content with lobbying to have leisure centres in nationalist areas closed down, unionists also proposed selling off the Dunville Park – the only green area in the Lower Falls. And that was against the background of a report into expenditure on Council parks which showed that while £4.1m was spent per annum in parks in unionist areas, just £480,000 went on similar facilities in nationalist areas.

Jim Rodgers also turned his beady eye to the nationalist West Belfast Economic Forum and tried to block £60,000 funding to the body on the basis that it was 'a one-sided nationalist group'. Funding wouldn't be released, he vowed in the *Belfast Telegraph*, until 'there was proper representation on the forum by Shankill Protestants'. 'It is deeply worrying that unionist politicians are obstructing our funding at this time', said Ruth Taillon of the West Belfast Economic Forum.

> It certainly must raise questions about whether these councillors are prepared to treat all sections of the community fairly. The local councils have only recently had responsibility for allocation of economic development funding restored to them. They now have control over a portion of the rates as well as a major involvement in the allocation of European and central government funds for economic regeneration. If the Council is going to discriminate against certain groups because they are based in nationalist areas or play party politics with the funding of community groups, then it should not be entrusted with public funds.

It was only after a high-profile campaign by the Forum at home and among groups in the US which the Council was canvassing for investment that the threat was lifted and the grant paid. Increasingly, and despite their slender majority, it was becoming impossible for City Hall unionists to force through blatantly bigoted decisions without falling foul of unsympathetic government ministers and senior civil servants trying to create a culture of partnership in Belfast, and the US opinion-makers they were trying to court.

Fred Cobain defended the continuing ban on Sinn Féin members holding committee chair positions with the claim that some democratic mandates were more equal than others. 'There are some democratic mandates which ought not to be fully recognised', he said. There's no evidence that Cobain knew enough about George Orwell to realise the literary resonances of his all-are-equal-but-some-are-more-equal-than-others statement. As a result of that claim, he found himself in hot water with the Council's economic ambassadors who were assuring US business leaders that discrimination was a thing of the past. Fred dismissed howls of protest from the Council's new American friends. 'This is Belfast not Washington', he snapped. Winning friends and influencing people in the US was a double-edge sword for the Council which rolled out the red carpet for a dizzying variety of US delegations only to see them peopled with leading Irish-Americans such as Californian Senator and veteran civil rights campaigner Tom Hayden (who adamantly refused to stand for the Loyal Toast at Council banquets). Likewise, when Mayor Thomas Menino of Boston was invited to Belfast in May 1995 to address the Council, he took time out to tour the Falls Road, meet with pupils from the government-blacked Irish language secondary school, Meánscoil Feirste, and accept the gift of a bodhrán from Sinn Féin councillors. On another occasion, New York State Comptroller Carl McCall, who occupied the highest position ever to be held by an African American in the state government, delivered the most eloquent address on equality of opportunity ever heard in City Hall before making way for the New York City Comptroller Alan Hevesi –

who made no secret of his support for the MacBride Principles and his admiration of Gerry Adams. Unionists, skulking at the back of the Great Hall during the civic dinner sneaked out the back doors during Carl McCall's moving speech. Sadly there were no reporters present to record the speech and when I wrote to Carl McCall's office later to request a copy, I was told there wasn't one as the speech had been delivered off the cuff. And from the heart. I was ecstatic as I wandered the corridors of City Hall aimlessly after the dinner, convinced that the rousing address was the clearest signal yet that the days were numbered for unionism's ancien régime. True to his Paisleyite roots, Peter Robinson was sure the end was nigh: 'The Tricolour could fly over City Hall', he predicted as analysts studied the projected voting figures for the May 1997 poll.

And there were other straws in the wind: though Sinn Féin never got the pogroms stained glass window it wanted, a party suggestion that a commemorative window to the dead of the Great Famine be installed did pass through Council, despite unionist objections. In a stirring contribution to the Council debate which would have done Goebbels proud, Sammy Wilson contended that the Famine hadn't impacted on Belfast and that if the window went in, it would be used as a stopping point on Sinn Féin guided tours of City Hall for their visitors. He was right about the last part as the striking window, finally unveiled in 1999, is not only a striking piece of art but also the only tangible evidence in City Hall of a nationalist ethos. Meanwhile, on the economic sub-committee, though Reg Empey and Alasdair McDonnell monopolised the positions of chair and deputy chair, there was a willingness to support Sinn Féin initiatives to bring jobs to the developing areas of Belfast and countless opportunities for us to set the jobs agenda for the city.

But that hop, skip and a jump towards equality had been bought at a terrible price. I walked in the valley of death and I was shit-scared. Before every meeting, I would don my Sinn Féin-supplied flak jacket, though I could never work out which was the front, with reinforced Velcro to protect the heart, and which was the back. As a consequence, I was never sure if it was better for me to be shot in the back or the chest. Getting to City Hall required a different route every time, including disregarding the traffic signs to nip across Donegal Square South into City Hall from Linenhall Street. When possible, I would use a car other than my own or hitch a lift to City Hall, in the knowledge that a fixed routine is the assassin's friend. Unionists were always uncomfortable with the role of Sinn Féin councillors as potential victims though they relished their own role of cheer leaders to the loyalists gunning for Sinn Féin members and their families. Some had the decency to turn away shamefaced when I would go into the Members' Room and take off first my overcoat and then the heavy flak jacket, draping them over the coat stand as if it was the most normal way in the world to go to work. Thankfully, none of the unionists needed to wear bulletproof vests but, though under little or no threat, the majority carried personal issue weapons. In my ten years at City Hall, barely a month went by without a gun or bomb attack on Sinn Féin members and their families, on party offices and councillors' homes. Yet security measures available to unionists, bulletproof windows, anti-booby trap devices for cars, and lights activated by sensors, were all denied Sinn Féin councillors on the basis, according to the Secretary of State, that the party supported terrorism.

Sinn Féin councillors fell back on their own devices. Some councillors built porches to give them an extra door of defence, while most placed reinforced plastic behind the front door which was, councillors were promised, strong enough to stop low-calibre bullets. There was a rumour that the glass on one of two bullet-proof vehicles used by Sinn Féin had been tested by firing two Armalite bullets at its driver-side window. They didn't pierce the exterior of the lumbering Cadillac which used more petrol per mile than a Council bin lorry. Everyone in Sinn Féin put a steel gate on the stairway to prevent intruders (whose usual method was to sledgehammer doors in the night) from making it to the bedrooms.

I invested in bulletproof glass for some of the windows in my Falls home – though it was somewhat disappointing to see the logo on the £1,000-plus pane of glass announce that it was merely 'bullet-resistant' – and had friends install the new window frames needed to hold the heavy material. The reinforced glass made a steel pull-down shutter I had installed on the inside of the window redundant. How anyone would escape during a fire with the gate on the stairs blocked and the window covered by an iron shutter didn't bear thinking about. When I was removing the cumbersome steel shutter, it suddenly uncoiled and gave me an almighty whack on the chest which knocked me on my backside. If it had have connected with my face or skull, it could have caused serious injury, the irony of which wasn't lost on me. The front and back doors had drop bars placed across them at night to thwart loyalists using sledgehammers – though I always felt the heavy iron bars posed more of a danger to children than to potential assassins. As a compromise, I placed just one on the back door and kept the other beneath my bed as a last-ditch means of defence. Lights outside the house were linked to a mini-camera in the door so that visitors could be identified, but I knew enough about the loyalist gun-gangs to realise that any attack was more likely to take place as I went to or returned from a Council meeting: Councillor John Davey from South Derry had been shot dead in February 1989 as he returned from his monthly Council meeting in Magherafelt. Operating with easy availability of RUC files, and with a blind eye being turned to their activities, loyalist gun-gangs could effectively strike with impunity. Councillor Eddie Fullerton was shot dead in his County Donegal home in May 1991, party worker Pádraig Ó Seanacháin was gunned down on his way to work in August of that year, and the same month Sinn Féin activist Tommy Donaghy was shot dead as he arrived at his workplace in County Derry. Lecturer and councillor Bernard O'Hagan met his death in September 1991 as he arrived for work at the Magherafelt College of Further Education, while Upper Bann election candidate and student Sheena Campbell was gunned down by the UVF in October 1992. They were just some of the Sinn Féin members and supporters, others include

Danny Cassidy, Malachy Carey and Peter Gallagher, who lost their lives in the government-backed loyalist onslaught.

Sinn Féin members' only defence against under-car bombs was to check under the car before getting in and then jump on the back bumper in the hope that any detonator would be triggered. Invariably, I would start and turn the car before allowing the children to get in for the school run. But while my Beechmount bunker offered me relative safety, others were defenceless in the face of an onslaught being carried out by loyalists in consort with the RUC. Though a loyalist gang was spotted in May 1993 walking outside my home and taking photographs from a van, I always believed that the reason I was never attacked was that that RUC never shunted me onto the loyalist target list.

Others paid a horrific price so that republican ratepayers could have their views represented in City Hall. Sean Lavery, the 21-year-old student son of Councillor Bobby Lavery, was shot dead in August 1993 when loyalists sprayed the family's Antrim Road home with automatic fire. Bobby Lavery had been upstairs at the time of the shooting. Fatally wounded, his son raced up the stairs towards his father only to collapse dying in his arms. Bobby's brother Martin had been murdered by loyalists the previous December as he wrapped presents in his Crumlin Road home. The latest attack came on the evening of the first ever nationalist parade into Belfast city centre – another landmark in the march to equality – and was seen by loyalists as 'revenge' for that achievement. Fr Des Wilson branded the murder 'the British answer' to the successful climax of the Belfast City Centre Or Bust campaign by nationalist marchers:

> During the Great March of Sunday 8 August 1993 there were many voices which prophesied: 'There will be reprisals for this…The British government has to allow this march but they will have their revenge.' It was not long in coming. The cowardly killing of a young man as he watched TV in the home of his family was the British answer. The blood of that young man is on the hands of the government and also of all

those who for the past eight years have criminalised the political party to which his father belongs.

The previous month, Twinbrook councillor Annie Armstrong had just returned home from a Council meeting when a gunman fired eight shots through her front door and into the living room where her eight-year-old daughter was watching TV. Shortly before these attacks, Secretary of State Patrick Mayhew had refused a request from Bobby Lavery to be included in the Key Persons' Protection Scheme which would have enabled him to install bulletproof windows at his home.

SDLP councillors, whose homes were attacked around the same time, were granted additional security measures immediately. The official line was that Sinn Féin's 'support for terrorism' precluded it from support under the Key Persons Protection Scheme. In practice it meant that republican representatives were sitting ducks for loyalist gun gangs equipped not only with weapons smuggled into the country by British Army agent and UDA Intelligence Officer Brian Nelson but with RUC files detailing the car number plates, addresses and even photographs of Sinn Féin councillors. Solidly working class and famed for his hands-on constituency work – if a constituent complained of leaking roof, he would be just as likely to climb up on the roof himself to repair the slates as to contact the Housing Executive – Bobby Lavery bore his loss with frightening stoicism. By the time his home was next attacked in December 1993, Bobby had installed heavy metal plates at the inside of his windows which swung into place each evening. None of the bullets penetrated the home-made defences. When the NIO still refused to permit the installation of security measures at the New Lodge's councillor's home after the second attack, his lawyers took Sir Patrick Mayhew to court. During the judicial review in December 1993 of Mayhew's block on security measures at the Lavery home, it emerged that just a month before the murder of Sean Lavery, £65,000 had been spent by the NIO on installing security measures at the home of SDLP councillor Jonathan Stephenson – who lived less than a mile from Bobby's house. He had been among four SDLP representatives in Belfast whose homes were bombed by loyalists in July of that year.

But it would be wrong to say the RUC were totally inactive in the face of a murder campaign carried out by UFF and UVF paramilitaries, whose leaders were invariably working for Special Branch handlers. After loyalists launched a rocket attack on Sinn Féin's Andersonstown headquarters in February 1994, Joe Austin was arrested for insisting he be allowed through an RUC cordon to speak with distressed Sinn Féin office workers. A fortnight later, two workmen carrying out repair work to the premises were shot and injured in a copycat attack. Even the SDLP mused publicly at the astonishing ease of movement which loyalists now apparently enjoyed in the heart of Andersonstown. Alex Maskey had also been arrested after loyalists shot up his home in January 1994 and charged by the RUC with assault. Though convicted on the charges, a higher court reversed the decision due to inconsistencies in RUC evidence, leading to the award of damages to the Sinn Féin councillor. However, the RUC could argue that in arresting Alex Maskey, they were simply following their traditional route of response to attacks on his home. After the 1987 attack in which he was shot in the stomach and seriously injured, his wife Liz was arrested by the RUC as she made her way to the hospital.

In April 1994, a second Sinn Féin centre in West Belfast was wrecked in a loyalist rocket attack. In the same Sevastopol Street offices in February 1992, an RUC man had shot dead doorman Paddy Loughran, advice worker Pat McBride and local man Michael O'Dwyer. Also in April 1994, Teresa Clinton, the wife of Sinn Féin candidate Jim Clinton was shot dead by loyalists in an attack on her Lower Ormeau home. Gunmen smashed in a reinforced window with a breeze block before shooting her 16 times as she watched TV. North Belfast councillor Gerard McGuigan, who the NIO also refused to include on their Key Persons' Protection Scheme, had a close shave with death on two separate occasions. He was in bed when a grenade was thrown into the living room, causing extensive damage, but miraculously escaped unharmed. On a previous occasion, he had been sitting supping tea in the kitchen when loyalists sprayed the living room with automatic fire. The following month, a Sinn Féin hunger strike parade was blocked by the RUC as it tried to make its way to City Hall in a half-hearted attempt to reintroduce the ban on city centre rallies which had been shattered the previous year. Republicans insisted they would take to the streets the next Sunday and every Sunday until the march was allowed to City Hall. Seven days later, the RUC relented and allowed the march to proceed unhindered to the city centre. However, as the parade made its way down the Falls Road, loyalists using automatic rifles opened fire on demonstrators, including my good self. Ronnie Flanagan, then the senior RUC man in Belfast, assured the press that the loyalists had been simply firing into the air. I later took journalists back to the spot of the attack where they managed to photograph the walls on the Catholic side of the peaceline where the bullets had lodged after, thankfully, clearing the marchers' heads by a foot.

As the bell went for the final lap of the four year term, Sinn Féin appeared to be in an unassailable position. On the backfoot, unionists had spent the previous three and a half years infighting and fire-fighting. Defensive, shambling, and often hysterical, they had spent the previous 40 months chasing shadows. Their own worst nightmare, a non-unionist majority in City Hall, now seemed on the cards though some traditionally astute observers still predicted that the sea-change wouldn't come until the 2001 elections. It was as we stood on that very cusp of a new era that Pat McGeown died.

When Pat failed to turn up for the monthly meeting of Council of 1 October, Tom Hartley and Fra McCann went to his New Lodge flat to check if he was ill. They found him dead on the settee surrounded by the Sunday papers. The heart disease which had plagued him since the hunger strike had finally taken its toll. Pat made little of the grim prognosis he had been given by specialists who were treating him for a heart condition unknown outside of parts of the developing world where malnutrition is rife. On one occasion, an eminent cardiologist had told him to stay off the cigs and his favourite tipple, red wine, and avoid stress if he wanted to stay alive. For his next check-up, Pat arrived sporting his flak jacket. The shocked consultant made some enquiries about the line of work he was in which necessitated the wearing of body armour before giving him absolution to drink and smoke as long as he switched careers. His had been a gruelling life. At the age of 25, he had endured 47 days on hunger strike during the 1981 protest, his family permitting medical intervention only after he slipped into unconsciousness. He told friends later that his last memory before falling into a coma was of the trolley carrying the body of INLA prisoner Mickey Devine being pushed past his cell. Pat had urged the Derry man to try and hold on until after the Fermanagh by-election called on the death of Bobby Sands which was being contested by prisoners' candidate Owen Carron. He told *Biting At The Grave* author Padraig O'Malley: 'I said to him, "Hold out for the ten days. After the by-election I don't see any point in us continuing the hunger strike and I'll be saying that quite openly".' Tragically Mickey Devine died on the day of the by-election – which Owen Carron won. Pat McGeown later recalled waking up to discover a female nurse bending over him with an injection needle. The tip of the needle had bent because the nurse, unable to find a vein capable of accepting the injection of vitamins, had hit bone.

On his release from jail, he had been re-arrested and charged in connection with the killing of the two British corporals during the funeral of Caoimhín Mac Brádaigh in March 1988. Those charges were subsequently dropped. A hugely evocative press photo from the time shows him leaving the Crown Court in the company of his solicitor Pat Finucane. The eleventh hunger striker had outlived his comrades by fifteen years, but his loss was felt just as keenly by the nationalist and republican community of Belfast. His death was doubly cruel, coming as the city he loved stood on the verge of the political change he had spent his life working for.

14.

A Perverse Practice

Growing up, I always thought vetting was a career pursued by hardy folk with Barbour jackets normally found with an arm buried up to the shoulder in a cow's birth canal. As it turned out, vetting in Ulstah was a political carnival of reaction in which everyone from the lowliest carmudgeony civil servant to the highest media mogul had a role to play.

At its peak, political vetting and community censorship were blunt instruments of political warfare, designed by the British and Irish governments to gag the enemy and effectively give a media megaphone to the ally. It was a farcical business, albeit with a deadly bottom line.

British government policy – modelled on the groundbreaking Section 31 censorship pioneered by that United Irelander (admittedly, belatedly) Conor Cruise O'Brien in the Republic – was to forbid Sinn Féin any form of recognition which could provide it with credibility. After the 1988 Ballygawley bus bombing, in which eight British soldiers lost their lives, Margaret Thatcher introduced broadcasting restrictions to ban Sinn Féin representatives from the airwaves.

Built around the blunt broadcasting prohibition was a battery of policy positions and administrative arrangements throughout every level of government which sought to deny Sinn Féin the legitimacy of its electoral mandate.

Government ministers were first out of the blocks, refusing to meet with West Belfast MP Gerry Adams and elected republican councillors. Senior civil servants also built a cordon sanitaire between themselves and the nasty Sinn Féiners. Such worthies as the Chief Executive of the Housing Executive, Victor Blease, were unavailable to meet Gerry Adams during his Westminster tenure, as were Permanent Secretaries of the main government departments. In an astonishing feat of eugenic engineering, the civil service created a complex pecking order which not only governed which level of official could contact Sinn Féin but also the degree of contact. Some of the Stormont Castle suits were empowered to actually break bread with Sinn Féin representatives, while others were permitted to restrict the contact to formal correspondence. Ministers would never respond to letters from Sinn Féin but would have a junior private secretary respond, preferably signing off with an unintelligible scrawl.

Immediately after my election to the Council in October 1987, I contacted the local Belfast Action Team head, David Bass, a Quaker with an admirable record of community endeavour. As a 'BATman', David was tasked with heading up a series of Department of the Environment policies in disadvantaged areas such as West Belfast. In the DoE pecking order, he wasn't exactly the Sultan of Brunei, but David told me he would have to check if government protocol actually allowed him to sit down face-to-face with a Sinn Féin councillor. Channels of communication having been cleared, I subsequently sat down with David to discuss the weighty matter of the corncrake population on the Bog Meadow.

My own introduction to political purdah came in 1988 when the West Belfast Irish language group Glór na nGael – which I had jointly founded with a parcel of republican rogues in the Felons' Club in Andersonstown in 1983 – received its 'Dear John' letter from Douglas Hurd. The bitter irony for the committee was that I had just flown the coop and resigned from the committee weeks before the axe fell. Someone, it seems, had forgotten to file an up-to-the-minute briefing with the civil servants schooled in the works of Dostoevsky who were charged with the task of pulling the funding plug on groups seen to be close to Sinn Féin.

With the Conway Mill, the funding blow came simultaneously with the setting up within eyesight of Twin Spires, a church-backed, pro-government enterprise park. Money denied to Conway Mill was pumped into state-of-the-art buildings at Twin Spires. A blind man riding by at midnight couldn't fail to get the message: while projects sympathetic to Sinn Féin were starved of funds, the pro-government groups were deluged with cash.

In the case of Glór na nGael, the executioner's song was spun only after the government had set up the Ultach Trust, a refuge for zealously anti-republican and pro-British government Irish speakers. Uncle Tomás Irish speakers became increasingly frustrated at the ability of republicans to popularise An Ghaeilge in working class areas of the North. Their frustrations boiled over after Glór na nGael, chaired by my good self, won the national Glór na nGael competition for the area in Ireland which does the most to promote the Irish language. I travelled to Maynooth in 1988 to pick up the prize from President Patrick Hillary, but already the fix was in. One Ultach Trust poltroon had warned the committee of Glór na nGael that as long as I was associated with the committee it couldn't expect to get 'as much as a grant for a coffee table'. Shortly afterwards, the government declared the political vetting equivalent of thermonuclear war on the battling Irish language group which ran a string of nursery schools. Funding was stopped and the group smeared with the allegation that it was no more than a front for illegal activities. A deadly accusation then as now, though the hand-in-glove relationship between the political vetting over vellum folders and cups of coffee in government offices and the gunning to death of republicans – such as Conradh na Gaeilge stalwart Pádraig O Cléirigh in North

Belfast in 1992 – by loyalist gun-gangs never seemed to cause the thought police among Gaeilgeoirí any qualms.

Short of assassination, the broadcasting bans represented the most insidious form of political censorship aimed at the nationalist community. Many journalists who took to the new restrictions like a porter drinker to pigs' feet were as keen to interpret the gag as widely as possible as they were to publicly pretend that they did, in fact, oppose press censorship.

Indeed, so worried were some of the BBC hacks about the broadcasting ban that they voted down – with the assistance of their equally righteous comrades in RTÉ – a proposal at the NUJ annual conference in Glasgow in 1989 to allow Brother Ó Muilleoir to speak. When push came to shove, the BBC broadcasters would point the finger at their censorious colleagues in RTÉ who for 25 years vigorously pursued a policy of demonising republicans. When I read a lesson at an Irish mass in Belfast in 1989 which was broadcast on Raidió na Gaeltachta – listened to, undoubtedly, by the proverbial one Donegal sheep farmer and his trusty mutt – RTÉ issued a profuse apology to its shell-shocked listeners: 'It was not known that Mr Ó Muilleoir was a member of Sinn Féin, and if it had been, then he would not have been used.' And we couldn't even threaten RTÉ that we'd refuse to pay our licences! Not that the same threat made much impression in the BBC. In 1991, the popular current affairs radio programme 'Talkback' commissioned a documentary style skit on the great wheelie bin debate which was engulfing Belfast as the old steel bins were replaced with shiny black plastic receptacles on wheels. Since the broadcasting restrictions didn't forbid a councillor from speaking on matters relevant to constituency matters, I penned for the programme a self-deprecating satirical piece. 'It is no coincidence that the words, 'wheeled bin' when spelt backwards spell Ned Dellhew, the notorious unionist firebrand and former Lord Mayor, who caused a furore in the forties with his plan to move the city zoo to the Falls Park, minus the cages, as part of a unionist plan to eradicate the problem of people walking on the grass', was about as seditiously funny as it got. It was canned. Keith Baker, Head of News and Current Affairs – and a man, one suspects, of limited humour – wrote to me:

> We were of the opinion that however satirical and tongue-in-cheek your contribution may have been, it did in essence reflect a Sinn Féin view and as such was affected by the restrictions.

But it wasn't all plain sailing for the broadcasters who – despite their public protestations – attempted to make censorship run smoother than it ever did in Stalinist Russia or McCarthyite America. Left-wing activist and respected commentator Eamon McCann put his own job with the BBC in jeopardy when he addressed a string of protests against the ban, while Seosamh Ó Cuaig of Raidió na Gaeltachta in Galway put his name to a case in the European courts protesting against Section 31. The belief at the time was that RTÉ in Dublin couldn't come up with a reporter willing to put his or her head on the block. The truth of that report was never established but I can vouch for the resolve of those solid defenders of the right to free speech in the RTÉ chapel of the NUJ. When I stood for the Council by-election in Belfast in 1987, I rang the Chapel Father – none other than Charlie Bird – to ask that he black the poll since he couldn't interview the only member of the NUJ in the race. There was a lot of humming and haaing and clearing of the throat but zero action from my fellow union members.

Many clever manoeuvres were used to circumvent the broadcasting restrictions. As they didn't ban a Sinn Féin representative speaking on behalf of other organisations, I set up a stable of one-man groups to protest council cutbacks, promote the Irish language and demand the demolition of dilapidated housing stock in my constituency. Such moves did have some limited success, but there was no effective way to counter the deadly effect of the broadcasting ban. When Councillor John Joe Davey was shot dead by loyalists at his South Derry home, BBC reporters sent to the scene filmed the reaction of rival SDLP councillors, who, of course, failed to raise the burning issue of collusion, rather than Councillor Davey's party colleagues. For loyalist gun-gangs working hand-in-hand with the RUC and British forces, the broadcasting ban was a leg-up. How much easier it was for loyalist gun-gangs to carry out attacks on Sinn Féin members, their supporters and ordinary nationalists when the policies of censorship had stigmatised and dehumanised their community.

The BBC didn't emerge from all this unscathed. There was justifiable suspicion about the bona fides of journalists called into nationalist areas to report the aftermath of loyalist attacks who often refused to interview the victims of those same attacks or their relatives and colleagues. More than once, I had stand-up rows with reporters about their blanket ban interpretation of the broadcasting restrictions, invariably only to be told later via a back door channel that in fact the journalist I had upbraided was a staunch opponent of the Hurd broadcasting order! Rather amusingly, BBC Head of Programmes Pat Loughrey rejected my charges that he was acting above and beyond the call of duty in relation to the broadcasting restrictions. 'I cannot agree that the BBC denies free speech in any way', he wrote to me in 1992 at the very height of the ban. Most of our rows centred on the flagship radio show, 'Talkback'. Between the introduction of the broadcasting ban in 1998 and April 1992, I was interviewed just once by the daily current affairs programme even though I was involved in a propaganda blitz on the City Fathers throughout that period. The Irish language department of the BBC, renowned for its obsequiousness, failed to interview a Sinn Féin representative from 1990-1992 even though Shinners headed up almost all the main Irish language groups in the North.

Pickets and parades took place on the anniversary of the ban each year, though the RUC prevented marches from going from West Belfast to the BBC headquarters because they would have to travel through the city centre which was then a no-go area for republicans. Other avenues of protest were explored. I bought a portable television set and wrote off to the BBC informing them that I wouldn't be buying a TV licence in protest at the ban. They couldn't have cared less – despite the welcome demand by unionist politicians that I be jailed (if not disembowelled) for this outrageous assault on the rule of law. Seven years later, I still have the Malaysian Akura set – quite a recommendation for its reliability – but as I haven't yet bought a licence, I'm still waiting for my dramatic day in court in defence of free speech. By gagging Sinn Féin representatives, the two governments hoped to make them fade into the background as the increased coverage of their SDLP opponents brought their primary colours into every sitting room. And, in some ways, it worked. Coupled with the ongoing political vetting of community groups and economic projects, the campaign to send Sinn Féin to Coventry made the party less attractive to its voters. À la Nicaragua, where ordinary people weighed down with the crippling effects of the US economic embargo eventually jettisoned the Sandinistas, so did many weary nationalists shift away from Sinn Féin or, at least, fail to become enthused enough to vote for the party. Conversely, those who stayed solid became even more committed to republicanism, grew more inured to criticism and became totally alienated from the authorities. Such a mix made the core republican constituency undefeatable; victory, however, would prove equally elusive.

From the mid-eighties until the early nineties, government funds were doled out in West Belfast in a bid to shore up the opponents of Sinn Féin and inform the local populace that support for republican ideals would translate into an empty plate at dinner time. The Knights of Columbanus, fervently religious gentlemen who dress up in uniforms astonishingly similar to those of the Ku Klux Klan, were ready recruits to the new policy. With the encouragement of Down and Connor Bishop and amateur political counter-insurgent Bishop (later Cardinal) Cahal Daly, the Knights and their clerical chums became the vehicle for government investment. Enterprise parks were built on green-field sites via committees made up largely of 'yes' men and women – usually compliant Catholics unlikely to challenge church or government edicts –

professionals who were also members of the Knights of Columbanus, and SDLP apparatchiks. Normal criteria of value for money were brushed to the side and the need for feasibility studies into the new developments dispensed with so that the retail and commercial centres could be developed. Political expediency is, of course, not the best business principle and ten years after the huge exercise in community control, many of the ventures have been found out. Some are burdened with debt they can't pay back while others, such as the Dairy Farm Centre in Twinbrook in West Belfast, were sold off to the private sector for 25 per cent of their original cost. Rumours are rife that the centre, sold at a knockdown price, will be bulldozed by its new owners to make way for a private housing development.

A Northern Ireland Audit Office report into the Dairy Farm debacle in 1995 revealed that the Auditor General for Northern Ireland was decidedly unimpressed with the political priorities cited by civil servants to justify their wasteful policies. The Auditor General noted that there was no evidence of a feasibility study having been carried out before work on the centre began. No formal business plan was completed and cash flow projections were not submitted until work was almost complete and the costs of the project had soared from the original approved estimates of £3.3m (described as at best 'an educated guess' by the DoE civil servants involved in the development) to £5.4m.

Decidedly unwelcome at the official opening of each of these developments were Sinn Féin politicians or their voters. Hapless SDLP councillors were given a PR gift by being allowed to officiate at the ribbon-cutting ceremonies while government ministers were fêted by their new-found pals in the Catholic Church. The night before the opening of Dairy Farm, arguably the single biggest disaster approved in the funding free-for-all, I overheard a representative of the statutory agencies congratulate a local cleric (who has since moved on to greener and debt-free pastures) on the excellent job he had done in keeping the centre 'free of those sort'. Keeping out 'those sort' extended to ensuring that anyone perceived by the local clergy to be a hush-puppy Provo couldn't even take out a lease on a shop unit. As 80 per cent of the local populace were Sinn Féin supporters, the policy of saving the people from themselves wasn't likely to succeed. The Audit Office report found that, while original proposals containing an ice-rink were regarded as unfeasible, its replacement, a bowling alley, lasted less than a year. 'The final projections, when received, showed that the project would incur a deficit of approximately £325,000 in the first five years', said the report. Despite evidence of gross incompetence within the DoE, even within its brief of shafting Sinn Féin, no heads rolled. (It was hardly surprising then that the profligacy of DoE civil servants with public money continued unchecked. In January 1997, during government attempts to close a youth club in Andersonstown for the want of £20,000, it emerged that the DoE had authorised the spending of one and a half million pounds on golf tournaments for wrinklies at Portrush between 1993 and 1997, under a programme called 'Positively Belfast'. An additional £300,000 went on a boat race up the Lagan.)

It wasn't only at Dairy Farm that the DoE masterplan went awry. It was disasterville as well for the Knights in the Work West enterprise centre on West Belfast's Glen Road. At the opening of the project, prominent Knight Paddy Byrne boasted that the work unit project had been the brainchild of the secretive religious organisation which earned its stripes in government circles by opposing the MacBride fair employment principles in the US. Work West board member Byrne told the opening reception: 'You are now witnessing the manifestation of a seed that was sown at a local council of the Knights of Columbanus some four years ago.' The new centre, he added, was 'a tribute to the work of the Knights'. At the tenth anniversary of Work West in 1999, the Knights still hankered after the halcyon days of political vetting; they refused to invite the local MP to their anniversary bash. But the fact that the anchor tenant in the centre was the *Andersonstown News*, a community newspaper as opposed to the policy of political vetting as the Knights are to women priests, somewhat undermined their original plan. First as a journalist and then as joint publisher of the *Andersonstown News*, I was present at both events. I might have begrudged the Knights my £1,500 in monthly rents – a sum which was effectively keeping the centre afloat – but for the fact that they had apparently fallen on hard times. Out of favour with government, who had now extended the hand of friendship to the community and their elected representatives, the Knights were now a rather pitiful bunch who had resigned themselves to the fact that the vast majority of the work unit tenants had failed to be converted away from nationalism.

Conway Mill in the heart of the Lower Falls bore the brunt of the political vetting policy. It was the Mill, headed by the indefatigable people's priest Fr Des Wilson, which first fell foul of the political vetting strategy. In 1986, Home Secretary Douglas Hurd wrote to the committee of the former mill, now home to education and job projects, to the effect that funding was to be stopped because it was seen to be furthering the aims of terrorists. What it was actually doing, of course, was more unforgivable than mortar-bombing the local barracks; the go-ahead community activists behind the plan to refurbish the dilapidated old mill were allowing local people a say in their educational and economic future. The economic embargo of the Mill was to persist until May 1995 when Stormont Minister for the Economy Baroness Denton lifted the boom on the eve of a high-powered jobs conference in Washington D.C. aimed at cementing the peace process with jobs. As the dowager's plane touched down, a letter was slipped through the letter box in the Mill offices informing the committee that the formal campaign of political vetting was over. The Mill was out of the X-files just in time to spike the guns of Irish-American politicos who were set to pounce on the British for maintaining their political vetting policies intact almost a year after the IRA's 1994 ceasefire.

'They tried to destroy us and they failed', said a vindicated Des Wilson as he took up his place at the Washington shindig. Sadly, over four years since the funding ban was quashed, the

Mill has yet to receive funding for its ambitious regeneration plans.

Nine months after the IRA ceasefire, the British were still resiling from ministerial contact with Sinn Féin. Worse, the ban on meetings with officials of the Department of Economic Development – which extended from the chief executives to the doormen – remained in place. This was a refinement on the traditional British policy of refusing to allow senior officials to meet with Sinn Féin and was the first time any department had instituted a blanket ban on contact. As part of the cat and mouse game with Sinn Féin, ministers never responded directly to correspondence, having private secretaries or clerks respond on their behalf. Staff were encouraged to address Sinn Féin representatives with the blunt 'Dear Sir' rather than the more courteous 'Dear Councillor'. While officials would include their title at the bottom of letters, they reduced their signatures to a scrawl so that names were indecipherable. I accused the NIO of permitting the practice in all replies to letters concerning Catholic areas and, after the *Sunday World* published copies of the scrawled signatures and invited readers to guess what they actually were, it was discontinued.

The ban was partially lifted in December 1994 when John Major reluctantly allowed Sinn Féin councillors serving on council economic development committees to attend an economic conference in the Europa Hotel. I had prepared an affidavit for our solicitors in preparation for a court challenge to the block when the British finally bowed to pressure and agreed to allow Sinn Féin limited access to the event. Gerry Adams was still not to be invited to an event for party leaders, lest by his presence he would upset the great and the good attending the opening festivities. Sinn Féin responded by picketing the entire event, describing its partial invitation as an elevation from third-class to second-class citizenry. I was among a small group of representatives who attended for opening comments from Sir Patrick Mayhew before walking out – much to the delight of the media who were camped outside. To their credit, many US politicians stayed away from the Europa shindig because of the row or, like New York City comptroller and justice campaigner Alan Hevesi, made it their business to break from the conference in order to meet with Gerry Adams and nationalist community groups. Neither was it lost on the British that their refusal to recognise Sinn Féin's mandate had moved the focus of the event from John Major to the issues of parity of esteem and discrimination.

Even SDLP economic affairs spokesman Sean Farren was predicting that the controversy would overshadow the push for jobs because investors will be asking why certain people have been excluded from the conference. A worried leader writer in the *Belfast Telegraph* commented:

> By snubbing the party (Sinn Féin) over this conference, the Government is handing republicans another propaganda weapon. Sinn Féin can argue that it is the second biggest party in Belfast and has majority representation in the west of the city, which is one of Northern Ireland's most deprived areas. It is also involved in planning the regeneration of the city through Belfast City Council's economic development programme which is government-funded...At a time when nationalists, of all shades, are demanding parity of esteem, the government's action will be viewed dimly by that section of the community.

As political soothsayers predicted his imminent demise, Major continued to play the peace process for all it was worth by inviting mayors and chairs of councils from across the North to Downing Street in January 1995. Again, despite holding 12 per cent of the vote across the North and boasting more votes in Belfast than any other party, Sinn Féin was locked out – though since there was only one SDLP representative among the 27 council leaders on the invitation list, Sinn Féin relished the opportunity to brand it an orange tea party. To hammer home the point that discrimination was hardly likely to be on the agenda of the discussion on job creation between Major and the council heads, Sinn Féin Belfast councillor Una Gillespie and equality campaigner Oliver Kearney went to Downing Street on the day of the meeting to hand in a letter protesting continued

discrimination against nationalists. Belfast Lord Mayor Hugh
Smyth had earlier refused to meet with nationalist
representatives to ensure that their concerns about the failure of
the government's Targeting Social Need policies to impact on
jobless figures were aired at the meeting. 'Discrimination
against nationalists has been a root cause of unemployment and
deprivation', said Oliver Kearney. 'It is unfortunate, therefore,
that in a meeting to discuss economic regeneration,
discrimination should once again be practised against
nationalists.' On the same day, Sinn Féin staged a picket of
protest outside City Hall, an increasingly frequent sight as the
party fought to remove the restrictions on its right to represent
its voters.

Community activists came together in City Hall in April 1995
to consider how best to tackle the continuing political vetting
while at the same time Sinn Féin supporters occupied the Motor
Tax office in Belfast in protest. On the announcement of the
first ceasefire, UUP Deputy Leader John Taylor had predicted
it would be ten years before his party dealt fully with Sinn Féin
– a timetable they were to cling to. It was clear that the British,
under John Major, had a similar timetable. But their refusal to
deal on an equal basis with the party became increasingly
untenable as the EC, Irish and US governments opened up the
door to Sinn Féin. Belfast City Council played its own
surprising part in combating the political vetting regime when
it permitted in August 1995 a £1,000 grant towards a feasibility
study into the regeneration of the Conway Mill and agreed to
send along a cross-party delegation – which was led by Reg
Empey – to view the project. When the EC unveiled its package
of economic measures to support the peace process, it insisted
on establishing partnership boards to dispense the booty. Parties
were to be represented on the local and Northern Ireland board
according to their political strength while community, trade
union and business representatives were also accorded places as
of right. It was a progressive gerrymander which left Belfast
unionists seething for a while before they decided to get on with
it and sat down with Sinn Féin representatives – and members

of community groups who they had previously got the boot into – to carve up the peace pie.

While the British might reluctantly concede that discrimination was one of the causes of the economic underdevelopment of nationalist areas of Belfast, they had no hesitation in maintaining their own battery of discriminatory policies which ensured that the representatives of those people most likely to be unemployed were treated as second-class citizens. Incredibly, the first meeting between Industrial Development Board officials and Sinn Féin councillors, including myself, didn't take place until June 1995.

Throughout this period, Sinn Féin bombarded new Economy Minister Baroness Jean Denton with requests for face-to-face meetings and then threatened her with legal action when she didn't respond to the letters quickly enough. But the British were unmoved. Ministers kept the party at arm's length, permitting officials to engage in 'exploratory dialogue' with Sinn Féin on 9 December 1994 and only allowing contact between ministers and party members taking part in official Council delegations from 15 January 1995. In February, Denton finally replied to letters requesting meetings that I had sent the previous November and December by insisting that it would be 'inappropriate' for her to meet with Sinn Féin councillors to discuss ways of ensuring our hard-pressed constituencies benefited from the predicted peace dividend. Writing on her behalf, Private Secretary Gerry Mallon explained:

> Ministers would regard it as inappropriate to agree to the meetings you have requested in advance of progress in exploratory dialogue between representatives of the government and Sinn Féin...This dialogue is, amongst other things, intended to allow an exchange of views on how Sinn Féin would be able, over a period, to play the same part as the current constitutional parties in the public life of Northern Ireland.

I had to write to Mallon to confirm that this letter also amounted to the continuation of the ban on meetings with DED and IDB officials – a fact he readily confirmed on 17 February.

Rather cheekily, I invited Secretary of State Sir Patrick Mayhew to address a meeting on political vetting in the

Conway Mill in March which was hosted by the Sinn Féin members of the Council Economic Development Sub-Committee. Among those who took up the offer to address the conference were PUP spokesman Billy Hutchinson, union leader Inez McCormack and Irish government advisor Martin Mansergh, both of whom rapped the British government's exclusion policies. Sir Patrick was less impressed with Sinn Féin insistence that participation in the event would help replace the old agenda of discrimination with a new agenda of partnership and community development. Apologetic officials wrote to inform me that such an engagement would also be 'inappropriate'. It was only in late April 1995 that the decision to permit contact with officials and ministers was announced (though meetings took another three months to arrange). While meetings with ministers were still beyond the Pale, that policy was becoming increasingly untenable as we engaged in a round of talks with the main economic agencies. In truth, the party councillors had come to know many of the officials from these bodies through involvement in the Council's Economic Development Sub-Committee. The situation where officials could sit down and talk to Sinn Féin across the sub-committee table – as IDB representatives did with myself and my colleagues on 2 December 1994 – but not meet us outside the meeting room as Sinn Féin representatives was the source of much embarrassment for the civil servants. One would like to think that some of those officials within the DED made their own protest against the bans and the very cynical way in which concessions were drip-fed to Sinn Féin according to a very strict timetable. If they did, and some, particularly in the Training and Employment Agency were clearly annoyed at the restrictions, the evidence remains in government filing cabinets.

The Ministerial boom was finally lifted in August 1995 – a year after the IRA ceasefire – when I joined a Sinn Féin delegation at a meeting in Stormont with Baroness Denton. Three weeks previously, Mitchel McLaughlin had led a Sinn Féin delegation into a meeting with the Permanent Secretary at the DED, Gerry Loughran, and his most senior colleagues. Suffocated with formal protocol the meetings were memorable in retrospect only because Mitchel forbid me from wearing football shorts and gutties to the pow wow with the DED heads. 'We want these people to take us seriously', he reminded me. A fair point but not having the time to dash home to change, I had to call to the nearby home of my younger – and slimmer – brother where I borrowed a shirt and a pair of suit trousers which were so tight that I spent the meeting in excruciating agony.

At the time of our meeting, Catholics made up around 43 per cent of the population of the North but accounted for 70 per cent of the unemployed. Though the Denton meeting was welcome, even if the Minister's patronising approach was difficult to stomach, there was never any real willingness among the Department of Economic Development to take the urgent action needed – huge investment, task forces, goals and timetables for the employment of nationalists – to make redress for three generations of systematic discrimination. After our initial tête-à-tête, relations between the Minister, her top DED officials and Sinn Féin became embarrassingly warm. Before I set off to the US in February 1996 for an economic and political mission with Gerry Adams – and just days before the balloon went up at Canary Wharf – Baroness Denton called me at home to discuss the best strategy to adopt when encouraging US business people to invest in the North, while frequently the British would instruct their top officials to attend Sinn Féin luncheons and conferences to discuss economic matters.

The meetings with Sinn Féin served another purpose: they sounded the death knell for the North and West Belfast Economic Working Group, a sham economic body set up by the British with the support of the SDLP to marginalise Sinn Féin in both areas and present the illusion of economic activity. The Group was a poor cousin of a real jobs task force and about as useful as a chocolate fireguard, but it did give SDLP MP Joe Hendron an excuse to get his picture in the paper. Announced with a publicity fanfare by the newly-elected SDLP West

Belfast MP in December 1993, the Economic Working Group, the public was assured, would include community representatives. It would also, insisted Joe Hendron, supersede the hitherto 'piecemeal' approach of government agencies. 'We will be there to promote jobs for West Belfast', he told *The Irish News*. Noble sentiments which weren't reflected in either the group's activities or its membership. As it turned out, Joe Hendron got to handpick the community representatives. Not surprisingly, he chose two of his colleagues, Margaret Walsh and SDLP South Belfast councillor Alasdair McDonnell who was Deputy-Chair of the Council Economic Development Sub-Committee. Margaret Walsh (who is today a well-liked councillor for the SDLP in Lower Falls) was to remain on the group which first met in March 1994 while Alasdair McDonnell handed his seat over to the Chief Executive of the SDLP-backed Phoenix West Belfast Development Trust (of which, more anon). It was only when I pressed the British organ grinder to release the minutes of the Economic Working Group – a request which was immediately refused – that I realised that it was so inept and ineffective that the government wanted to keep its deliberations secret. When I stumbled upon minutes of one meeting of the secret Working Group – which had been provided to one Group member, the Belfast City Council Economic Development Officer, and were thus, unbeknownst to the DED, available on request to all councillors – my low opinion of the group was confirmed. I followed up with a demand that the Working Group be scrapped and replaced with a real task force, with teeth. The decision to ban Sinn Féin members from membership of the Economic Working Group meant that it suffered from a credibility deficit right from the off. It also meant its real priority wasn't to provide West Belfast with the 3,200 jobs it needed just to bring unemployment levels there down to the city average or to give the area the same type of funding as went into the privatisation of Shorts and Harland and Wolff (£1.2bn), but to prop up British political policy.

The Working Group was the architect of its own woes as well, not least because it met only slightly more frequently than

Ian Paisley and Gerry Adams. In 1994, it met six times but in 1995 came together just twice. Its standards improved dramatically in 1996: it met three times. Interestingly, in 1995, when the block on meetings between Sinn Féin and the economic agencies was lifted, both the IDB and LEDU were keen to wash their hands of the body, dismissing it as the progeny of the by-then dearly departed Economy Minister Tim Smith. If the Group's star burnt briefly, it didn't burn particularly brightly. Having laboured mightily, the Working Group did in 1997 bring forth a report on the economic travails of North and West Belfast – to add to the long list of other worthy reports on job creation. I did eventually get to see all the minutes of the Group, though access was restricted to reading through the documents in the city centre offices of the Industrial Development Board. In July 1995, Baroness Denton wrote to me to state that my request to see the minutes of the group would be considered at its next meeting. Unfortunately, the dynamic Working Group didn't actually meet for another year. But when it did eventually come together, members were told they had no choice but to release the minutes. Fascinating reading the minutes made too, with more references to deflecting Sinn Féin criticism of the Group and how best to resist my demand to see its minutes than job creation. As I pored over the minutes on a sunny spring day in 1997 on the top floor of the IDB's oft-bombed offices, Chief Executive Bruce Robinson dropped by to say hello and initiate an interesting discussion on the equality agenda, in terms of job provision and consultation, which, he predicted, would dictate future economic policy. It was the equivalent of a graveside speech for the doomed Economic Working Group.

Shortly thereafter, the group was taken out and put to sleep by its British government creators who no longer needed bogus economic groups now that contact with Sinn Féin was not only permissible but essential. It was a scene being played out across the North as senior civil servants, admittedly dancing to a new tune, sang the praises of partnership and inclusion and decried political discrimination because it was counterproductive, increased division and fed the bigotry of bodies such as local councils. Not that they committed such sentiments to print, but I do recall a very senior civil servant at the official opening of the Twin Spires enterprise centre on the Falls Road drag me into a conversation he was having with Fr Matt Wallace, a key figure in many government-backed regeneration bodies. 'We've tried you boys for 20 years', he said to Matt Wallace, adding, as he turned to me: 'Now it's time to give these boys a chance.' Hundreds of jobs were lost directly as a result of political vetting policies which were designed to disadvantage Sinn Féin but in reality hurt the party's constituents who already lived in the most economically depressed areas. By channelling funds through church groups, community activists had been excluded from decision-making and self-development while funds and patronage had been accorded to groups not on merit but on the basis of their sympathy with the government.

Discrimination was no sounder a basis for economic progress in West Belfast than it was in the shipyard. But some groups depended for their very existence on their hostility to Sinn Féin. Indeed, the Economic Working Group was in turn the baby of the Phoenix West Belfast Development Trust which prided itself in churning out anti-republican statements and providing an electoral springboard for Joe Hendron. Wallowing in government funding, the Trust rented lavish offices in a West Belfast shopping centre where its chairman and chief executive – both hailing from South Belfast – railed against Sinn Féin. Always one for the mix, I applied to the Trust for membership in 1993 – after all it portrayed itself as a body open to all. However, even one dissenting voice was one too many for Chief Executive Eamon Hanna. He wrote to me explaining that my £5 membership fee and application form wasn't good enough to allow me entrance to the select body. Instead, I would have to sign up to the virulently anti-republican Phoenix analysis of our economic woes. As Eamon spelt out in a letter in January 1995, after my application had been considered by the Board, this meant that the two greatest obstacles to economic development in West Belfast were 'government neglect' and the IRA. Government neglect was summed up with one sentence in Eamon's letter, the latter subject took up one third of the letter. Phoenix, in their wisdom, 'suggested there was a clear conflict of interest between that of Phoenix and Sinn Féin and that membership of both organisations could cause unnecessary confusion'. I wrote back to Phoenix commending them on their analysis and asking them to cut to the quick and say whether they were accepting my application. That involved another Board meeting because, as Eamon explained in a second letter, my views were at variance with theirs. As it happened, I hadn't expressed any view on matters economic or political other than to commend their own analysis, but that apparently didn't amount to the 'clarification' on my political opinions which their chief executive, in his second letter, now insisted was essential. On 9 February, Eamon Hanna wrote again, sending back my fiver, and stating that the board had rejected my application. It was one of the clumsiest instances of political vetting I was to experience but gave me a golden opportunity to protest to all and sundry that I was banned from the Trust, a charge which, as Sinn Féin was given its place in the sun, hurt a group purportedly committed to the regeneration of West Belfast. Perhaps it was just as well that my membership application was blocked because, as political circumstances changed and the need to ostracise Sinn Féin was no longer a government priority, funding for the Trust dried up and members engaged in some ugly in-fighting. It wasn't a pretty sight to see the Trust, penniless and friendless, flit its lavish shopping centre redoubt and disappear up its own behind, having created not one job.

The Ministerial block on contact with Sinn Féin was reinstated after the breach of the IRA ceasefire in February 1996 – though meetings with even the most senior officials weren't put on ice – but by then Baroness Denton was to have more pressing matters to worry her than Sinn Féin requests for meetings. Documents leaked to *The Irish News* put her at the very eye of a fair employment storm. Fair Employment was part of Denton's portfolio as Minister for the Economy, yet it emerged that she had ordered the transfer of a Catholic staff member in her private office who had suffered sectarian harassment. The chain of events began in June 1994 with the appointment of a Catholic man to the post of private secretary to the Baroness at the Department of Agriculture. In April 1995, a Catholic woman with 15 years' unblemished service, who later became the victim of sectarian harassment, was appointed to the private office at Executive Officer II level. Three weeks after her appointment, the woman was told she was doing a good job and was given the sensitive position of diary secretary in recognition of her good performance. Also in May, Alvina Saunders, a Protestant who also worked in the private office, was promoted from Executive Officer II to Executive Officer I. Baroness Denton recommended that Mrs Saunders take over the position of private secretary. This was done and the Catholic man, who would normally have held the post for another year, was shifted. On July 11 1995, Alvina Saunders watched the TV in the minister's room and, according to internal civil service documents, provided other staff with 'running commentary' on events at the first siege of Drumcree. She reported 'with some pleasure' to colleagues that the Orangemen had been allowed to parade triumphantly through the nationalist estate. The Catholic woman felt 'genuinely harassed' by the incident.

On Friday 28 July, a senior official at the Department of Agriculture went to the then head of personnel and told him that 'the minister had asked' that the Catholic woman be transferred because she was 'not fitting in'. (Fair employment guidelines are adamant that the victim of harassment should never be moved from post as a method of resolving disputes.) The personnel director decided to do nothing in the short term until he could explore the matter. On the same day at 4pm, the Catholic woman was told by Alvina Saunders that she was being moved and was instructed to leave the office at once. On 31 July, the Catholic woman visited the director of personnel and told him that a transfer so soon from the private office would 'send a message to all in the department that she had not been up to the job'. When she told him about the incident of sectarian harassment, he asked her to write a note outlining her side of the story and said he would explore opportunities for a suitable posting elsewhere. He didn't offer her the option of staying on in the private office while Mrs Saunders was transferred pending an investigation – which would have been normal fair employment practice. The Catholic woman was subsequently transferred to the Tourist Board and began proceedings under the Fair Employment legislation.

In February 1997, the FEC revealed that the Department of Agriculture had agreed to pay the Catholic woman £10,000 damages and admitted that she had suffered sectarian harassment. Later that month, *The Irish News* was leaked documents which linked Baroness Denton's private office to the case and named the harasser as her private secretary, Alvina Saunders. Then with the portfolio of Economy Minister, Baroness Denton declined all comment on the case and pointed the finger of blame at her civil servants. However, further information was leaked to *The Irish News* to the effect that Denton had personally ordered the transfer of the harassment victim. Only then did she break her silence but, in a letter to *The Irish News*, Denton expressed no regrets over the incident and offered no apology to the victim. Neither was there any explanation from the minister as to why it had taken her ten days to admit she had moved the victim of sectarian harassment from her office after press officers had expressly said that she was not involved in the transfer decision. It was sweet revenge for fair employment campaigners traditionally faced with British government spokespersons who argued that there was no need for the MacBride Principles because the existing legislation, overseen by successive economy ministers, was sufficiently robust. While the British government reluctantly ordered an inquiry into the affair, Sinn Féin took great delight in pointing out that the scandal was threatening jobs. With ministerial contact again banned (and it would remain so until shortly after the IRA ceasefire was reinstated in July 1997), Mitchel McLaughlin travelled to the US in March 1997 warning that leading US Congressmen would be seriously concerned at the involvement of the Economy Minister in the affair. When former Ombudsman Maurice Hayes finally published his inquiry report, he included a string of recommendations on tightening up fair employment practices within the civil service and gave Denton's behaviour short shrift. However, he failed to throw any light on reports that members of staff in the private office who were married to RUC officers received better treatment than their Catholic colleagues. For her part, the Baroness was to limp on as Economy Minister, stoutly resisting calls for her resignation over the matter, until the Tories were routed at the April 1997 elections.

But it wasn't only in economic and political circles that the McCarthyites flourished. In fact, if censorship was ignorance writ large, some self-styled leaders of opinion proved themselves dunces. In late 1993, the Fortnight Educational Trust, an off-shoot of the 'liberal' magazine *Fortnight*, hosted a conference with 60 different workshops in Dublin under the title 'Imagining Ireland'. Every political party with the exception of Sinn Féin was invited. When I threatened to personally picket the event, Trust head Gordon Guthrie responded that he had recently attended a Sinn Féin public meeting and believed the party was not exhibiting enough new thinking to be invited. Strange-but-true fact: Ian Paisley jnr was on the guest list. As it happened, Mr Guthrie's comments came at the very time that new thinking in Sinn Féin was laying the foundations for the IRA ceasefire of August 1994 and the most important political development in a generation. Under pressure from a who's-who of guest speakers, including Joe O'Connor, the imagination-challenged Trust backed down and issued an invite to Sinn Féin. There was a less than sophisticated system to select the unfortunate Sinn Féin speaker for the dreary gathering of *Fortnight* glitterati: the unfortunate republican representative who drew the shortest straw.

14.

A Place at the Table

If nationalists were to fail in their bid to snatch a famous victory at the May 1997 election, it wasn't going to be for the want of trying.

Emboldened by Gerry Adams' success in recapturing the West Belfast seat in the Westminster elections just a fortnight previously, Alex Maskey rallied the troops with a prediction that this indeed could be the election which would see unionists lose their grip on City Hall. 'Hopefully this election will see a Council returned which is willing to end sectarianism forever and build a new future where respect is paid to everyone in the city', he said. Alex Attwood scented victory in the air. 'On 21 May, nationalists will have the chance to make history by breaking unionist power and maximising opportunity for equality.'

Having jumped ship and decided not to stand for the 1997 elections, I made way for a younger candidate. There had been a brief flurry (to be precise, about 30 seconds) of Sinn Féin protests at the loss of an indispensable member of the City Hall team before we all settled down to ensure the election of my successor Michael Brown. His runaway success was a fair indication of the way the political wind was blowing in Belfast. A virtual unknown, Michael romped in with a larger vote than I had ever secured. Rather nervously, I pointed out to colleagues that this was obviously down to my work on his election team rather than any reflection on the previous incumbent! (In September 1999, I got to see Michael Brown in action in the chamber. He made much the same points I would have made myself during a debate on flags and emblems – but with one tenth of the words and one hundredth of the hyperbole.)

As the Sinn Féin vote surged to its highest point ever – and continued the rise it had enjoyed in every Council election since 1983 – the party snatched an extra seat in Upper Falls. There were gains too in the virgin territories of outer North Belfast and Laganside where, previously, middle-class voters had steered clear of Sinn Féin. When the two-day count finished, Sinn Féin had an astonishing 13 seats to its credit. With the Official Unionists, the party was the joint biggest in City Hall. In North Belfast Bobby Lavery was joined by his brother Danny who won a seat in the Castle ward, an area previously marked 'there be dragons' by republican cartographers. In the same electoral area, SDLP chairman Jonathan Stephenson exited politics having, just weeks earlier, made an unsuccessful and undignified effort to hot-foot it from North Belfast and obtain a nomination in the safer territory of South Belfast. The SDLP similarly lost out to Sinn Féin in the Laganbank area of South Belfast – which includes the strongly republican Markets and Lower Ormeau areas.

More importantly, when the votes were stacked up, the unionists had lost their majority. With 13 seats for Sinn Féin, seven for the SDLP and six for the Alliance Party, the unionists now found themselves on the wrong side of the 26-25 Council split. And within the ranks of the unionist camp were three members of the Progressive Unionist Party (Billy Hutchinson and David Ervine joined Hugh Smyth) who promised not to view Council affairs through Orange-tinted glasses. For the count at City Hall – and in an intriguing little twist, I remained a councillor until the last new councillor was returned in the two-day count – I donned the most garish Orange tie I could find in Dunnes Stores and paraded like a peacock from one nail-biting count centre to the next. At every turn, Sinn Féin supporters were celebrating unprecedented electoral performances. Sour-mouthed Official Unionists and sullen DUP stalwarts studied the evidence of their political demise on the electoral tally boards. On the other side of the house, only the PUP contingent – in every respect a mirror image (bar their Orange rosettes) of the working class, bedenimed Sinn Féin supporters – were in high spirits. It was quite a change in a council where in 1977 the bitterly anti-republican SDLP candidate Paddy Devlin had polled an astonishing four quotas in the heart of West Belfast.

The loss of City Hall, the jewel in the unionist crown, was of inestimable historic and symbolic importance to nationalists and unionists alike. In the time warp unionists wished to make of City Hall, the clock was stuck permanently at 1690, but now they had been brought crashing into a new era. A generation previously, when gerrymandering was outlawed, unionists had lost Derry. Now the winds of change were blowing through Belfast too. The two largest cities in a state set up to break the spirit of its Catholic inhabitants and reduce them to second-class ciphers were lost to unionism. As they surveyed the aftermath of the May 1997 elections, nationalists could rightly say: we have arrived.

Horse-trading for the position of Lord Mayor got underway as soon as the 26 non-unionist councillors had been handed their seals of office. Sinn Féin, yesterday's poor cousins, were today's kingmakers. After striking a defiant posture and insisting they would have to be included in the handout of committee and Mayoral goodies, Sinn Féin joined with the Alliance Party and the SDLP to return Alban Maginness as the first Catholic and first nationalist to hold the position of Lord Mayor in Belfast City Council. Ungracious to the last, unionists voted against the North Belfast barrister at the June annual general meeting of Council and, when he romped home, vowed to boycott his inaugural dinner – from which the divisive Loyal Toast was banned. Going into the election, the DUP had warned its supporters: 'Use your vote or lose your city'. The simple fact that there weren't enough unionists in Belfast any more to recreate a civic Jurassic Park was apparently lost on the

Paisleyites who won just seven seats – and later saw one of that number jump ship and join the UUP. For the almost 30,000 people who had voted for Sinn Féin, the record was still stuck: 'The DUP doesn't care about the 30,000 people who have voted to destroy this city', Sammy Wilson told the June council meeting. 'Sinn Féin are lepers and will remain lepers. We should lock them out. They should be squashed and kept outside.' Pointing to the Lord Mayor's chair, he declared: 'They will never occupy that chair.' Sadly for Wilson, his political gravitas had been undermined somewhat by the publication in the *Sunday World* of holiday snaps his girlfriend had taken in France which showed him romping through verdant pastures wearing only his birthday suit.

Affable and assured, Alban Maginness was the perfect ambassador for the bright new Belfast which was rapidly displacing the suffocating sectarian city of yesteryear. 'I am aware of a great sense of history in the position I hold and in this building, but it is remarkable to think that no Catholic has ever been Lord Mayor of Belfast, that no nationalist has ever been allowed to be at home in these chambers', he told the *Andersonstown News* as he relaxed in the sumptious surrounds of the Lord Mayor's parlour – minus the ceremonial Union Jack which he promptly took down. Trumpeting his election as 'a triumph of tolerance', he promised to represent all the citizens of the city while tackling the sensitive legacy of a century of unionist domination. The symbols and flags of one political and religious tradition which bedecked City Hall were, he declared, 'political ivy surrounding local government without being essential to it'.

Oblivious to the semaphore signalling from a Lord Mayor keen to build bridges, unionists decided to abandon the game and leave with the ball, except they didn't own it anymore. Miffed, Fred Cobain announced a campaign of non-co-operation with the Lord Mayor. In reality that amounted to reversing even further into a unionist *cul-de-sac* and emerging only to decry the slice of the pie being won by nationalist areas. But that they should have been half as concerned about their own constituencies. For while unionists fumed at grants being allocated to nationalist groups or tried to close facilities in nationalist areas, they traditionally ignored their own patch. Thus were the strongly loyalist Shore Road, Crumlin Road, Shankill Road and Lower Newtownards Road the most dilapidated and underdeveloped of all the city's thoroughfares. These were people who wouldn't give a nationalist a snowball if they owned the Alps but now they were watching Alban Maginness' every move so that they could hurl allegations of bias and discrimination at him. In fact, the Lord Mayor proved unfazed by the unionist whingeathon – refusing even to raise to the bait when they boycotted his Christmas dinner. Unimpressed, Alban Maginness adhered to his agenda of throwing open the doors of the Lord Mayor's parlour – literally and metaphorically – and quickly put his feel-good stamp on an office which had previously been the preserve of dour, died-in-the-wool bigots.

For unionists hankering after the Belfast of old when the Council chamber had two categories, first class and Catholic, the loss of their once impenetrable majority was a rude awakening indeed. On the very night of the Lord Mayor's election, the SDLP proposed and won Sinn Féin and Alliance support for a move to do away with the appointment of Aldermen. Though nowadays enjoying no more power than a councillor, unionists coveted the position of Alderman and fought among themselves to be among the 12 councillors who were allowed to use the title. Just days later Ulster Unionist guru Michael McGimpsey found himself booted off the Senate of Queen's University to make way for the SDLP's Alex Attwood. Nationalists – with their Alliance colleagues along for the ride – were discovering that a majority was a wonderful thing. When the DUP launched a do-or-die assault on new fair employment policies being introduced to the Council to ban the gratuitous display of the Union Jack – branded 'an attack on the whole British tradition' by Robin Newton – the non-unionists listened politely and then voted the measures through.

And there were other changes too; Sinn Féin members took their seats on the Council trips' gravy train (also known as crucial economic missions to the US and Canada), and when the Irish language national fest, An tOireachtas, came to Belfast for the first time in its century-old history, the Lord Mayor made history by addressing delegates entirely in Irish (and having his comments broadcast live on Raidió na Gaeltachta). Skipper Maskey was nominated by a sub-committee to represent the Council on the powerful Harbour Commissioners' board, only to be made to walk the plank by the unionists and the Alliance when the position came up for ratification at full Council. That was a clear signal that the election of a nationalist Lord Mayor and the securing of a non-unionist majority didn't mean it was all to be plain sailing for Sinn Féin. However, with the reintroduction of the IRA ceasefire in July 1997, moves to ensure a fairer share-out of City Hall positions received a fillip.

In February 1998, the death occurred after a lengthy illness of veteran Sinn Féin councillor Paddy MacManus. A dedicated and industrious constituency worker, his death brought yet more signs of the changing times. At a special council meeting to mark his death, councillors from both sides of the chamber spoke reverentially of his solid contribution to the work of the Council. When the vacancy in Oldpark created by his death came before the next full meeting of Council, unionists made no attempt to object to the co-option of his party colleague and former councillor Sean McKnight. 17 years previously, unionists had forced a by-election in the same area following the murder of independent nationalist Larry Kennedy – and won it. By March 1998, they no longer commanded a majority in the Oldpark electoral area. Similarly, the anti-Irish language lobby threw in the towel and finally admitted defeat in their efforts to prevent the establishment of a Cultural Diversity Committee at City Hall. When the body was set up in January 1998, unionists launched a rearguard action to hijack the Committee for the sole promotion of Ulster Scots. Despite sniping from the unionist trenches, the first street signs in Irish – and in Ulster Scots – were to go up within a year. A weighty report on cultural diversity, to include the thorny issue of flags and symbols, was due to be published before the end of 1999. In February 1998, the High Court ruled against a Sinn Féin bid to have their prohibition from Committee chairs and outside bodies declared illegal. It was the party's first setback in the courts and may have, some years previously, raised the spectre of a unionist backlash. Pat Finucane had cautioned against taking any court cases which might be lost for fear that unionists would take a legal ruling in their favour to further harass Sinn Féin representatives. But by 1998, unionism was rapidly becoming a spent force. The court clash was no more than a rehearsal for the more important political battle to be fought in the Council chamber where nationalists now had the numbers (Sinn Féin alone had 30 per cent of the vote across the city) – with Alliance support – to change existing standing orders governing appointments. And there was no doubt that the Alliance Party was committed to sharing chair and outside body positions, even though such a democratic dispensation would mean fewer plum positions for their own members.

Evidence of rising nationalist spirits, bolstered by the IRA ceasefire, came on St Patrick's Day 1998 when 50,000 people descended on the city centre for the first-ever Saint's Day carnival in the heart of Belfast. Unionists who had refused for one hundred years to sport as much as a sprig of shamrock on St Patrick's Day were, they told a biddable media, outraged at the sight of young people waving Tricolours during the festivities. The fact that the annual Lord Mayor's parade had been turned into a Union Jack-fest complete with RUC band and RIR majorettes was, of course, another matter altogether. Older residents of West Belfast can recall a time when the RUC was called to Falls and Dunville Parks on Sundays to tackle youngsters flouting the city by-laws by playing ball. In fact, up until the sixties, the swings at Dunville were padlocked on the Sabbath. Perhaps nationalist senior citizens, more than anyone, realised the pivotal importance of the green gridlock which gripped Belfast city centre that St Patrick's Day. One can only imagine the sense of desolation experienced by flabbergasted unionists as they watched this green tide coming in. In 1981, supporters of the H-Block prison protesters were battered by the RUC for trying to organise a 50-strong rally at City Hall. Up to 1993, the hallowed ground in front of City Hall was off-limits for republican protests. Yet, in the blink of an eye, the same city centre was playing host to a mammoth celebration of Irishness. If the nationalist game plan was 'festina lente' – to make haste slowly – the pace was still too hot for unionism.

Yet it wasn't a one-way street for nationalists, as preparations for St Patrick's Day 1999 were to show. Building on the success of their 1998 extravaganza, the West Belfast Festival Committee applied for a promised £50,000 grant from City Hall. However, unionists led by Sammy Wilson and the PUP's Billy Hutchinson blocked the grant, insisting that the event wasn't sufficiently inclusive to satisfy loyalists who for the past century had refused to as much as acknowledge the Patron Saint's Day. Indeed, in the North of Ireland, St Patrick's Day isn't a public holiday which tells its own story of how the day was regarded by unionists who like to give themselves a fortnight off over the Twelfth of July.

Billy Hutchinson justified his decision to vote against the St Pat's Day grant because the previous year two youngsters had clambered up on Queen Victoria's imposing statue outside City Hall and placed a Tricolour and a Saoirse prisoners' flag in her granite grasp. In unionist-speak, that amounted to 'triumphalism'. What exactly the flag flying above City Hall every day of the year amounted to wasn't exactly clear. But unionists who thought the organisers would, cap-in-hand, back down and ban the Tricolour from the '99 parade had obviously got their centuries mixed up. The green mardi gras was an even bigger success in 1999, even though it was run on a shoe-string. Though distressed by the loyalist murder of human rights' solicitor Rosemary Nelson just days previously, nationalists turned out in their thousands to celebrate the hottest St Patrick's Day for 30 years.

Rare unionist successes during the term usually came when Sinn Féin and the SDLP found themselves at loggerheads or when both parties were unable to put enough lead in the Alliance pencil to ensure they would stand up to a unionist assault. The obvious lesson – and one taken on board by nationalist groups – was to ensure that maximum support was won for initiatives before they went to the vote, with councillors on the majority side of the chamber being briefed intensively. Whatever about Alliance Party reservations over the nationalist agenda in City Hall, the election of David Alderdice as Alban Maginness' successor in June 1998 showed that the party was committed to a culture of change in City Hall. Boyish ('He's 32 on the outside but inside he's 85', quipped one wag) and enthusiastic, the new Lord Mayor was keen to visit those areas where previous mayors of his religious persuasion had never been seen. He was on hand to open the West Belfast Festival, meet pupils of Irish-medium schools and cut the cake at the Andersontown pensioners' Christmas party.

However, the perennial problems of City Hall – not least the enduring imbalance against Catholics in the workforce – remained apparently immune to the power-shift within the Council. By 1998, just 16 per cent of craftworkers came from the nationalist community while only six of the 25 directors were Catholics.

Whatever about their religious persuasion, the credibility of several senior Council officials took a battering over their handling of the contract for a major West Belfast development. In a no-punches-pulled report into the scandal, the Ombudsman found the Council guilty of 'gross maladministration' over the awarding of the £1m tender to build a Travellers' site in the Upper Springfield area. It emerged that the tender had gone to a builder who was carrying out work at the home of Client Services Director Mervyn Elder – one of the most powerful officers in City Hall – rather than to the successful contractor. Mr Elder had gone against the recommendation of his own officers and the advice of independent consultants that the contract should go to Tyrone firm Connolly and Fee. He encouraged members instead to award the contract to JDC Joinery, the firm which was contracted to carry out work on his own home. 'The award of public sector contracts is an area of work which must be undertaken within clear procedures which should provide equity of treatment', declared the Ombudsman in his August 1998 report, adding: 'These procedures must be sufficiently robust to prevent any tenderer gaining an unfair advantage in a competitive situation and to ensure that the public interest is best served.'

The spotlight turned on the contract debacle after Andersonstown builder Liam Napier, who unsuccessfully bid for the tender, lodged a complaint with the Ombudsman. The investigation of that complaint opened a council can of worms. While the Commissioner of Complaints awarded damages of just £2,000 to Liam Napier, he found that the most aggrieved party were Connolly and Fee builders of Coalisland whose tender had been the unanimous choice of the Council's professional advisers. Following publication of the Ombudsman's report, Maurice Connolly launched his own legal battle amidst predictions that the Council could find itself having to pay out damages of up to £1m.

The Ombudsman found that, in accepting the tender of JDC Joinery, the Council had ignored the recommendations of its own Head of Property Services, Robin McMullen, that the tender be awarded to Connolly and Fee. 'The Council's handling and processing of the subject contract was flawed by gross maladministration, allied to inefficiency and poor administrative practice, all of which fell woefully short of the standard citizens have a right to expect from public servants', reported the Ombudsman. Council documents showed that councillors had refused to accept a recommendation from the Head of Property Services in October 1994 that the contract be awarded to Connolly and Fee after an intervention by Mervyn Elder. The Head of Client Services told councillors he wanted a hold on any decision until he had checked out claims that there were problems with a Connolly and Fee project at Andersonstown Leisure Centre. It subsequently emerged, as Mervyn Elder conceded during the Ombudsman's investigation, that Connolly and Fee had never carried out work on the leisure centre. However, during this delay in awarding the contract, JDC Joinery submitted further information to the Council about its tender. Effectively the company was allowed two bites at the contract cherry. At the subsequent November meeting of the committee, Mervyn Elder presented the Client Services Committee with additional information from JDC Joinery – which had been submitted after the tender deadline. However, he failed to inform the committee that JDC Joinery were building an extension to his own home or that they had contacted him after the October meeting with information favourable to their bid. The Committee decided to accept the JDC tender, prompting the Ombudsman to note that the company's tender had led 'a charmed life'.

Meanwhile, the work at Mr Elder's home which had been originally estimated by JDC Joinery to cost £8,286 was revised upwards during the Ombudsman's probe to £15,000.

On the advice of Council lawyers, an all-party group, headed by Lord Mayor Alban Maginness, was set up to consider disciplinary action against Mervyn Elder and Robin McMullan. Before that group's recommendations had been presented, Robin McMullan took early retirement. Mervyn Elder was subsequently issued with a final written warning for his 'serious misconduct' in the case. While some critics of the Council's contract shenanigans felt both men had escaped lightly, the reprimand was a bitter blow in particular for Mervyn Elder who had won plaudits from nationalists and unionists for his even-handed approach to Council business. Certainly, I had found that during the height of the unionist harassment campaign in the late eighties, he had resolutely refused to join in the anti-Sinn Féin free-for-all. Indeed, at committee meetings, he made a point of involving the Sinn Féin councillors in discussions, much to the disgust of the ruling unionist caucus.

Meanwhile, significant progress was being made in the Dome of Delight.The most important breakthrough came when the new majority parties united to introduce the principles of proportionality into Council business. In early 1999, Alliance, SDLP and Sinn Féin representatives sat down to share out top jobs and positions on outside bodies between all the parties according to their political strength. Only the positions of Lord Mayor and Deputy Lord Mayor were outside the remit of a sweeping agreement which transformed the higher echelons of the Council. And even those two symbolically powerful posts were subject to a different round of horsetrading.

Unionists whinged mightily over the new set-up, even though it would give them representation equal to their strength. With 13 seats, Sinn Féin found itself picking up five committee and sub-committee chairs when the committee annual general meetings were convened in June of 1999. The City Hall atmosphere was rich with the irony of it all as Fra McCann – once barred from the Leisure Services Sub-Committee – took up the position of Leisure and Community Services supremo. Sean McKnight, once tossed off the committee of the Markets' Community Centre by irate unionists, found himself chairing meetings of the most powerful body on the Council after the full Council itself: the Policy and Resources Committee. New boy Danny Lavery took up the reins of the Town Planning Committee. Just a few years previously, SDLP and Sinn Féin councillors had been excluded from planning's 'inner sanctum'. There was no mistaking the mammoth impact the new deal had on City Hall. For 16 years, the ban on Sinn Féin from holding committee chair positions had been an article of faith for City Hall unionists. Overnight it was gone.

Somewhat nervously, the Alliance Party stood over the new deal. 'Greater proportionality was important to reflect the different concerns and different political insights in a divided city', Councillor Tom Campbell told the press. For Alex Maskey, the new structures 'drive a nail into the coffin of discrimination and injustice'. David Ervine stood aside from the wailing unionist pack to offer qualified support for the move on the basis that the PUP had 'argued consistently for inclusion'.

The biggest fillip for Sinn Féin came in June 1999 with the election of veteran standard-bearer Marie Moore as Deputy Lord Mayor. An active republican since the sixties, Marie took to the new post with some aplomb. Ignoring unionist begrudgery – which extended to the incoming Lord Mayor Robert Stoker barring her from his inaugural dinner – she presided over a dizzying whirl of events in nationalist areas of the city. Sporting her mayoral chain and being ferried from one civic event to the next in a chauffeur-driven BMW, she was the toast of nationalist Belfast. Yet it was also a case of the more things changed, the more they stayed the same, as the Council insisted in imposing the Loyal Toast on civic dinners being hosted by the Deputy Lord Mayor – a practice she managed to side-step. Similarly the Union Jack continued to fly over City Hall on every single day of the year and the acceptance of the nationalist tradition into the cold house of City Hall was not yet complete. An official City Hall guide book inadvertently illustrated the extent of the problem for the new nationalist power bloc on the Council when it extolled the virtues of the British and pro-unionist items of interest to the tourist. These include 'a stained window memorial to the Officers, NCOs and men of the North Irish Horse', 'portraits of King Edward VII and Queen Alexandra', a table 'commemorating the granting of the charter to Belfast by King James I', 'a stained glass window to the 36th (Ulster) Division', stained glass windows in the Council chamber of 'the Royal Arms and those of Lord Dufferin of Londonderry', 'two chairs used by King George V and Queen Mary at the opening of the first Parliament of Northern Ireland', portraits of Queen Victoria, King Edward VII and the Earl of Shaftesbury, in the Great Hall portraits of King William III, Queen Victoria and King Edward VII, in the Reception Room a stained glass window showing 'the Royal Arms of Edward VII' (him again!), and a massive painting 'Reading of the Proclamation of King Edward VII, 1901'. There was much more, of course, which didn't make it into the guide book. It was a minor miracle that nationalists managed to draw breath at all in the stiffling, British-only atmosphere of City Hall.

Hopes were high though that further strides towards recognition of the city's proud nationalist tradition would be taken in late 1999 when an all-party Council committee was due to publish its report into the culture of City Hall and the celebration of the city's diverse heritage. But the real prize being eyed by Sinn Féin was the Lord Mayor's position. No single development could be more debilitating to Orange unionism and more uplifting for new nationalism than the election of Alex Maskey as Lord Mayor of Belfast. June 2000 will tell that particular tale.

The Great Escape or just bad timing? Cold feet or career-move? Three years after having slipped the net and left Belfast City Council, I'm not entirely sure myself. But in early 1997, I had made my mind up to leave the Council in the May election and take up a new job as managing editor of the *Andersonstown News* group of newspapers (which today includes the *North Belfast News* and the Irish language weekly, *Lá*). It would be gratifying to imagine that I had written a small footnote in the history of Belfast but the reality is that yesterday's bread is soon forgotten. And that's how it should be. As cataclysmic change gripped Belfast City Hall in the weeks and months after the May 1997 elections, there were times when I regretted foregoing the opportunity to be a part of the new dispensation. But there were periods too when I marvelled at my ability to remain relatively mute for ten years in the face of insults and invective from political pygmies. How did I do that? I don't know, but I suppose humour helped. Alex Maskey still enjoys telling the (surely aprocrophal) tale of how an exasperated Tish Holland approached him in the early days of City Hall and told him that the abuse she was receiving from councillors had her at the end of her tether. 'I told her to just chin the next one who gives you trouble', he recalls. 'Two minutes later, I looked round and she had just floored Máirtín.' Or the time when the inimitable Eric Smyth refused to heed the Lord Mayor's insistence that he stop guldering and sit down – even when he was told he was breaching Council standing orders. 'These are my standing orders', bellowed back Smyth as he brandished aloft his Bible. And then there was the sight of Dixie Gilmore making his lumbering way into City Hall in his Lord Mayor's finery while behind him minced a camp City Hall official whistling, for the amusement of other councillors, 'I Wish I Was In Dixie'!

I took a seat in the public gallery for the September 1999 meeting of full council in order to remind myself of just what I was missing. The ambience of the chamber was stuffier than I had remembered it. Business also seemed to move at a snail's pace, with interminable delays for votes to be formally recorded by clerks who called out each councillor's name by rote and totted up the 'For' and 'Against' responses. In the eye of the storm ten years previously, such votes had seemed to take just moments to complete. Now they compounded an already soporific atmosphere.

True, Sammy Wilson was in high dudgeon as, like a crackly '78 record, he recited a long list of unionist woes, headed by the flying of Tricolours from St George's Market in the city centre. Yet this time his targets weren't Sinn Féin but the Alliance and SDLP members who flanked the huge Sinn Féin contingent, which now fills two blocks of seats and spills into a third. It would be a long time before the unionists forgave the Alliance Party in particular for making its bed with the SDLP and Sinn Féin rather than crossing the chamber to unite with the parties who traditionally held sway in City Hall. Surprisingly for a man who had made his career out of sectarianism, Wilson's deplored the 'one-sided sectarian attitude' of the Alliance Party. But for all his ranting, Wilson possessed all the power of a busted beach ball. Twice he rose to berate the parties sitting opposite him. Twice his motions were rebuffed by 27 votes to 17. His colleagues rose half-heartedly to the task of vilifying their opponents. Chris McGimpsey ventured that the SDLP and 'Sinn Féin/IRA' were involved in the same business of destroying the Britishness of the unionist people but that one used 'syntax while the other used Semtex'. Though the debate covered the wearily familiar territory of flags and emblems, it was a resigned and subdued performance from the unionists. On my first visit to City Hall in 1987, I had been overawed and terrified. The most frightening thing about City Hall on my latest visit was the horrendously steep seating in the public gallery.

The unionists were oblivious to my presence as they sat beneath the protruding gallery, but I nodded hellos to the Sinn Féin benches. As I got up to leave, Chris McGimpsey pitched himself into another assault on the parties sitting opposite. Their crime this time was, allegedly, to want to tear down the statue of unionist firebrand Henry Cooke in Belfast city centre. 'It's a pity Máirtín Ó Muilleoir isn't here', he said, 'for he would appreciate the fact that the Rev Cooke was a fluent Irish speaker.' To his bemusement, his comments drew guffaws from the councillors sitting opposite him who pointed out that I was, in fact, present – and not just in spirit.

As I made my way out of the splendid City Hall building, I allowed myself a smile at having, perhaps, taken just the smallest of chips out of unionism's Wall of Jericho. In a city both woebegone and wonderful, terrifying and terrific, hurtful and hurt, it had been a privilege to serve the most magnificent of people. In the city they loved, nationalists wished only for a seat as equals at the table, so that they too could sing Belfast.

A Note on Sources

The vast majority of quoted sources are taken from the Belfast dailies, *The Irish News*, *Belfast Telegraph* and *News Letter*, as well as from the *Andersonstown News*.

The *Sunday World*, and to a lesser extent, the Sunday Life, also played a prominent role in exposing the seamier side of City Hall life. Jim McDowell in particular, now Northern Editor of the *Sunday World*, entertained readers of *The Irish News* with his missives from the Dome of Delight, most of which ended him up in hot water with the unionist old guard. For fear of cluttering the text, I haven't included the date or source of each quote, except where, as in the case of Frankie Millar, I felt the statements were so outrageous that a reader would only believe they were true if they were accompanied by their original source.

I have also made extensive use of my own press cuttings' files, which were compiled during my ten years on the Council, as well as using the resources of the Central and Linen Hall libraries. I kept a copy of every letter I ever sent or received as a public representative, knowing they would come in useful at some stage, and in my latter years on the Council, the trusty computer has kept on file a daily record of all letters and statements that I wrote.

On a few cases, I have relied on contemporaneous notes jotted down during Council meetings, but in the main accounts of full meetings of Council have been taken from press reports. On some occasions, in particular in my account of the battle against political vetting, I have relied heavily on copies of letters sent to me. Comments by judges ruling on court cases taken against unionist discrimination are based on the official text of the relevant rulings.